DANIEL
GOD'S MESSENGER TO OUR TIMES

A detailed commentary on one of the Bible's most authenticated books

GEORGE PYTLIK

ILLUMIN●SITY

Illuminosity™ Press
www.illuminositypress.com

DANIEL: GOD'S MESSENGER TO OUR TIMES
by George Pytlik

ISBN 978-0-578-05376-9

Copyright©1995, 1997, 2002, 2003, 2010 by George Pytlik

All rights reserved. No part of this book may be reproduced, stored in a retrieval system, or transmitted in any form or by any means — electronic, mechanical, photocopying, recording, or any other — except for brief quotations in printed reviews, without prior written permission from Illuminosity Press.

The primary Scripture translation used throughout this book was especially produced for this publication and is protected by the copyright of this book.

Scripture quotations marked NIV are taken from the Holy Bible: New International Version®. NIV®. Copyright © 1973, 1978, 1984 by International Bible Society. Used by permission. All rights reserved.

Scripture quotations marked NASB are taken from the New American Standard Bible, Copyright © 1960, 1962, 1963, 1968, 1971, 1972, 1973, 1975, 1977, 1995 by The Lockman Foundation. Used by permission. (www.Lockman.org)

Scripture quotations marked AMP are taken from the Amplified® Bible, Copyright © 1954, 1958, 1962, 1964, 1965, 1987 by The Lockman Foundation. Used by permission. (www.Lockman.org)

Scripture quotations marked NLT are taken from the Holy Bible, New Living Translation, copyright 1996, 2004. Used by permission of Tyndale House Publishers, Inc., Wheaton, Illinois 60189. All rights reserved.

Scripture quotations marked NKJV™ are taken from the New King James Version®. Copyright © 1982 by Thomas Nelson, Inc. Used by permission. All rights reserved.

ILLUMIN●SITY

Illuminosity™ Press

145 Tyee Drive
PO Box 862
Point Roberts, WA 98281
info@illuminositypress.com
www.illuminositypress.com

Table of Contents

Foreward v
Part 1: A Book for Our Times vii
01 Introduction: A Most Authenticated Book 15
02 Who Was Daniel? An Example of Genuine Faith 25
03 The setting: A Devout Nation Exiled to a Pagan Land 31

Part 2: The Narratives 51
04 Daniel chapter 1: Exiled to Babylon 53
05 Daniel chapter 2: The Man of Metal 65
06 Daniel chapter 3: Bow or Burn 89
07 Daniel chapter 4: The Insane King 107
08 Daniel chapter 5: The Kingdom Falls 129
09 Daniel chapter 5: Politically Incorrect 147

Part 3: The Prophecies 165
10 Daniel chapter 7: The Four Wild Beasts 167
11 Daniel chapter 8: The Persian Wars 189
12 Daniel chapter 9: Time of the Messiah 205
13 Daniel chapter 10: Spiritual Forces at War 227
14 Daniel chapter 11: Earthly kings at War 245
15 Daniel chapter 12: The End of the World 271
16 Resources 291

Foreward

Daniel is a book for our times. Daniel, the man, was a model of true faith, committed to God in a culture that did not honor Him nor value the integrity Daniel stood for. His example gives us encouragement that God is in control, even when everything seems to be going against us.

Daniel and his friends faced certain death at the hands of tyrant leaders, yet their faith did not waiver. Daniel lived in a world of bigotry against his beliefs, yet remained firm in his convictions even into old age, never allowing the pressures of the environment around him to soften his relationship with God.

The legacy he left is a source of remarkable strength for our faith, including many prophecies that have played out accurately, even to an exact day in history. Fulfilled prophecy is evidence of Scripture's divine authorship. God told us that only He can foretell the future, challenging others to try:

> "And who can proclaim as I do? Then let him declare it and set it in order for Me, since I appointed the ancient people. And the things that are coming and shall come, let them show these to them." — Isaiah 44:7 (NKJV)

Many of the prophecies given to Daniel were so detailed, critics have no choice but to claim that they were written after the events took place.

Daniel motivates us to walk the talk. In our modern times, we find the Bible, and the Christian faith, increasingly under attack. Not only from outside, but even from those expected to uphold its message and significance. Daniel serves as an inspiring example of how God honors those who don't shy away from convictions when pressure becomes uncomfortable. Or unbearable.

Not only did Daniel influence the people around him, including the conversion of the tyrant king of the pagan Babylonian empire, but his influence extended all the way to our current time. Today, we are still inspired by his example, perhaps more than ever.

This study began as a Bible Education class I was teaching at my church. I'm grateful to dozens of pastors and Bible teachers from across the country who contributed useful insight as I posted content online prior to the final production of this material in book form.

SUPPORTING MODERN-DAY DANIELS

For the past few years, I've provided communication assistance to The Pocket Testament League, a ministry that encourages Christians to Read, Carry and Share the Word of God. League members take up the challenge to read a portion of Scripture daily, carry a Gospel of John with them wherever they go, and prayerfully seek a chance to give it away before the end of each day. I love the spirit and significance of this ministry. Many of the League's most active, most faithful members are those without financial means to donate for their evangelism resources. Like Daniel when he began his ministry, many are just teens, with a vision to stand firm under pressure and to reach their world with the message of God's love and faithfulness. They are truly Daniels of our age.

A portion of the proceeds from every copy of this book is donated to the League to sponsor evangelism so that these modern Daniels may order Gospels of John to freely give away to others. For more information about the League, visit www.pocketpower.org/7115

George Pytlik, May 2010

PART 1

A Book for *Our* Times

October 28, 2008

Rutherford Appeals To U.S. Supreme Court On Behalf Of Football Coach Prohibited From Bowing Head During Team's Pre-Game Prayer

WASHINGTON, DC — Attorneys for The Rutherford Institute, acting as co-counsel for Coach Marcus Borden, have asked the U.S. Supreme Court to protect the high school football coach's right to silently bow his head while his players offer a pre-game prayer.

In appealing to the high court, Institute attorneys argue that public school administrators, faculty, coaches and staff do not violate the Establishment Clause when they make gestures of silent respect in response to constitutionally protected student-initiated religious acts.

"If this ruling is allowed to stand, it will mean that high school teachers across the United States will have no free speech or academic freedom rights at all," said John W. Whitehead, president of The Rutherford Institute. "This undermines a time-honored tradition that has less to do with religion than it does athletic tradition. It's a sad statement on our rights as Americans that schools are no longer bastions of freedom."

The American Football Coaches Association has also filed an amicus in support of Borden, declaring that "when the federal courts interpret the Constitution in a way that intrudes into the locker room, invades the player-coach relationship, and undermines a coach's ability to maintain an atmosphere of mutual respect and team unity by showing deference to the prayers of this nation's youth, that concerns the AFCA."

The case arose in October 2005 after officials at East Brunswick High School adopted a policy prohibiting representatives of the school district from participating in student-initiated prayer. The policy prevented high school football coach Marcus Borden from bowing his head in a silent gesture of respect while his team offered a pre-game prayer, a regular part of the team's pre-game activities for over 25 years.

In July 2006, U.S. District Judge Dennis Cavanaugh declared that the school district violated Borden's constitutional rights to free speech, freedom of association and academic freedom when they prohibited him from silently bowing his head and "taking a knee" with his players while they engaged in student-initiated, student-led, nonsectarian pre-game prayers. However, the school district, aided by Americans United for Separation of Church and State, challenged the court's decision before the U.S. Court of Appeals for the Third Circuit, insisting that Borden has no constitutional rights of expression or academic freedom in connection with his duties as a teacher and coach. The appeals court ruled in the school's favor.[1]

March 3, 2009

Supreme Court rejects appeal of New Jersey high school football coach

WASHINGTON, DC — In a blow to athletic coaches across the country, the United States Supreme Court has refused to weigh in on the question of whether or not high school football coaches have a right to silently bow their heads as a sign of respect while their student players offer a pre-game prayer.

In refusing to hear the case of high school football coach Marcus Borden, the Supreme Court has let stand a lower court ruling with chilling ramifications for coaches and teachers everywhere— namely, that Borden has no constitutional rights of liberty, expression or academic freedom in connection with his duties as

---

1   The Rutherford Institute (*www.rutherford.org/KeyCases/Borden.asp*). Used with permission.

a teacher and coach. Attorneys for The Rutherford Institute, acting as co-counsel for Coach Borden, had urged the U.S. Supreme Court to affirm that the liberties secured by the U.S. Constitution guarantee Borden's right to offer a simple, silent gesture of respect, whether he does so by silently bowing his head or taking a knee while his players say their pre-game prayer.[2]

August 4, 2009

School officials may be jailed for prayer

PENSACOLA, FL — Jail may be in the future for two Pace High School administrators if a federal judge rules they violated a court order forbidding the promotion of religion in Santa Rosa County schools.

Principal Frank Lay and Athletic Director Robert Freeman face criminal contempt charges for "willfully violating the court's temporary injunction order" after they prayed at a school function, according to a court order of contempt.

The injunction was issued Jan. 9 after the American Civil Liberties Union sued the Santa Rosa School District in August 2008 on behalf of two Pace students and their parents who said religion was forced upon them at school.

On Jan. 28, Lay encouraged Freeman to lead a prayer before a meal at the dedication of a new field house during a school-day luncheon. Freeman complied. Santa Rosa Superintendent of Schools Tim Wyrosdick later told Lay to avoid such activities because they violated the court injunction.

The incident was brought to the attention of U.S. District Judge M. Casey Rodgers after the ACLU noted the episode in a separate case it filed in the spring against School Board employee Michelle Winkler, who had her husband pray at a school event.

---

2   The Rutherford Institute (*www.rutherford.org/KeyCases/Borden.asp*). Used with permission.

The U.S. Attorney's Office will prosecute the case, but representatives couldn't be reached for comment Tuesday.

Lay, Freeman and Winkler also couldn't be reached for comment.

Lay and Freeman will appear in court Sept. 17. If convicted, Lay and Freeman could each face up to six months in jail or a $5,000 fine.[3]

August 15, 2009

Preacher threatened with arrest for reading out extracts from the Bible in public

MANCHESTER, ENGLAND — A street preacher is at the centre of a row over freedom of speech after police threatened to arrest him for reading the Bible in public.

Lawyers acting for Miguel Hayworth, 29, have demanded an explanation over the alleged intimidation and abuse of power by three officers.

Andrea Minichiello Williams, the director of the Christian Legal Centre, has written to Peter Fahy, the Chief Constable of Greater Manchester, over the incident. She claims that Mr Hayworth and his father, John, 55, were unlawfully and unfairly treated as they preached Christianity in the city at the end of July.

"They were clearly told that reading the Bible and preaching can be offensive and that they could be arrested," she wrote. "Furthermore, they were subjected to abuse and intimidation. They were told that they were being monitored and filmed," she wrote.

Mr Hayworth, a voluntary worker who is married with two children, has been a street preacher in the Manchester area for five years and he is often accompanied by his father. He said that he

---

3   from *The Panama News Herald*. Used with permission.

and his father had decided to preach from 11am at St Ann's Square in Manchester instead of their usual place on nearby Market Street.

He was reading passages from the Old and New Testaments while his father distributed leaflets containing the message of the gospel.

"At 2pm, I was approached on more than one occasion by several police officers who falsely accused me, stating that I was inciting hatred," he said. "One plain-clothed officer, who was with the other two uniformed officers, said: 'It is against the law to preach and hand out tracts: preaching causes offence and handing out tracts is harassment and could result in an arrest.'"

Mr Hayworth said that at about 2.30pm a second officer confirmed that his colleague had accused the preacher of inciting religious and racial hatred and wanted to warn him that this was an arrestable offence.[4]

March 22, 2010

Refusing to Hear Nurre Case, U.S. Supreme Court Lets Stand Ban on Instrumental 'Ave Maria,' Fails to Protect Student Artistic Expression

WASHINGTON, DC — Public school officials prohibited the performance of an instrumental version of Franz Biebl's "Ave Maria" at a high school graduation simply because the superintendent feared it might be religious. The U.S. Supreme Court has refused to hear the case.

Justice Samuel Alito publicly dissented with the high court's rejection of the appeal. In voicing his disapproval, he was harshly critical of school officials.

"When a public school purports to allow students to express themselves, it must respect the students' free speech rights," stated Alito

---

4   from *The Daily Telegraph* © Telegraph Media Group Limited 2009. Used with permission

in a six-page opinion on the case. "School administrators may not behave like puppet masters who create the illusion that students are engaging in personal expression when in fact the school administration is pulling the strings."

In 2006, members of the senior high woodwind ensemble at Henry M. Jackson High School in Snohomish County, Wash., elected to perform an instrumental arrangement of German composer Franz Biebl's "Ave Maria" at the school's graduation ceremonies. School officials had adopted a custom of allowing the senior members of the high school's top performing instrumental group, the woodwind ensemble, to choose a song from their repertoire to perform as a farewell during graduation ceremonies. Previous selections included "On a Hymnsong of Philip Bliss," a popular composition based off the hymn "It is Well Within My Soul." Thus, having previously performed "Ave Maria" at a public concert, Kathryn Nurre and the other seniors in the wind ensemble unanimously chose to perform it again at their graduation ceremony on June 17, 2006. No lyrics or words would be sung or said, or printed in ceremony programs.

Despite the absence of lyrics, the superintendent refused to allow the ensemble to perform "Ave Maria" at graduation, allegedly because she believed the piece to be religious in nature.

The Rutherford Institute had asked the Supreme Court to weigh in on the case in December 2009.

"Free speech in the public schools is on life support," said John W. Whitehead, president of The Rutherford Institute. "With this decision, the Supreme Court may have pulled the plug. It's a sad day for freedom in America."[5]

---

5   The Rutherford Institute (*www.rutherford.org/articles_db/press_release.asp?article_id=818*). Used with permission

01

INTRODUCTION
A MOST AUTHENTICATED BOOK

> **As soon as you began to pray, AN ANSWER WAS GIVEN, which I have come to tell you, for you are highly esteemed."**
>
> —Daniel 9:23

As **Alexander the Great marched aggressively towards Jerusalem, a procession dressed in dazzling white led by the high priest greeted his army, encircling his officers.**

Alexander bowed low before the Name of God inscribed on the high priest's head piece. His officers wondered if he had gone insane.[1]

Alexander explained that he had seen Jaddua the high priest in a vision in which God promised success in his campaign against the Persians.

As Alexander was escorted into the city, Jaddua showed him the book of Daniel, in which the Greek empire had been specifically identified 200 years earlier as the instrument that would overthrow the Persians.

As he saw his military success described in advance of it happening, Alexander was so amazed and delighted that he not only spared the city, but agreed to many requests made by the Jewish people.[2]

AUTHENTICATED BY HISTORY

Written during some of the most dramatic events of antiquity, the book of Daniel enjoys a status as one of the most authenticated books of the Bible. But because it contains so many detailed prophecies, critics are desperate to find ways to discredit its authorship.

It was quoted extensively by early historians such as Josephus, and in the Maccabean accounts, and was translated into Greek, the world's trade language, in 270BC as part of the Septuagint.

Jesus authorized the works as having been penned by Daniel himself.

Copies of both Daniel and the Septuagint dating back to 200BC have been found in some of the caves of the Dead Sea Scrolls at Qumran, identical to copies dated centuries later.

---

1 Josephus, *Antiquities of the Jews: From Esther to the Ptolemies*
2 *ibid*

A UNIQUE BOOK

The book of Daniel is unlike any other book in the Bible. The first half includes narrative stories of historical events that show us how we are to demonstrate real faith in God when the world around us presses in with demands to conform.

The fourth chapter of Daniel was written by the Gentile king of a pagan nation, remarkable when you consider how reverently the Jews protect their holy Scriptures. That they would so embrace the testimony of this ruler — not just any king, but the one who exiled their nation — as to include it in the *Tanach*, is a testament to Daniel's influence.

The last half of Daniel is filled with prophecies of the future so detailed that critics have no choice but to claim that the book must have been written after the history it describes took place.

BRINGING THE BIBLE TO LIFE

This study is designed to bring the book of Daniel to life. Many people, especially today, think of the Bible as dull or outdated. Not so. It soars with wonder, joy and drama from beginning to end! As you study Scripture, you see into the very heart of God.

This book was meant to be enjoyed and understood without requiring a Bible college background. Detail is added to give you a thorough understanding of the content and of various viewpoints held by Bible teachers, but most of the comments are meant to keep things simple and easy to read.

FIGHTING BACK AGAINST FALSE TEACHING

One great concern with modern study tools is the growth of false teaching brought on by self-proclaimed liberal-thinking 'Bible experts.'

The Bible was meant to be understood by ordinary people, and is beautiful in its clarity. But Liberal scholars, who don't hold to the foundational truths of Scripture, want to rewrite the biblical text into a new, more politically correct narrative.[3]

Prominent Bible commentaries today will, at times, suddenly proclaim of a statement in Scripture, "this is doubtful." Nothing in the Bible is doubtful! Many things once questioned were later proven accurate by archeological or scientific discoveries.

Post-modern textual criticism, practiced by those who reject the inerrancy of Scripture, leads to many doctrinal errors. A recent rash of atheist manifestos has accelerated rejection of biblical truth, further eroding acceptance of the Bible as the genuine Word of God. Many Christians are deeply concerned about such distortions, but don't know how to recognize them nor how to respond. This book attempts to be as detailed as possible when discussing areas of disagreement, to equip you for discernment. If there's a great deal of scholarly disagreement, the issues are discussed to give you a deeper understanding.

A foundation of scriptural truth

The content of this study is based on a traditional evangelical Christian world view. Five foundational principles are presented here so you fully understand them before you embark on this journey:

1 **THE BIBLE IS THE INSPIRED WORD OF GOD.** This means that the original Scriptures as written in Greek, Hebrew and Aramaic are perfectly recorded, just as God intended. Every word is meant to be there. It is "God-breathed."[4] Nothing is left to chance

---

3   Luke Timothy Johnson, *The Real Jesus*
4   2 Timothy 3:16

or accident by the human writers. The Holy Spirit designed every word to be part of an intricate message system given, through the Jewish people, to the whole world.

Yet some passages are not always perfectly translated into other languages, including English. As a result, text we encounter may be unclear or confusing. See the sidebar on the next page for details on how this impacts the study.

Never doubt your Bible. Use more than one translation to get a better idea of what may be meant when passages don't seem clear. During the Reformation, many people died cruel deaths simply for making the English-language Bible possible. You are able to honor them when you make the most of the wealth of resources available today.

2 TODAY'S DANIEL IS THE SAME BOOK HE ORIGINALLY WROTE. Some people, unwilling to accept that God can reveal history before it happens, insist that Daniel was written after the events it foretold. They argue that its authorship in more than one language is proof. This is absurd, since the entire book was translated into Greek as part of the Septuagint more than 100 years before many of the events it describes took place. Copies of Daniel found in the caves of Qumran among the Dead Sea Scrolls predate many of the prophecies described in Daniel and are identical to versions found centuries later, proof that there were no changes made during the intervening years.

3 GOD REVEALS THE FUTURE TO DEMONSTRATE HIS EXISTENCE. With some 27% of all Scripture verses made up of prophecy, this aspect of the Bible is vitally important as part of God's message and has a distinct purpose. He uses prophecy to prove His existence, as He revealed to Isaiah:

> Thus says the Lord, the King of Israel, and his Redeemer, the Lord of hosts: 'I am the First and I am the Last; Besides Me there is no God. And who can proclaim as I do? Then let him declare it and set it in order for Me, since I appointed the ancient people. And the things that are coming and shall come, let them show these to them.'
> —Isaiah 44:6-7 (NIV)

Prophecy is a powerful way to bring people into an encounter with the living God. Furthermore, He appears to reveal the most intimate prophecies to those who follow Him most closely. Daniel and the apostle John, two figures who were each declared to be especially loved by God, were given the most detailed prophecies of all.

4 **GOD CHOSE THE JEWISH PEOPLE AS HIS INSTRUMENTS OF REVELATION TO THE WORLD.** They are His chosen people, those with whom He has both a beautiful, unbreakable covenant relationship and for whom He has a comprehensive plan.

Much anti-Semitism has resulted from misunderstandings about the role of the Jews in history. The Christian church has not replaced God's plan for Israel, as some teach, but merely interrupts it until the *times of the Gentiles* described by Jesus[5] are complete. This is covered in Daniel chapter 9.

While part of Daniel is designed to show future history in a Gentile context, the ultimate purpose is to show it through the lens of Israel, with the Jews as the focal point of all history.

5 **JESUS CHRIST IS THE PROMISED MESSIAH, THE KING.** He was revealed throughout the Old Testament, with more than 300 specific prophecies ranging from His ancestry to the place of His birth, from details of the crucifixion to His ultimate position as King of kings.

---

5   Luke 21:24

Only through a personal relationship with Jesus Christ can we be accepted into God's perfect kingdom of Heaven and granted eternal life in the presence of God. Without a genuine commitment to follow Jesus, we remain mired in sinful rebellion against God and cannot be given access to Heaven. Another writer of Scripture, who was also loved by God and who walked with the Messiah, explained this relationship in detail in the book of John.

APPLYING THIS STUDY TO YOUR LIFE

Daniel is a remarkable book, incredibly relevant to the times we live in. You're encouraged to apply this study to your own life. As you reflect on Daniel's account, think about how the issues he faced relate to the issues we're living through in our times. You'll be surprised by the similarities.

Ask God to give you insight and wisdom to understand how you can live your life more like Daniel. Trust Him to help you respond as Daniel did when you find yourself in difficult situations, especially those outside of your own control.

A blank page following each chapter can be used for notes, or to write discussion questions and answers for use in a group Bible study. Take advantage of that space to integrate your own thoughts into your study of this fascinating book of Scripture. When you're finished, you'll have a renewed passion for God's Word, and for living a life that honors God in every way.

Insight

The Bible as originally written in Hebrew, Aramaic and Greek is perfect in every way. Yet translated versions may be less than perfect interpretations of the original text.

There are sometimes printer errors. One published Bible accidentally left out the word "not" in one of the commandments.

Some versions intentionally change clearly written words or meanings. A recently-published Bible uses politically correct terminology to avoid gender-specific references like Father or Son, arguably an imperfect version of God's Word as originally written.

The Jehovah's Witnesses have published millions of copies of a Bible containing intentional modifications, such as changes to John 1:1, designed to support their view of Scripture.

Why would God allow differences to exist? Perhaps only to ensure that we never get complacent. Knowing there are differences, intentional or not, keeps us on our toes and ensures that we think about what we read.

How does this relate to our study of Daniel?

As you go through the study, you'll discover words and phrases used in various translations that might convey slightly different things from one version to another. Scripture is never wrong or questionable, as some claim. The translators have simply applied their own world view when translating some of the more difficult ideas or concepts expressed. As Baptist theologian J.L Dagg pointed out, the fact that there are so few differences in the entire Bible is impressive proof of its accuracy.[1]

---

1 J. L. Dagg, *A Manual of Theology*

02
WHO WAS DANIEL?
AN EXAMPLE OF GENUINE FAITH

The name Daniel means "God is my judge." After being taken as a Jewish captive to the pagan world of Babylon, his name was changed to Belteshazzar which means "may Bel protect his life" or "prince favored by Bel" (Bel was a Babylonian god).

Jerusalem may have been his birthplace, though this is mere opinion. He was likely of royal blood, because he was among the nobles and princes taken captive by Nebuchadnezzar following the first Babylonian siege of Jerusalem in 605BC, the fourth year of Jehoiakim. He was likely in his mid-teens at the time. It was a long trip from his beloved holy city of Jerusalem to Babylon, some 1,600 km (1,000 miles) through the desert trade route. Now essentially a slave in a pagan nation, he was put into a three-year training program to learn the skills necessary to serve the king of Babylon as one of the educated group of scholars known as the wise men.

Daniel quickly distinguished himself through his discernment and deep commitment to God.

Recognizing that his gifts of intelligence, physical condition and wisdom came directly from God, he continually emphasized that everything we have, including popularity or political power, is a gift that can be taken away by God at any time.

Ezekiel, a Jewish prophet taken captive a few years later, used Daniel as an example of true righteousness. In a conversation with Ezekiel about the fate of Jerusalem, God placed Daniel with Job and Noah in purity of faith. He said that even if these three men were in Jerusalem their righteousness would save only them and not spare the city its coming destruction:

> "Son of man, if a country sins against me by being unfaithful and I stretch out my hand against it to cut off its food supply and send famine upon it and kill its men and their animals, even if these three men — Noah, Daniel and Job — were in it, they could save only themselves by their righteousness, declares the Sovereign LORD."
> —Ezekiel 14:13-14 (NIV)

After interpreting a dream for Nebuchadnezzar, the king promoted Daniel to a senior position. He continued to interact closely with king Nebuchadnezzar throughout his reign. Jewish tradition holds that Daniel looked after the king during his seven years of insanity. He had such an impact on Nebuchadnezzar that the king eventually published a personal testimony as a royal affidavit of his conversion, recognizing the God of the Jews as the one and only true God.

Several kings later, Daniel still served Babylon's ruler, though he had no interaction at all with Belshazzar, the co-regent under Nabonidus, until the final day of the Babylonian empire. The end of chapter 8 suggests that he was working in some capacity for Nabonidus.

HOW OLD WAS DANIEL?

Daniel never gives his age anywhere in his accounts.

His narrative covers a span of 73 years. He was certainly past his early childhood when taken captive by Nebuchadnezzar, though still in his teens.

Some scholars insist that he refers to himself and his companions as "children" in Daniel 1:4, but he was not a young child. Children do not have well developed physiques and most of chapter 1 deals with issues surrounding physical appearance, so it must be assumed that the exile took place while he was in his mid teens. This would make him nearly 90 years of age when his book comes to a close.

After the fall of Babylon to the Persians, Daniel so impressed the new king that he was groomed for the position of Prime Minister. This caused considerable political turmoil. A plot by his enemies succeeded in getting him marked for execution by having him thrown into a lions' den. God miraculously spared his life.

Tradition has it that Daniel died in the Persian city of Susa which would eventually become the capital city of the Persian empire. It is believed from language structure that Daniel completed his memoirs in 532BC.

His fluent use of both the Chaldean (Aramaic) and Hebrew languages are a testament to his intelligence and wisdom. He wrote his account in both languages.

The portion dealing with Gentile history was recorded in the Gentile language of the day, Aramaic, beginning and ending with nearly identical visions given first to Nebuchadnezzar and then to Daniel.

The portion dealing primarily with the Jews as the focal point was written in Hebrew, the language of the Jewish people.

BLENDING DIFFERENT CULTURES INTO ONE EMPIRE

The early empires often absorbed other cultures in short periods of time, resulting in a blending of national identities. This mixing of cultures created many complexities, making adherence to a strict legal code important in dealing with conflict. We will see this played out several times in the life of Daniel.

Shown above is a detail from the Code of Hammurabi. Written by an early king of the first Babylonian empire more than 1,000 years before the time of Nebuchadnezzar, its 3,600 lines of cuneiform writing are engraved on a pillar nearly 3 meters (9 feet) tall.

✏️ Application — My Notes & Bible Study Questions

03

THE SETTING
A DEVOUT NATION EXILED TO A PAGAN LAND

Taken from his home while just a young man, Daniel was thrust into a pagan culture 500 miles to the East. Babylon. The center of the Chaldean empire.

Babylon was vastly different from Jerusalem. Instead of an old, comfortable city with narrow winding streets, Daniel found himself in a metropolis that stretched as far as the eye could see with streets like modern-day highways, straight as an arrow.

The walls of Babylon were legendary, difficult to imagine even today. According to historian Herodotus, they towered 300 feet into the sky, the height of a 30-story building. More than 200 watchtowers along the length of the city wall extended even higher, some to 137 meters (450 feet).[1] Historians aren't sure if Herodotus actually saw the city, or relied on eyewitness accounts, because some numbers seem exaggerated. He described the walls as measuring 88 km (55 miles) in circumference. A description by Ctesias (quoted by Diodorus Siculus) put the circumference at 65 km (41 miles). In the early 1900's, German archeologist Robert Koldewey measured the excavations and found the wall to have a circumference of 17

BABYLON RECONSTRUCTED

For nearly 25 years, Saddam Hussein sponsored the archeological reconstruction of Babylon at a cost of more than $750 million. The project broke many rules of archeology by building over the original site, and was a fraction of its original scale.

Shown in the postcard above is part of Sadam's reconstruction of Babylon, including the Ishtar Gate. Nebuchadnezzar's palace was also rebuilt.

---

1   Herodotus, *The History,* Book 1: Clio

Insight

The site of the city of Babylon lay abandoned for two millennia, its magnificent bricks stolen (or recycled, depending on your perspective) over centuries by locals for house construction.

Shown below is the archeological site of Babylon as it looked before Saddam's reconstruction began. To the right is a photo taken in 1932, showing the still-prominent bas relief designs on the walls of the Ishtar Gate.

In 1902, German archeologist Robert Koldewey began a lengthy project to rebuild the Ishtar Gate, which now stands in a museum in Berlin. See chapter 16 for more images of Babylon.

km (11 miles).[2] This was certainly only a part of the original wall, because other cities were much larger than that. The Bible says Nineveh was so large that simply visiting the city required three full days.[3]

With Babylon straddling the Euphrates river, its outer wall rose up directly out of the water. There were actually two walls, with a deep moat between them. Any army that would have breached the first wall would then have to attack the second from inside the river. One of those two walls was wide enough to run chariot races four-abreast. Because of this incredible wall, the city was considered militarily unconquerable.

The Processional Way formed the main gateway into the city, leading to the Ishtar Gate. This road was as wide as a modern-day freeway, remarkable considering that the most sophisticated vehicle using it would have been a chariot. The impressive Ishtar Gate towered 12 meters (almost five stories) high, and was covered with Babylon's famous blue glazed bricks, adorned with 575 relief images of various animals, including the dragon god Marduk and the lion of Babylon.

The royal museum where Nebuchadnezzar kept artifacts from nations he had conquered was just outside the city walls, next to the famed 'hanging gardens of Babylon,' a masterpiece of engineering and one of the seven wonders of the ancient world. Not actually hanging, they were called that because the abundance of foliage overhanging each level of a series of massive waterproof terraces, according to ancient historian Diodorus.[4] Below the gardens, slaves turned giant pumps to bring irrigation from the river through three shafts up to the garden levels.

---

2   Reader's Digest Books, *The Last Two Million Years*
3   Jonah 3:3
4   Diodorus, *Geography*

In the center of the city was a ziggurat, or pyramid, said to be a partial reconstruction of the Tower of Babel. An inscription found at the base of the tower, signed by Nebuchadnezzar with his royal seal, declared that the tower was the most ancient monument of Babylon, and confirms the biblical story of the confusion of languages at the original construction of the Tower of Babel.[5]

> "Since a remote time, people had abandoned [this tower], without order expressing their words."
> —Inscription, Tower of Babel in Babylon

Centuries later, Alexander the Great briefly considered rebuilding the tower, but concluded that it would be too much work just to clean up the debris.

CHALDEAN RELIGIOUS PRACTICES

Throughout Babylon were temples. The largest honored the chief god of the empire, the horned dragon-shaped god named Marduk. Its image was seen everywhere. Many other gods were also honored, including gods related to the sun, the moon and the goddess of fertility (Ishtar). The people of Babylon regularly offered sacrifices to their favorite gods. Into this environment came Daniel and the thousands of other Jews, honoring not a plethora of gods but a single True God.

According to Herodotus, women were required to serve as temple prostitutes at least once in their lifetime.[6] During that time of service to the fertility goddess, they would not be allowed to leave the temple. The report claimed that attractive women would quickly finish their duty and go home within a few days but some women might be there for months. In general, however, women were treated quite respectfully for a male-dominated culture of that time period.

---

5   Grant Jeffrey, *Unveiling Mysteries of the Bible*
6   Herodotus, *The History*, Book 1: Clio

💡 Insight

Chaldean Empire 605-539BC

Assyrian Empire when conquered by the Chaldeans/Babylonians in 605BC.

Final size when overthrown by Persia 539BC.

THE SHRINKING EMPIRE

Babylon was already 1,000 years old when Nabopalassar conquered the Assyrians with his son, Nebuchadnezzar. Their Babylonian, or Chaldean, empire was large, but it never replaced the scale of the Assyrian empire. Shown above is a comparison of it's initial size, and what it looked like when the Persians took control some 70 years later. Under the weaker leadership of the kings who succeeded Nebuchadnezzar, it had lost much influence.

NEBUCHADNEZZAR, THE GREAT KING

The king of Babylon at the time Jerusalem was besieged was Nabopolassar. His son Nebuchadnezzar was a military general who had just swept away the remains of the huge Assyrian empire, though his father, who was quite ill, remained in Babylon. Assyria had been assisted by Egypt, and Egypt controlled Jerusalem, so Nebuchadnezzar now turned his attention on the Jews. As Jerusalem surrendered to him, he learned that his father had died and that he was now the king of the Chaldean empire.

NEBUCHADNEZZAR
This image of Nebuchadnezzar was originally the eye in a sculpture of the Babylonian god Marduk. Archeologists noticed that it contained an inscription referring to Nebuchadnezzar as "once the king of Marduk."

Most of what we know about Nebuchadnezzar comes from the Bible. We know that he had a huge ego like many other ancient kings, driven to impulsive decisions and quick to fly into a murderous rage. He couldn't stand being in a position where he was not completely in control. He would roast his officers over a slow fire when they displeased him. Scripture says he had two false Jewish prophets, Ahab son of Kolaiah and Zedekiah son of Maaseiah, roasted alive.[7] Like the Assyrians before him, he often treated the military officers of enemy nations with horrible cruelty, even having their skin removed from their backs.

After Judah's king Zedekiah rebelled against him, Nebuchadnezzar had Zedekiah's sons killed while forcing him to watch and then gouged out his eyes so the last thing the Jewish king saw was his family being executed.

---

7   Jeremiah 29:21-22

LANGUAGE AND CULTURE

Babylon was a trading center, a busy city, filled with travelers from around the world. It was an economic powerhouse. People took out loans in the form of goats or cattle and paid back with animals as well. Interest charges on loans ranged from 20-50%. Clay tablets discovered by archeologists, from a Chaldean firm named Murashu and Sons, are full of detailed business records including warranties on purchased goods.[8]

Spurred on by a letter of encouragement from Jeremiah, the Jewish people took advantage of the setting to become prosperous. It was a remarkably advanced economic climate. You could even buy insurance. But in the last years of Nabonidus, just before Babylon fell to the Persians, inflation had risen to 200% as a result of excessive spending by the kings who followed Nebuchadnezzar.[9]

The Chaldeans were one of the most sophisticated cultures in the ancient world. Their knowledge of astronomy, mathematics and physics was rich and detailed. Their interest in astronomy was not scientific, but tied to astrology, which was important to Babylon. Every change of planetary objects was recorded and compared to events happening on earth. These would then guide the king in his decisions when the same celestial conditions were repeated. There were many pagan arts related to fortune telling. Dreams were important to the Chaldeans and seen as messages from the gods.

The language was called Chaldean. Also known as Aramaic, Chaldean written letters of the alphabet were similar to Hebrew letters and placed on scrolls using ink.

---

8 Werner Keller, *The Bible as History*, Second Revised Edition
9 Robert Ingpen & Philip Wilkinson, *Encyclopedia of Mysterious Places*

Akkadian was another Babylonian language (today referred to as cuneiform writing), that involved triangular shapes drawn into clay tablets with a stylus. The clay would be baked to become a permanent document. A complex language, special education was required to learn Akkadian, and this formed some of the special training of Daniel and his Hebrew friends after they first arrived in Babylon.

The journey taken by the Israelites from Judah to Babylon was a long and arduous one covering about 1,000 miles through the trade route. Dry and dusty, they would have faced thirst and hunger. Many no doubt perished along the way. Arriving in Babylon would have seemed like entering an oasis. 70 years later, when they were released, most did not bother to make the trip back.

Daniel was taken captive to Babylon as the Chaldean empire took hold of the world stage, but to fully grasp his story it helps to step back and look at the events leading up to the Jewish exile.

In terms of history, the Babylonian or Chaldean Empire was one of a series of empires that intimately affected the Jewish people. The Babylonians burned down the temple and destroyed the city of Jerusalem. The Persians would help rebuild it. The Greek (or Macedonian) Empire would desecrate the temple and the Romans would destroy it a second time.

Most Bible scholars agree that Daniel was taken captive in 605BC, after Nebuchadnezzar's first siege of Jerusalem (three different events affecting the holy city culminated in the destruction of the city and temple 19 years later). The Jews were in Babylon for 70 years, eventually released by king Cyrus of Persia, who had been specifically named by Isaiah some 150 years earlier.

💡 Insight

Historical dates are usually difficult to pinpoint because there were no modern-style "year" references. Instead, all dates were measured against known events such as the throning of a king (i.e. "in the third year of Zedekiah"). To figure out what year an event took place, we must compare it to other events we know about.

Fortunately the Babylonians were pretty detailed in providing astronomical information that allows dates such as Nebuchadnezzar's regnal years to be very clearly understood.

Determining biblical dates is made even more challenging because the Jewish calendar is broken into two versions, the original month order and the religious calendar based on the re-ordering of months as God commanded at the time of the Exodus (the seventh month, Nisan, became the first month). If an account says an event happened in the 'first' month, we must determine if the writer was using the secular or religious calendar.

On top of that, different cultures had different ways of measuring events. Babylonians did not count the partial year in which a king gained his crown as a year of reign, while the Jews of Judah did. So the Jewish account would say in the "fourth year" of a king while the Babylonians would say it happened in the "third year" of that king. Babylonians and some other nations called the first year of a king his "year of ascension" or "the year he became king."

A DIVIDED KINGDOM CRUMBLES

After the civil war at the end of king David's life, the nation of Israel would never return to its former unified glory. Though the nation enjoyed great strength under Solomon, trouble brewed under the surface, leading to a civil revolt that eventually divided the kingdom into two parts.

The northern kingdom of Samaria, usually called **Israel**, was led by a series of evil kings, eventually falling to the Assyrians.

The southern kingdom of **Judah** also experienced its share of evil leaders, though not as many.

Mannasseh's lengthy and evil reign of terror was followed by Josiah's goodness. Mannasseh had plunged the nation into its lowest point of spiritual decay, turning the people away from God and silencing all voices of righteousness. It is said that he had the prophet Isaiah sawed in half. His son Josiah, though just a young boy, worked hard to turn the nation back towards God.

> "Josiah was eight years old when he became king, and he reigned in Jerusalem thirty-one years. He did what was pleasing in the LORD's sight and followed the example of his ancestor David. He did not turn aside from doing what was right." —2 Chronicles 34:1-2 (NIV)

Josiah's treasurer found the Book of the Law in the neglected temple. Josiah was shocked when he read the Law and saw how far the nation had fallen from God's commandments. It is possible he had no knowledge of the Law until this point.

> "When the king heard what was written in the law, he tore his clothes in despair." —2 Chronicles 34:19 (NIV)

Josiah recognized the seriousness of the penalties God was about to bring upon the nation. He asked if it could be averted. God said no, but affirmed He would delay it until Josiah's death.

> "I will not send the promised disaster against this city and its people until after you have died and been buried in peace. You will not see the disaster I am going to bring on this place." —2 Chronicles 34:28 (NIV)

But even Josiah failed in his faith when he went against pharaoh Neco at Carcemish on the Euphrates river while Neco was battling general Nebuchadnezzar of Babylon. Neco sent him a message declaring that God had given him this mission, but Josiah refused to believe this and continued fighting anyway, disguising himself in battle on the plain of Megiddo.[10]

God punished him for his disobedience. Josiah was fatally wounded in the battle. He died in Jerusalem.

The people crowned Josiah's younger son Jehoahaz as his successor instead of the rightful son, possibly because of strong anti-Egyptian feelings. Egypt controlled Jerusalem, and it was felt that the older son was too friendly towards Egypt. Yet within weeks the nation would lose control over its throne, forced to adapt a vassal king appointed by the conquering nation.

Jehoahaz was deposed by pharaoh Neco after three months and taken to Egypt as a prisoner. Eliakim, his older brother, was made vassal king instead, and Neco changed Eliakim's name to Jehoiakim. Jehoiakim would reign eleven years.

GOD'S PROMISSORY NOTE

God had previously commanded that the land was to enjoy a year of rest every seventh year, a **Sabbath of the land**. During that year you could pick food for individual consumption but you were not to harvest the land or cultivate the fields.

---

10   2 Chronicles 35:21-22

God said that if the Jews failed to give the land this rest, He would force the land to have the rest He had called for by removing the people who lived upon it. For 490 years the land had not received its Sabbath years. 70 years were owed to God and He was about to claim them.[11]

> The LORD said to Moses on Mount Sinai, "Speak to the Israelites and say to them: 'When you enter the land I am going to give you, the land itself must observe a sabbath to the LORD. For six years sow your fields, and for six years prune your vineyards and gather their crops. But in the seventh year the land is to have a sabbath of rest, a sabbath to the LORD. Do not sow your fields or prune your vineyards. Do not reap what grows of itself or harvest the grapes of your untended vines. The land is to have a year of rest." —Leviticus 25:1-5 (NIV)

JUDGEMENT FALLS

When the battle of Carcemish was finished, Nebuchadnezzar came to Jerusalem. After a brief siege, Jehoiakim surrendered and was put in bronze chains to be taken to Babylon. Nebuchadnezzar heard about his father's death and changed his mind about Jehoiakim, installing him back on the throne as a vassal king for the next seven years as he rushed back to take the throne of Babylon before civil unrest set in back home. Daniel was taken at this time.

Five years later, in 600BC, Jehoiakim rebelled against Nebuchadnezzar, possibly believing that Neco would win another battle against the Babylonian king. Jeremiah warned him that this was foolish, but the king of Judah refused to listen to the prophet, and even called for him to be arrested.[12] He burned the scrolls of Jeremiah and listened to the advice of his false prophets instead, who claimed that Nebuchadnezzar would leave him alone.

---

11 Leviticus 25-26
12 Jeremiah 36:26

> "Whenever Jehudi had read three or four columns of the scroll, the king cut them off with a scribe's knife and threw them into the fire pot, until the entire scroll was burned in the fire. The king and all his attendants who heard all these words showed no fear, nor did they tear their clothes."
> —Jeremiah 36:23-24 (NIV)

They were wrong about their predictions. Jeremiah had been right. Nebuchadnezzar was not about to stand for rebellion by a vassal king, and acted swiftly to set things straight. He marched on Judah in the month of Kislev (December), to lay siege against it.[13]

THE ROYAL LINE OF DAVID ENDS

Jehoiakim died during Nebuchadnezzar's siege. Now Jehoiachin, the son of Jehoiakim was made king. He is also called *Jekoniah* and *Coniah* in different books of the Bible. His reign would be just three months and ten days.

Though his reign was short, he was filled with evil. His emphasis on idol worship and evil deeds was so severe that God pronounced a blood curse on the line of Jehoiachin, declaring that none of his descendants would ever sit on the throne of David.

God said He would treat this man, this direct royal descendant of the line of David, as if he were childless!

> "As surely as I live," declares the LORD, "even if you, Jehoiachin son of Jehoiakim king of Judah, were a signet ring on My right hand, I would still pull you off. I will hand you over to those who seek your life, those you fear — to Nebuchadnezzar king of Babylon and to the Babylonians. I will hurl you and the mother who gave you birth into another country, where neither of you was born, and there you both will die. You will never come back to the land you long to return to."

---

13 Date confirmed by the *Babylonian Chronicles*, cuneiform tablets now in the British Museum

> This is what the LORD says: "Record this man as if childless, a man who will not prosper in his lifetime, for none of his offspring will prosper, none will sit on the throne of David or rule anymore in Judah."
> — Jeremiah 22:24-30 (NIV)

This was significant, because the promised Messiah was to come from that same royal line, and it was long recognized that He would take the throne of David. How could God proclaim a physical end to the royal line of David and still fulfill His prophetic promise to put the Messiah on David's throne?

Compare Matthew's genealogy (of Jesus) through Joseph to Luke's genealogy through Mary. Both come from the line of David, both grant a proper title to Jesus, yet they manage to avoid the blood curse placed on Jehoiachin.

Matthew's genealogy goes through Jehoiachin and ends with Joseph. Though the father of Jesus, he is not His *birth* father. Thus Jesus inherits the right to the throne through His father's genealogy without being blemished by the blood curse.

Luke's genealogy goes to David and then turns off slightly to move through Nathan rather than Solomon, ending up with Mary, the birth mother of Jesus. Thus both parents came from the line of king David, just as God promised. Jesus received the legal right to the throne through His earthly father, but His blood is untouched by the curse on the line of Jehoiachin.

On the second day of the month of Adar (March 16, 597BC)[14], Nebuchadnezzar captured Jerusalem, bound Jehoiachin in chains and led him away as a captive, along with more of the treasures from the Temple.

Jehoiachin was brought to Babylon and kept there as prisoner for 37 years. He was released on the 27th day of the 12th month and

---

14   Date confirmed by the *Babylonian Chronicles*, cuneiform tablets now in the British Museum

enjoyed dining at the Babylonian king's table for the rest of his life, but as prophesied he never returned to Israel.

Nebuchadnezzar installed Jehoiachin's uncle Mattaniah as king, making him swear an oath of loyalty and changing his name to Zedekiah. At this time the Babylonians took many treasures from the temple, along with 18,000 more captives, including Ezekiel.[15]

Zedekiah reigned eleven years. In his fourth year, he was summoned by Nebuchadnezzar, possibly to check on his loyalty.

At that time, the prophet Jeremiah sent a letter of encouragement to the captives, telling them they would stay in Babylon for 70 years. He encouraged them to make the most of their time in that foreign culture.

ZEDEKIAH REBELS

In his ninth year, Zedekiah rebelled against Nebuchadnezzar and was besieged for 2-1/2 years. During this time, the prophet Jeremiah was put in prison as a suspected deserter.[16]

THE CONTRADICTORY PROPHECIES

Two prophecies were given to king Zedekiah that appeared, at first glance, to be contradictions.

He was told that he would never see his homeland again. At the same time, he was told he would be taken to Babylon, yet never see it. God told him that he would die in Babylon.

"Even Zedekiah will leave Jerusalem at night through a hole in the wall, taking only what he can carry with him. He will cover his face, and his eyes will never see his homeland again. Then I will spread out My net and capture him in My snare. I will bring him to Babylon, the land of the Babylonians, though he will never see it, and he will die there. I will scatter his servants and guards to the four winds and send the sword after them."
—Ezekiel 12:12-14 (NIV)

The fulfillment of this prophecy, and of Jeremiah's prophecy that he would be carried captive to Babylon, are described in several places, but the most detailed is in Jeremiah 39.

---

15   2 Kings 24:14-16
16   Jeremiah 37:14-15

Ezekiel was given an interesting prophecy about Zedekiah in which he declared that the king would never see his homeland again, would be taken to Babylon but would not see it, and would die there. Jeremiah had also prophesied that Zedekiah would be taken captive to Babylon.

As the siege of Jerusalem came to an end and the Babylonians entered the city, God's judgement upon the nation came to a close. This represented the third and final Babylonian captivity.

On the ninth day of the Jewish month of Av in the year 587BC, general Nebuzaradan plundered the holy temple and the palace, then set fire to both.

> "And on the ninth day of the fourth month of Zedekiah's eleventh year, the city wall was broken through. Then all the officials of the king of Babylon came and took seats in the Middle Gate: Nergal-sharezer of Samgar, Nebo-sarsekim a chief officer, Nergal-sharezer a high official and all the other officials of the king of Babylon.
>
> When Zedekiah king of Judah and all the soldiers saw them, they fled; they left the city at night by way of the king's garden, through the gate between the two walls, and headed toward the Arabah.
>
> But the Babylonian army pursued them and overtook Zedekiah in the plains of Jericho. They captured him and took him to Nebuchadnezzar king of Babylon at Riblah in the land of Hamath, where he pronounced sentence on him.
>
> There at Riblah the king of Babylon slaughtered the sons of Zedekiah before his eyes and also killed all the nobles of Judah. Then he put out Zedekiah's eyes and bound him with bronze shackles to take him to Babylon.
>
> The Babylonians set fire to the royal palace and the houses of the people and broke down the walls of Jerusalem. Nebuzaradan commander of the imperial guard carried into exile to Babylon the people who remained in the city, along

with those who had gone over to him, and the rest of the people." — Jeremiah 39:2-9 (NIV)

Judgement day had come to Jerusalem. Zedekiah escaped through a hole in the wall, racing towards the Jordan river in hopes of reaching the desert.

At daybreak, the Babylonians overtook him near Jericho. They brought Zedekiah and his family before Nebuchadnezzar at his headquarters in Riblah, a city to the north. He denounced the Jewish king as a traitor and an ungrateful wretch.

While Zedekiah was forced to watch, Nebuchadnezzar executed his sons, then his eyes were gouged out with a spear. He was bound in bronze shackles and taken prisoner to Babylon, where he was presumably put on public display before being executed.

Some 470 years after it was built with such care and joy by Solomon and his people, the temple lay a smoldering wreck, devoid of hope, glory, or people to worship within its walls.

Although Daniel had already lived in Babylon for 19 years when the temple was destroyed, this is a fitting place to begin our study of the incredible book of Daniel.

THE LION OF BABYLON
A prominent symbol of Babylon, related to the goddess Ishtar, was a lion. Pictures of the Lion of Babylon graced the gates of the city. The lion was a symbol that had also been used prominently in the Assyrian empire. Even in modern times, the lion appears on Iraqi currency (below).

THE OMINOUS DAY

The destruction of the first temple took place on the ninth day of the month Av, known as **Tisha B' Av**.

This day, which usually falls in late July or early August on the secular calendar, has ominous relevance in Jewish culture, because of the many disasters that have fallen upon the Jewish people on that day throughout history. Even the prophet Zechariah referred to it as a day of mourning.[13]

The day has its origins as the day on which the Hebrew spies returned from the Promised Land with their report. Except for Caleb and Joshua, they gave a negative report striking fear into the hearts of the people.

- The first temple, built by Solomon, was destroyed on this date in 587BC.

- The second temple, built by Herod, was destroyed on this date in AD70.

- Simon Bar Cochba's army was decimated by the Romans on that day in AD135, and its flagship city, Betar, was destroyed.

- In AD136, Jerusalem itself was burned, the Temple area plowed, and the fate of the Jews sealed for millennia.

- England expelled all Jews on that day in 1290.

- It was the day on which the Spanish Inquisition was launched, when King Ferdinand of Spain signed the Alhambra Decree expelling 800,000 Jews in 1492.

- Russia unleashed persecutions against the Jews after WWI was declared on that same date in 1914.[24]

---

13   Zechariah 7:5
14   Grant R. Jeffrey, *Unveiling Mysteries of the Bible*

Application — My Notes & Bible Study Questions

PART 2
The Narratives

04

DANIEL CHAPTER 1
EXILED TO BABYLON

As the book of Daniel opens, we see how this young man of faith deals with the first challenges of his new pagan environment. His example is one that should be an inspiration to all of us.

Nebuchadnezzar, the son of Nabopolassar the king and at this time the military general of Babylon, has just defeated the Assyrians and sent the Egyptians retreating. A ruler of immense power, he now turns his attention on Jerusalem.

Daniel 2:38 says that the beasts of the fields and the birds of the air were under his command. Jeremiah also records that God called Nebuchadnezzar, the king of a hostile pagan nation, *His servant* and gave command of the wild animals to this king.

> "Now I will give your countries to King Nebuchadnezzar of Babylon, who is My servant. I have put everything, even the wild animals, under his control."
> —Jeremiah 27:6 (NLT)

We don't know how much awareness Nebuchadnezzar had of his power over wild beasts, but we do know that he had a blazing temper and a massive ego. His officers were terrified of disappointing him in any way. In these early chapters of Daniel we see the impact of his character flaws.

Daniel, on the other hand, is a sharp contrast to the impulsive arrogance of the king. He is steadfast, trustworthy, humble and completely committed to a power greater than himself: the God of the Hebrews. Despite the turmoil and upheaval of the actions that brought these Jews of noble background into Babylon hundreds of miles from home, Daniel is determined to follow God. He refuses to lose his focus or be distracted by events. He remains consistent in his commitment to his faith.

DANIEL 1:1

> 1 In the third year of the reign of Jehoiakim king of Judah, Nebuchadnezzar king of Babylon came to Jerusalem and besieged it.

The Babylonians measured a king's reign from the first full year, beginning with the start of the year. The partial year prior to that is called *the year of ascension* or *the year he became king*.

The Jews (those of the southern kingdom of Judah) measured a king's reign from the day he became king. This explains why Daniel (writing from Babylon) says it was the third year of Jehoiakim when Jeremiah says it was in the fourth year of Jehoiakim.

DANIEL 1:2

> 2 And the Lord gave Jehoiakim king of Judah into his hand, with some of the vessels of the house of God. He carried them into the land of Shinar [Babylon] to the house of his god and he took the vessels to the treasure house of his god.

The Babylonians invaded Jerusalem three different times. This was the first event, which took place in 605BC, following the Battle of Carcemish, where Nebuchadnezzar defeated the Egyptians.

When a king would conquer a nation, it was common practice to take the most sacred things from that country to his own land and place them in the temple of his gods. This was a visible symbol of power and control over the conquered people group. Nebuchadnezzar's *treasure house of his god* was a museum just outside the city walls near the Ishtar Gate in Babylon.

The Babylonians honored many gods. The names of their gods were associated with people's names, street names, and many other names throughout the culture.

The chief god of Babylon was Marduk, a dragon-shaped god with horns. There were others treated with almost equal reverence, including Ishtar, the goddess of fertility. The worship of Ishtar began long before the Chaldean empire and continued for hundreds of years afterwards. It was eventually transformed into the Christian celebration of Easter[1] by Roman emperor Constantine in an effort to eradicate pagan worship. Ancient myths claimed that Ishtar, in an earlier form known as Semiramis, came to earth in a giant egg which fell from the moon into the Euphrates river, explaining why eggs are part of the symbolism associated with Easter.

From the beginning, Daniel goes out of his way to make it clear that God is the one who calls the shots in life. He attributes the power of kings, a person's intelligence, wisdom, or the ability to interpret dreams, entirely to God. He gives God credit for everything, even the loss of Jehoiakim's kingdom.

The temple objects taken will play a role in the final destruction of Babylon many years later, when co-regent Belshazzar calls for them as part of a defiant party.

DANIEL 1:3-5

> 3 And the king spoke to Ashpenaz the master of his eunuchs, that he should bring in some of the sons of Israel, of the royal line and of the nobles;
>
> 4 youths in whom was no blemish, but handsome, skillful in all wisdom, having knowledge and understanding science, young men who had the ability to stand in the king's palace; and that he should teach them the knowledge and language of the Chaldeans.
>
> 5 And the king appointed for them a daily portion of the king's food, and of the wine which he drank. He ordered that they should be nourished three years, and that at the end of the three years they should be presented before the king.

---

1   *Encyclopedia Britannica, 1934 edition*

Some scholars interpret the reference to sons as **children**, which is accurate enough if you don't assume they are *young* children. It is clear from the emphasis on this passage that physical attributes play a large role in this selection process. Young children do not have well-developed physiques.

Ashpenaz, the chief of the royal officials, was charged with selecting, training and nourishing the candidates. Punishment for failure was harsh, so these officers took their responsibilities very seriously.

The Hebrew word **saris** is translated by some Bibles as **eunuch** (the NIV more accurately interprets this as *chief of the court officials*). Eunuch does not necessarily mean a castrated male as we commonly use that term (which came from the Greek). Joseph's boss Potiphar was also a *saris* and he was married, so he was not a eunuch as we generally think of that term. The word actually refers to an officer of the palace, though some, like those working in the harem, would be castrated to ensure that they were not tempted.

A HISTORY OF WINGED GODS

The Assyrian Empire that preceded Nabopolassar's Chaldean empire had many symbols of animals with wings, often with human faces. This winged bull, or Lamassu, from the time of Sargon II (now located in the Louvre) guarded an Assyrian king's tomb.

A similar image of a regal winged lion was adopted by Nebuchadnezzar as a symbol of Babylon. It played prominently throughout the culture and was used as the metaphor for the Chaldean Empire in the vision given to Daniel recorded in Chapter 8.

It should not be assumed that these young men actually ate *at* the king's table, though some Bibles do use that wording. The phrase simply means that they ate food which came from the royal storehouse, which was paid for from the king's budget.

Daniel and his friends would be learning the Akkadian language (cuneiform script) as well as some of the detailed scientific knowledge that had made the Chaldean empire so highly respected in that culture. Babylon was famous for its study of astronomy. Its "wise men" used the study of celestial objects to attempt to predict events on earth. According to historian Diodorus of Sicily, a room some 90 meters (about 300 feet) high at the top of the reconstructed Tower of Babel in the center of the city was an observatory for astrologers[2] (although Herodotus claimed it was used for fertility rites).

It should never be assumed that Daniel accepted or followed magical arts or other pagan practices, as we know from his character that he would never have allowed himself to fall into paganism. This perception (that Daniel engaged in pagan arts of astrology) comes from a common misunderstanding of the origin of the word **magi** or **magician**. The word interpreted **magicians** in some Bibles comes from the root word for the instrument used to create the complex Akkadian cuneiform wedge-shaped script.

RENAMING THE HEBREWS

The Babylonian names given to Daniel and his friends were distortions of their Hebrew names, inserting the name of Babylonian gods.

HEBREW NAMES

Daniel: "God is my judge"

Hananiah: "Yahweh has been gracious"

Mishael: "Who is like God?"

Azariah: "the LORD has helped"

BABYLONIAN NAMES

Belteshazzar: "may Bel protect his life"

Shadrach: "command of Aku" (lunar god)

Meshach: "Who is like Aku?"

Abednego: "servant of Nebo"

---

2   Reader's Digest Books, *Vanished Civilizations*

Daniel could certainly have learned about pagan practices without being involved in applying them, just as Christians may learn about other religious beliefs without accepting them as valid.

DANIEL 1:6-7

> 6 Now among these were, of the sons of Judah, Daniel, Hananiah, Mishael, and Azariah.
>
> 7 And the prince of the eunuchs gave new names to them: to Daniel he gave the name of Belteshazzar; to Hananiah, the name of Shadrach; to Mishael, he gave the name of Meshach; and to Azariah, the name of Abednego.

It was common practice to give new names to captives as a final sign of domination over them.

Imagine that your nation has just been subdued by a hostile force and you've been taken captive. The only thing you have left is your name. Taking that from you is designed to strip you of any remaining allegiance to your former citizenship or nationalistic association. In the case of Daniel and his friends, their Hebrew meanings were distorted to reflect the gods of the Babylonians instead of their previous relation to Jehovah, the God of the Jews.

DANIEL 1:8

> 8 But Daniel purposed in his heart that he would not defile himself with the king's food, nor with the wine which he drank: therefore he requested of the prince of the eunuchs that he might not defile himself in this way.

Jews were required to follow strict dietary laws (see Leviticus 11, Deuteronomy 14). Orthodox Jews classify wine as forbidden unless it has been prepared by Jews, so this may be why it's included in Daniel's list of concerns. But it could be that the bigger issue was food served being offered to idols prior to being brought in for consumption.

DANIEL 1:9

> 9 Now God caused the prince of the eunuchs to find kindness and compassion towards Daniel.

Daniel always gave the credit to God. He indicated that it was God who granted favor to Daniel in his relationship with the guards, not Daniel's personal charm or wisdom.

DANIEL 1:10

> 10 And the prince of the eunuchs said to Daniel, "I fear my lord the king, who has appointed your food and your drink. Why should he see your faces worse looking than the other youths that are your age? The king would then have my head because of you."

Ashpenaz's concern over the men's physical appearance gives interesting insight. The interview with the king was still a long ways off, but the guards were worried that there wasn't enough time to correct what they thought could be a problem of appearance. Did the king come by at times to check on them?

DANIEL 1:11-13

> 11 Then Daniel said to the steward whom the prince of the eunuchs had appointed over Daniel, Hananiah, Mishael, and Azariah:
>
> 12 "Test your servants, I ask you, for ten days. Let them give us vegetables to eat and water to drink.
>
> 13 Then look upon us, and compare our appearance to that of the youths that eat of the king's delicacies; and as you see fit, deal with your servants."

Daniel offered a test for ten days, allowing the steward in charge to draw his own conclusion. He would then accept whatever decision was made at that time. Not only did this demonstrate enormous faith in God, it reflects wisdom and grace.

As a devout Jew, Daniel was not a vegetarian. But the vegetarian diet he suggested is similar to what modern bodybuilding competitors use to make muscles more prominent.

DANIEL 1:14-16

> 14 So he agreed to this, and tested them ten days.
>
> 15 At the end of ten days their appearance was better, and they looked more physically developed, than all the youths that ate the king's food.
>
> 16 So the steward took away their food, and the wine that they should drink, and gave them vegetables.

This passage is often misunderstood because of less-than-ideal translations. Some English Bibles interpret the Hebrew word **bawri** as *fatter* which is a poor translation. The word refers to increased appearance of flesh, but doesn't necessarily mean fat. *Bawri* can just as accurately be interpreted as *more physically developed* or *more muscular*. While verse 10 does refer to faces, the Babylonians were primarily interested in physique; they wanted these teens to look muscular and powerful. In this context, the word means that the young men had the appearance of being more muscular, a common result of reduced water retention following a diet of this type. It's a healthy diet used by many people, including fitness competitors and body builders, for exactly that reason.

DANIEL 1:17

> 17 Now as for these four young men, God gave them knowledge and skill in all learning and wisdom. And Daniel had understanding of visions and dreams.

Notice again how Daniel attributed any skill, knowledge or wisdom he has to God. They were not the result of human effort.

The passage tells us that Daniel had *understanding of visions and dreams*, showing a pattern of dealing with such issues. Dreams were important in that culture, so this was a valuable skill.

DANIEL 1:18-20

> **18** At the end of the days which the king had appointed for bringing them in, the prince of the palace staff brought them before Nebuchadnezzar.
>
> **19** The king talked with them; and among them all were found none like Daniel, Hananiah, Mishael, and Azariah: therefore they were brought before the king to serve him.
>
> **20** And in every area of wisdom and understanding which the king questioned them, he found them ten times better than all the magicians and enchanters in his entire realm.

The end of the time set by the king for "bringing them in" would be, based on the context of the passage, the end of the full three years of the training program, since we were told earlier that they were to be presented to the king at the *end* of three years.

This interview must have taken place before the events of chapter 2 were completed, because Daniel is promoted at the end of that chapter to a senior position. The narrative of chapter 2 specifically places those events in Nebuchadnezzar's second year, which would be in the third year after he was crowned king, since Babylonian reckoning of a king's reign did not count the first year.

Verse 19 refers to the men *entering* or *beginning* their service to the king. The text says they were "brought before the king" in a separate event to begin their service. This may have involved a formal ceremony. In the next chapter, we'll see that Daniel is not among the wise men called before the king when he has his dreams, but Daniel is included among the wise men when the king decrees that they are all to be executed.

THE DANGEROUS AFFIRMATION

The king finds them **ten times better** than all the other wise men in the country. This is an interesting insight into Nebuchadnezzar's impulsive nature and tendency to exaggerate.

Obviously God had made these men vastly superior to others in the empire, but consider the magnitude of this statement. Ten times represents a one thousand percent increase. For the king to name these young foreign captives from Judah — essentially slaves — as being 1,000% 'better' than all the learned men in the empire, was an exceptionally bold thing to say.

Something about these young men made a spectacular impact on the king. Was it just their intelligence? Hardly. Scripture refers to "wisdom and understanding" but no doubt the impression went much deeper into their character. Leaders hold virtue and incorruptibility in the highest regard. Their integrity must have been so clearly superior to everyone else that they stood out dramatically.

What impact does your life make on those around you? Is your character of the highest quality? If you have diluted your impact through poor choices, make a decision now to put God first in all things. He will honor you, though it may not be easy.

The king's impulsive affirmation of Daniel and his friends would, unfortunately, prove to become a source of jealousy and hatred that would follow these four through their entire careers of service to the king. We will see more of Nebuchadnezzar's impulsive nature in the next few chapters.

DANIEL 1:21

> 21 **And Daniel continued there until the first year of King Cyrus.**

The final verse of Chapter 1 indicates Daniel's term of service. He would serve the entire remaining period of the 70-year Babylonian captivity, since the captives were released from Babylon in the first year of the reign of Cyrus.

Brought to Babylon as a teenager and beginning his service sometime later, this would make his age somewhere in the 80's by the time he retired.

Application — My Notes & Bible Study Questions

05

DANIEL CHAPTER 2
THE MAN OF METAL

Daniel's account gives us a fascinating glimpse into God's sovereignty. God has granted Nebuchadnezzar incredible power and majesty so that even the wild animals and birds of the air were under his control, yet the king was powerless over a simple dream, because he was unable to understand what it means.

In this chapter we see a sharp contrast between the king's response to his dilemma and that of Daniel when told he would be executed. The king turns to his own resources and brute strength in an effort to solve his problem, while Daniel turns immediately to God in an attitude of humility and peace.

DANIEL 2:1-3

> 1 In the second year of the reign of Nebuchadnezzar, the king dreamed dreams, and his spirit was troubled, and his sleep went from him.
>
> 2 Then the king commanded to have the magicians, astrologers, sorcerers and Chaldeans called to show the king his dreams. So they came and stood before the king.
>
> 3 And the king said to them, I have dreamed a dream, and my spirit was troubled to know the meaning of the dream.

Nebuchadnezzar's *second year* of reign was actually the third since his crowning, because Babylonians did not count the year he became king. It is possible that when these events began, Daniel had not yet completed his three-year training program. Daniel is not included among the wise men who are called before the king. However, not much later we see that he's included among the wise men affected. Since he's promoted to a senior position at the end of this narrative, the training program is certainly finished by the time the story plays itself out.

Dreams were important to people of the Chaldean Empire, and still are today throughout the Middle Eastern world. People in those cultures have long considered dreams to be messages from the gods.

The plurality of the word *dreams* in verse 1 suggests that the same dream was repeated over several nights, which would have indeed troubled the king greatly, since he could not understand what he was seeing.

DANIEL 2:4-6

> 4 **Then the Chaldeans said to the king in Aramaic, "O king, live forever! Tell your servants the dream, and we will show the meaning."**
>
> 5 **The king answered and said to the Chaldeans, "The word from me is certain: if you will not make known to me the dream, with the meaning of it, you will be torn into limbs, and your houses will be made a dunghill.**
>
> 6 **But if you describe the dream, and the meaning of it, you will receive of me gifts and rewards and great honour. Therefore show me the dream, and the interpretation of it."**

WISE MEN, OR JUST WISE GUYS?

The Chaldeans enjoyed a long-established emphasis on science, especially in the area of astronomy. Wise men constantly watched the heavens and recorded every observation to help interpret potential announcements and requirements of the many gods they served. Assyrian tablets have been discovered describing such things as the lunar eclipse in great detail.

There is little doubt that these "wise men" had also built a strong political hierarchy that acted as an alternative power base to that of the king himself. These men could very quickly usurp the throne of a weak or inept king.

From this point through the end of chapter 7, Daniel changes from the Hebrew language to the Gentile language of the day, Aramaic. This uses the same characters as Hebrew, just as Spanish uses the same characters as English. Chapters 2 through 7 deal primarily with Gentile history, while chapters 1, and 8 through 12, deal primarily with Jewish issues and are thus written in Hebrew. Chapter 4 is not only written in Aramaic but is written by a Gentile!

The term *live forever* was an early version of our modern-day greeting, *long live the king*. It didn't literally refer to an immortal life but was meant to honor the length or scope of the kingdom the king has established or represents.

Some English Bibles interpret verse 5 as *cut into pieces*. There is no actual reference to cutting instruments. The proper interpretation is *torn into limbs*. This may have referred to a form of ancient torture in which the victim was tied to four trees bent towards each other, then the binding was cut so they sprang apart and literally tore the body into parts. Of course, it may have meant taking off body parts, which was also a common ancient practice.[1]

The phrase *the thing is gone from me* appears in the King James translation in verse 5. That can be incorrectly understood to mean that the king had forgotten. That's not what Daniel meant. The Aramaic says something more like *the word has gone forth from me* or *the word from me is [assured or certain]*, indicating that Nebuchadnezzar was referring to his own words as a command of authority.

It was still early in the king's reign. Nebuchadnezzar had inherited these advisors from his father. He probably disliked them and saw them as little more than con artists. Chances are that, as a crown prince, he had seen much corruption in their ranks. His unreasonable challenge was an opportunity to prove them as fakes and get rid of them. What a way to trim the royal payroll!

---

1 Erika Bleibtreu, *Biblical Archeology Review: Grisly Assyrian Record of Torture and Death*

DANIEL 2:7-9

> 7 They answered again and said, "Let the king tell his servants the dream, and we will explain the meaning of it."
>
> 8 The king answered, "I know with certainty that you are only trying to gain time [because you see my word is gone forth from me].
>
> 9 But if you will not make known to me the dream, there is but one decree for you, for you have prepared lying and corrupt words to speak before me, hoping to delay things. Therefore tell me the dream, and I will know that you can show me the meaning of it."

Notice that the king accused them of a conspiracy. Clearly there was more to what they claimed than we see in the text. They've obviously told him in the past that they were capable of things such as knowing what someone has dreamed. Perhaps even when first assigning their jobs, the king tested them by asking if they had such powers. Whatever the history, they placed their feet firmly in their mouths and were about to pay the ultimate penalty.

Again the KJV Bible oddly interprets the king's reference to his own word of authority as *you see the thing is gone from me* which is quite a different meaning if one reads it as meaning that the king had forgotten the dream. That's not what is meant here.

DANIEL 2:10-11

> 10 The Chaldeans answered the king, and said, "There is not a man upon the earth who can show the king's matter. Therefore there is no king, lord, nor ruler, that asked such things of any magician, or astrologer, or Chaldean.
>
> 11 And it is a rare thing that the king requires, and there is no one else who can show it before the king, except the gods, and they don't live among men."

These men had no idea how true their statement was. Although they may have been quite devout, there was no basis on which to have a deep conviction of faith in their gods. They were just trying to save their skins. Yet what they said — that only God can reveal such things — was true and Daniel was now going to bring that truth into the light.

DANIEL 2:12

> 12 **This made the king angry and extremely furious, and he commanded to have all the wise men of Babylon destroyed.**

Why was the king's anger so aroused by their statement? At first glance, what they said doesn't seem like something that should upset him so much.

These men were suggesting he was not connected to the gods of the Babylonians. Their words were an insult to the king, because his role was traditionally seen as that of a servant managing the affairs of the gods on earth. He was *supposed* to be in touch with the gods! Their statement showed a lack of respect for his position.

Notice how impulsive Nebuchadnezzar is. When he has a problem, he resorts to brute strength to solve it. His rash solution would not actually solve his problem in any way. The only issue it does solve is to reduce the royal budget and rid him of corrupt advisors. Killing them won't explain the dream.

Until now, things have been unexpectedly comfortable for Daniel as an exile — a captive slave — living in a pagan land. But now he faces a true test of both his faith and his character. It is likely that this was a spiritual battle designed to remove him from the influence he will ultimately have over millions of lives to come.

At some point in your life, you've probably been on the receiving end of unfairness. But chances are, it didn't put your life at risk! Imagine how you would respond if you suddenly learned that you were placed on death row not for anything you did, but just because someone else had a temper tantrum. Think about your thoughts, your actions, the emotional upheaval as you would struggle to understand the purpose in such a bizarre situation.

It is during such times that our faith in God, our maturity in understanding the spiritual battle raging unseen around us, and the true depth of our character, are fully tested.

DANIEL 2:13-16

> 13 The decree went out that the wise men should be executed; and the officers of the king sought Daniel and his friends to be executed.
>
> 14 Then Daniel spoke with wisdom and tact to Arioch the captain of the king's guard, who had come to kill the wise men of Babylon.
>
> 15 He said to Arioch the king's captain, "Why is the decree so quick from the king?" Then Arioch explained everything to Daniel.
>
> 16 Then Daniel went in, and requested of the king that he would give him time, and that he would show the king the interpretation.

Daniel was unaware of the reason for the decree, showing that he was not included among the wise men who had been called before the king. This suggests that his three-year training program was not yet complete, though the timing must have been near the end of the training.

Note Daniel's response to news that he was headed for execution. He spoke with **wisdom and tact**, noticeably opposite to Nebuchadnezzar's response to a problem, and very different from the response the wise men had.

Daniel was able to speak personally to the king. This shows that the men he reported to trusted him. His ability to meet with the king might be the result of the favorable interview from chapter 1.

DANIEL 2:17-18

> **17** Then Daniel went to his house, and made the thing known to Hananiah, Mishael, and Azariah, his companions:
>
> **18** That they would seek mercies of the God of heaven concerning this secret; that Daniel and his friends should not perish with the rest of the wise men of Babylon.

Daniel's first action after speaking to the king was to call his friends and hold a prayer meeting. Sure, they were under pressure beyond their ability to fix, which usually brings people to their knees. But their prayerful response demonstrates their genuine faith in God. Daniel had been confident enough that God would provide an answer that he had personally met with the king asking for time.

DANIEL 2:19-23

> **19** Then was the secret revealed to Daniel in a night vision. Then Daniel blessed the God of heaven.
>
> **20** Daniel answered and said, "Blessed be the name of God for ever and ever: for wisdom and might are His.
>
> **21** He changes the times and the seasons. He removes kings, and sets up kings. He gives wisdom to the wise, and knowledge to those that have understanding.
>
> **22** He reveals the deep and secret things. He knows what is in the darkness, and the light dwells with Him.
>
> **23** I thank You, and praise You, O God of my fathers, who has given me wisdom and strength, and have made known to me now what we asked of You, for You have now made known to us the king's matter."

Daniel praised God for three characteristics: His **eternal existence**, His **wisdom** and His **power**. God is recognized as the source of all wisdom and the source of all power.

The essence of Daniel's prayer is prophecy and its interpretation. He recognized in the revelation of the king's dream and its message that God uses prophecy to prove that He is God, since only God Himself can tell the future. Prophecy is one of the primary reasons for the existence of the Bible. 27% of all Scripture verses are prophecy! This dream was only one of many visions and prophecies Daniel would receive in his lifetime.

DANIEL 2:24-25

> 24 **Therefore Daniel went in to see Arioch, whom the king had authorized to destroy the wise men of Babylon. He said to him, "Do not execute the wise men of Babylon: bring me in before the king, and I will show the king the meaning of his dream."**
>
> 25 **Then Arioch quickly brought Daniel before the king, and said to him, "I have found a man among the captives of Judah, who will make known to the king the meaning of his dream."**

COOL UNDER FIRE

We hear lots of stories of soldiers, police officers, pilots and others who remain cool under fire. These are usually people trained to handle dangerous situations.

Normally when an untrained person is placed in a high-stress situation they become unglued. If you were suddenly told that you would be executed for no reason, would you just calmly ask "why did the authorities issue such a harsh decree?"

How *would* you respond?

Note that Arioch attempted to take the credit for finding Daniel, as if it was only by his tireless efforts that this interpreter of the dream was found. He was looking for a promotion, but appeared to have been unaware that Daniel already talked personally to the king about this issue.

DANIEL 2:26-28

> 26 The king said to Daniel, whose name was Belteshazzar, "Are you able to make known to me the dream which I have seen, and the meaning of it?"
>
> 27 Daniel answered in the presence of the king, and said, "The secret which the king has demanded cannot be shown to the king by any of the wise men, the astrologers, the magicians, the diviners;
>
> 28 But there is a God in heaven that reveals secrets, and makes known to king Nebuchadnezzar what will be in the latter days. Your dream, and the visions of your head upon your bed, are these;

Daniel not only refused to take any credit for what he was about to tell, but used this as an opportunity to witness to the king about the God of the Hebrews. He told the king that God is capable of doing what man (and the Babylonian gods) could not, then proved it by telling the king his dream and its interpretation.

Daniel is not only going to interpret the dream itself, but even what the king was thinking as he lay on his bed, trying to fall asleep! Compare that to the uncommitted answer the 'wise men' gave to the king earlier.

As Daniel prepared to interpret the dream for the king, notice the tact and respect with which he treated this egotistical man. He was not condescending. He didn't talk down to this pagan leader. He lifted him up and treated him with love and thoughtfulness.

While the wise men appeared to separate the king from the gods by suggesting that he was out of touch with the god he served, Daniel affirmed the king's role by declaring that he was not only in touch with the true God, but that God cared about him personally. What a contrast to the insulting way the king was treated by his advisors!

DANIEL 2:29-30

> 29 As for you, O king, your thoughts came into your mind upon your bed about what should come to pass in the future. And he that reveals secrets makes known to you what shall come to pass.
>
> 30 But as for me, this secret is not revealed to me for any wisdom that I have more than anyone else, but for their sakes that shall make known the interpretation to the king, and that you might know the thoughts of your heart.

Daniel began by telling the king something he hadn't asked for: what he was thinking about before he went to sleep. This goes far beyond the ability to interpret a dream or even to know what the dream was.

He informed the king that his ability to tell and interpret this dream had nothing to do with Daniel's human skill but came from God alone. This dream and its interpretation was purely designed to show Nebuchadnezzar that God is sovereign by revealing the future, something only God can do.

DANIEL 2:31-33

> 31 You, O king, looked, and saw before you a great image of a man. This great image, whose brightness was excellent, stood before you; and the form of it was terrible.
>
> 32 This image's head was of fine gold, his chest and arms of silver, his belly and thighs of brass,
>
> 33 His legs of iron, his feet partly of iron and partly of clay.

The statue is a man, representing kingdoms of men. Four metals are shown in their order of value. They are secular symbols that a pagan king could identify with. In a later chapter, we'll see the same vision given to Daniel from God's point of view, as wild, voracious beasts.

A popular British television show called *Doctor Who* features one particular group of bad guys known as the Cybermen. They are men of metal, virtually unstoppable. They trample everything in their path. Bullets bounce off their armor plating. People run screaming from their advance. Even today we're terrified by the idea of metal beings.

Four kingdoms are represented by these metals:

- **Babylon** (the head of gold)
- **Persia** (the chest and arms of silver)
- **Greece** (the belly and thighs of bronze)
- **Rome** (the legs of iron later mixed with clay)

DANIEL 2:34-35

> **34** You looked until you saw that a stone was cut out without hands, which smashed the image upon its feet of iron and clay and broke them to pieces.
>
> **35** Then the iron, the clay, the brass, the silver and the gold was broken to pieces all at once, and became like fine dust on the summer threshing floors; and the wind carried them away, that no place was found for them. The stone that smashed the image became a great mountain, filling the whole earth.

The Rock is cut out of a Mountain, but without human hands. There are many references throughout the Scriptures describing both God and His promised Messiah — Jesus of Nazareth — as a rock or stone. As the "Son of God," the metaphor of a rock cut out of a mountain without the use of hands could not be more clear.

After the terrible and glorious yet-to-come Day of the Lord, the **Maschiach Nagid** (Messiah the King) Jesus Christ will take the throne of David. His kingdom will be an everlasting kingdom *filling the whole earth*.[2] Every knee will bow and every tongue confess that He is the Lord of lords and King of kings.[3]

---

2 2 Timothy 4:1
3 Isaiah 45:23; Romans 14:11

It's interesting that the rock, when it crushes these kingdoms of men, crushes all of them together, not just some of them or the last one, even though it says that the stone will smash the feet of iron and clay first. This reference to all the prior kingdoms still somehow being in place on that day, through the nationalities represented by them, is clarified in Daniel's vision described in chapter 8.

DANIEL 2:36-38

> 36 **This is the dream; and we will tell the interpretation of it before the king.**
>
> 37 **You, O king, are a king of kings: for the God of heaven has given you a kingdom, power, and strength, and glory.**
>
> 38 **And wherever people live, the beasts of the field and the birds of the air have been given by him into your hand. He has made you ruler over them all. You are this head of gold.**

MAN OF METAL

The metal man shown to Nebuchadnezzar may have held some similarity in styling to typical Babylonian dress. But the similarity would have ended there. Its appearance frightened the king. It had a head of gold, chest and arms of silver, belly and thighs of bronze, and legs of iron mixed with clay.

Babylon was a kingdom blessed by God in some unique ways (God Himself referred to Nebuchadnezzar as "His servant" in Jeremiah). The Chaldean Empire was used by God as an instrument of judgment for the nation of Judah. It was taken over by the Persians in 539BC.

DANIEL 2:39A

> ³⁹ **And after you shall arise another kingdom inferior to you.**

The Persian kingdom was at first a single kingdom (the Medes) but was then manipulated by Cyrus into a Persian-dominated coalition often referred to as the Medo-Persian empire. Although the Persians created a kingdom which was larger in size, it was not as impressive in its accomplishments or influence. It was destroyed by Alexander the Great around 330BC.

DANIEL 2:39B

> ³⁹ **After that will come a third kingdom of brass [or bronze], which shall rule over all the earth.**

Alexander's Greek kingdom swept the world rapidly. In just 11 years it grew substantially larger than the previous ones, covering the known world from Spain to India and down into Egypt. After Alexander died, his kingdom was eventually broken into four pieces. Much of the later prophecies of Daniel deal with the continuing battles between two of these kingdoms that continued on for hundreds of years.

DANIEL 2:40-43

> ⁴⁰ **Then a fourth kingdom will come that will be strong as iron. For as iron breaks into pieces and subdues all things, shall it break in pieces and bruise all these.**
>
> ⁴¹ **And the feet and toes you saw, partly of potters' clay and partly of iron, shows that the kingdom will be divided; but it will have the strength of the iron, just as you saw the iron mixed with miry clay.**
>
> ⁴² **And as the toes of the feet were partly of iron and partly of clay, so the kingdom shall be partly strong, and partly broken.**

Babylonian Empire:
605-539BC

Persian Empire:
539-330BC

Greek Empire:
330-64BC

Roman Empire:
64BC and never conquered

FOUR COMING KINGDOMS

Nebuchadnezzar was shown several future empires in his vision. The first was his own Babylonian (or Chaldean) empire. The second was the Persian empire. Then would come the Greek (or Macedonian) empire under the command of Alexander the Great. Finally would come the Roman empire, which from God's point of view, still exists because it was never conquered by a different religious or cultural authority. Even today, we still follow Roman structures of government, democracy, military strategy and even organized religion.

Of the four, Alexander's empire was the largest in total size under the control of one man. No other ruler after that would achieve the same kind of unified power.

In the future, another ruler arising out of a revived form of the Roman empire will gain massive control, even greater than that of Alexander, during which he will attack the Jewish people with a ferocity unseen ever before in history.

> 43 And as you saw iron mixed with miry clay, the people will mingle themselves but they will not be unified with one another, even as iron does not mix with clay.

The reference to iron smashing and breaking everything is remarkable, because unlike the kingdoms of Babylon, Persia and Greece, the Roman style was to crush the nations it conquered. This was unheard of at the time of Daniel. Previous empires had been highly sensitive to the cultures and people of the nations they conquered; they valued their strengths and showed respect for what had been established because it gave them strength. The Romans, on the other hand, simply destroyed everything and replaced it with their own systems and people using brute force.

Note the reference to the people of the Roman empire not remaining united. The Romans absorbed many diverse cultures, from the Egyptians to the barbarians in northern Europe. These cultures were not united but divided, eventually causing the empire to crumble into decay. Daniel explained that this last kingdom will feature nationalities very much intermingled in their gene pool, but very diverse in their philosophies and cultures.

The book of Revelation describes a revived Roman empire in the last days that will include ten dominant nations, making the ten toes even more relevant.

An interesting point made by some end-time scholars is the long-term existence of a ten-nation military alliance known as the Western European Union. These countries are members of both NATO and the European Union. What binds these ten nations together is their mutual defense obligation under the modified Brussels Treaty (known as the *Brussels Treaty Powers*). We should be cautious not to jump to conclusions that these are the ten toes meant by Daniel's vision, but it is interesting, and there is certainly potential that the WEU has such significance.

The coming one-world leader will arise from the ten nations represented by the ten toes and subdue three of them politically, but all kingdoms or nations will be crushed by Jesus when He returns on the Day of the Lord.

DANIEL 2:44-45

> **⁴⁴ And in the days of these kings the God of heaven will set up a kingdom that shall never be destroyed. That kingdom will not be left to other people, but it will smash to pieces and consume all these kingdoms, and it will stand forever.**
>
> **⁴⁵ For as you saw that the stone was cut out of the mountain without hands, and that it broke into pieces the iron, the brass, the clay, the silver and the gold; the great God has made known to the king what shall come to pass hereafter. The dream is certain, and the interpretation of it sure."**

Note the reference to the time **of these kings**. This specifically means the time of the ten kings represented by the toes of iron mixed with clay. The setting of the final dominion of Jesus will take place in the days of a revived Roman empire in which ten primary nations play a key role. The coming world leader will arise suddenly on the world stage, politically manipulate his way over three of those ten nations so that he controls them, then he will begin to rule with an iron hand, showing his true colors. There is more on this in later chapters of Daniel.

Psalm 2 is a conversation between the three figures of the Godhead, in which they discuss the folly of the final battle of Armageddon, when human armies set out to battle God. In this Psalm, God affirms to His Son, Jesus Christ, that the armies will be given over to Jesus and He will rule over the nations. Notice how closely the wording in that Psalm relates to this dream Nebuchadnezzar was given:

> "You will rule them with an iron scepter; you will dash them to pieces like pottery." —Psalm 2:9 (NIV)

Can you imagine anything more foolish than setting a human army to battle God? The Bible tells us that the coming world leader will do exactly that when the time comes. And he will be crushed by the stone cut from the mountain without human hands.

DANIEL 2:46-47

> 46 Then king Nebuchadnezzar fell on his face before Daniel, and commanded that they should offer him a sacrifice and incense.
>
> 47 The king said to Daniel, "It is true that your God is a God of gods, and a Lord of kings, and a revealer of secrets, seeing how you could reveal this secret."

The king did not worship Daniel, but bowed before him in respect to the God Daniel represented. Still, imagine this remarkable scene: the king of the world's greatest empire actually falling on his face before a captive slave! It was only the start of a great ministry Daniel would have reaching out to this pagan ruler.

The wording used does not say the king presented an offering *to* Daniel. Instead, the king presented to Daniel the items needed to make an offering to God. He equipped Daniel for making a sacrifice, something that had been impossible for him ever since he was taken from Jerusalem.

DANIEL 2:48-49

> 48 Then the king made Daniel a great man, and gave him many great gifts, and made him ruler over the whole province of Babylon, and chief of the governors over all the wise men of Babylon.
>
> 49 Then Daniel requested of the king, and he set Shadrach, Meshach, and Abednego, over the affairs of the province of Babylon. But Daniel sat in the gate of the king.

Although it was common practice for kings like Nebuchadnezzar to appoint the most qualified people to positions of power, it would have been unusual to place one of the Jewish exiles into a position of this nature.

The Israelites were essentially captured as slaves. The complex Babylonian code of law had clearly defined rules regarding slaves, and they did not treat slaves as equals to natural-born citizens. For example, "the slave is not regarded or spoken of as a man, but as a thing, and is reckoned in the same way as cattle."[4] For a king to put a slave into a high ranking position was unusual and politically unpopular, especially given the anti-Semitism which already existed in the geographical region of modern-day Iraq.

It upset the wise men to see these Jewish captives put into positions of authority over them, even though one of them had saved their lives. In Daniel chapters 3 and 6, we'll see very real examples of anti-Semitism, indicating that bigotry was alive and well among the wise men of Babylon.

CONQUERORS OF CLAY
The apostle John quotes Jesus as saying that the saints in Christ will be co-regents with Him in the final kingdom. Under His authority they (those who followed Christ in life) will assist in destroying the kingdoms shown in the vision of king Nebuchadnezzar. Notice the reference to the nations as "clay" vessels:

"To all who are victorious, who obey me to the very end, I will give authority over all the nations. They will rule the nations with an iron rod and smash them like clay pots."
—Revelation 2:26-27 (NIV)

---

4   Stewart Charles Bruce, *Modern Commercial Law is Based on Ancient Babylonian Codes*

💡 Insight

There are many references in Scripture to God as the "Rock" of salvation. Rock and stone are common metaphors used to represent God and Christ.

For example, the apostle Paul refers to Christ metaphorically as the "rock that followed the Israelites in the desert," indicating that the rock from which they received water was an idiom for Jesus.

Here are some of the most dominant themes of God and Jesus Christ represented as a rock in Scripture:

"You and Aaron must take the staff and assemble the entire community. As the people watch, command the rock over there to pour out its water. You will get enough water from the rock to satisfy all the people and their livestock."
—Numbers 20:8 (NIV)

This is an oblique reference to salvation through Christ. He called Himself the "living water" and said that everyone who drinks from the water he provides will never again thirst.

If you're thinking this seems contrived, look at the next verse.

"I don't want you to forget, dear brothers and sisters, what happened to our ancestors in the wilderness long ago... For they all drank from the miraculous rock that traveled with them, and that rock was Christ."
—1 Corinthians 10:1-4 (NIV)

The apostle Paul wasn't saying that the rock was physically Christ, but that it symbolized the way Christ provides for us at all times and that His salvation sustains us permanently.

"These are the words he sang: 'The LORD is my rock, my fortress, and my savior; my God is my rock, in whom I find protection. He is my shield, the strength of my salvation, and my stronghold, my high tower, my savior, the one who saves me from violence.'"
—2 Samuel 22:2-3 (NIV)

"The stone rejected by the builders has now become the cornerstone." —Psalm 118:22 (see also Psalm 89, 95)

The stone in this passage is a direct reference to Jesus Christ. He and His disciples quoted that same passage. It means that the Jewish religious leaders rejected Him but that He is in fact the cornerstone of salvation.

"Trust in the LORD always, for the LORD GOD is the eternal Rock" —Isaiah 26:4 (NIV)

"Therefore thus says the Lord GOD, "Behold, I am laying in Zion a stone, a tested stone, A costly cornerstone for the foundation, firmly placed. He who believes in it will not be disturbed."
—Isaiah 28:16 (NASB)

This is another reference to Christ. The word interpreted as *disturbed* means that those who believe in Jesus will not be judged or destroyed on Judgement Day.

"Jesus said to them, 'Have you never read in the Scriptures: 'The stone the builders rejected has become the capstone (cornerstone); the Lord has done this, and it is marvelous in our eyes'? Therefore I tell you that the kingdom of God will be taken away from you and given to a people who will produce its fruit. He who falls on this stone will be broken to pieces, but he on whom it falls will be crushed.'"
—Matthew 21:42-44 (NIV)

Jesus used Psalm 118:22 to explain why He was now offering His gift of eternal life to Gentiles. Initially he brought salvation to the Jews, but when they rejected Him it was given to non-Jews for a time. After the church is removed in the event called the Rapture, God's plan for the Jews will be completed as described in Daniel 9.

"Listen to me, you who pursue righteousness and who seek the LORD: Look to the rock from which you were cut and to the quarry from which you were hewn." —Isaiah 51:1 (NIV)

Insight (cont'd)

We are to act and live in a way pleasing to God. Are you living a life that God would approve of? Are you free from sexual immorality? Are you honest? Loving? Forgiving? Encouraging?

Being clay in the hands of the Potter

Clay always represents people in Scripture. It is a symbol of how we are shaped and molded by God through the experiences He gives to us. Here are some references to clay:

"Remember that you molded me like clay. Will you now turn me to dust again?"
—Job 10:9 (NIV)

"How stupid can you be? He is the Potter, and he is certainly greater than you. You are only the jars he makes! Should the thing that was created say to the one who made it, 'He didn't make us'? Does a jar ever say, 'The potter who made me is stupid'?" —Isaiah 29:16 (NLT)

"And yet, LORD, you are our Father. We are the clay, and you are the potter. We are all formed by your hand."
—Isaiah 64:8 (NLT)

We are clay in God's hand, but are only of value if we are soft and pliable. No wonder God often brings us to a point of true humility before we can be used by Him! In the case of king Nebuchadnezzar, God will later strike him down to a surprisingly low position before the arrogant king is pliable enough to give himself over to God's control.

How soft and pliable are you?

Is your response to godly discipline bitter and resentful, or do you allow difficulties in life to offer a measured evaluation of God's true purpose in putting you through them?

Application — My Notes & Bible Study Questions

06

DANIEL CHAPTER 3
BOW OR BURN

Daniel and his three friends, filled with grace and mercy, saved the life of every official wise man of Babylon. Are those men grateful? As we find so often in life, our faith in God doesn't remove us from strife but can throw us into the midst of it. The account in Daniel's third chapter is an inspiring example of how we can respond with faith when life isn't fair.

DANIEL 3:1

> 1 Nebuchadnezzar the king made an image of gold, ninety feet high and nine feet wide. He set it up in the plain of Dura, in the province of Babylon.

Daniel didn't specify what the giant statue was an image of. Scholars have long argued over this. For a number of reasons, it is highly unlikely that this was an image of Nebuchadnezzar himself.

The extreme dimensions of this gold-covered image do not allow it to be the image of a man unless it was distorted so much that it would be an irreverent likeness. It was exceptionally tall and narrow, measuring almost 9 stories high and just 9 feet in width — a tenth as wide as it is high. Even the skinny looking Oscar award, if enlarged to such a height would be much too wide. On a pedestal, it would require a stand 60 feet high. So what are the possibilities?

Except in Egypt (and later in Rome) it was considered blasphemy for any man — even a king — to set himself up to be equal to a god. Kings would associate themselves with the gods, but only as ambassadors of the gods, assigned to carry out their duties.

The name Nebuchadnezzar made him **the protector of Nebo's boundaries**. He was not equal to Nebo, but acted as Nebo's personal deputy in this role. This brought the king glory and honor simi-

💡 Insight

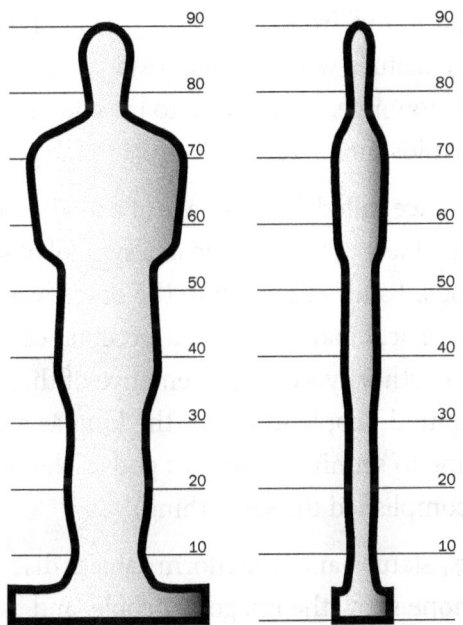

WHAT WAS THE IMAGE?

Some Bible commentaries claim that the king's idol was actually an image of himself. A quick mathematical test shows that this is simply not possible.

Daniel says the idol was 90 feet high but only 9 feet wide. Even a skinny image of a person, such as the Oscar statue shown above left would measure 28 feet wide.

Some scholars say it was on a pedestal, but this would result in a small statue atop a stand more than half the entire height, an unlikely proposition.

An image of a man so skinny it would be a mere 9 feet wide would look like the one on the right above. This would not be something reverent enough to be worthy of worship. Images of people — and especially rulers — from that time period were always properly proportioned. It may have been a horn shape, or the image of a weapon, since there are archeological records of such statues set up.

In any case, if its appearance was important, we would have been given a more detailed description.

lar to that given to the gods. In essence, the people worshipped their gods through the king.

Stelae have been found from that time period showing people worshiping large statues while the king stands nearby. This way the king is given honor generally given to the gods, but by distancing himself he avoids making himself equal to the gods.

An Assyrian practice called for an image of a weapon of their king to be set up as an object to be honored as a symbol of loyalty to the king and the gods. Failure to worship the object was considered insubordination. Participation showed acceptance of the deity and of the king's authority as a representative of that deity. It was a ritual that required people to honor the king as a god without requiring the king to set himself up as a god (a clever loophole in essence that accomplished the same thing).

In all the reliefs, statues and cuneiform tablets discovered from ancient times, none show the image of people, and especially not rulers, in proportions which are irreverent or abstract. They are always properly proportioned, even when stylized. So it is inconceivable that this statue would have been the image of a man stretched to such an extreme shape.

Historical records show that Nebuchadnezzar was dealing with a civil uprising in 576BC. If this event was related, it is reasonable to assume that the requirement to pledge allegiance to the gods of the king was designed to create the appearance of national unity.

Dura simply means *enclosed by a wall*. Many historians believe that the location of this statue was about six miles south of Babylon. But it may have stood near the summer palace, which was located a few miles north of Babylon at the intersection of two walls.

DANIEL 3:2-3

> 2 Then Nebuchadnezzar the king sent to gather together the satraps, prefects, governors, captains, treasurers, judges, counsellors and all the rulers of the provinces to come to the dedication of the image which Nebuchadnezzar the king had set up.
>
> 3 Then the satraps, prefects, governors, captains, treasurers, judges, counsellors and all the rulers of the provinces were gathered together for the dedication of the image that Nebuchadnezzar the king had set up; and they stood before the image.

It's easy to forget that building the statue involved a huge period of time. Building a statue 9 stories high doesn't happen overnight. Weeks of planning were followed by assignments of work detail to laborers. Design was followed by construction, followed by gold-leaf application. Once the completion date approached, the king would have sent invitations to military officers and top officials of all kinds to attend the dedication party from across the empire. This would have involved weeks of advance notice. So in total a few months were probably needed to make this come together, all designed to establish allegiance to the gods or chief god of the Babylonians through the king.

- **SATRAPS** were provincial governors looking after major divisions of the empire.
- **PREFECTS** were similar to governors, but they were responsible for conquered cities.
- **GOVERNORS** were civil administrators over provinces.

That the proclamation and invitation extended to so many officials, and that they are specified, indicates that this was an empire-wide ordinance, not just a local issue.

DANIEL 3:4-6

> 4 Then a herald cried aloud, "To you it is commanded, O people, nations, and languages,
>
> 5 That at whatever time you hear the sound of the horn, flute, zither, lyre, harp, pipes and all kinds of music, you must fall down and worship the golden image that Nebuchadnezzar the king has set up.
>
> 6 Whoever does not fall down and worship shall immediately be cast into the midst of a burning fiery furnace."

Note the inclusive reference to peoples (racial groups), nations (the nations making up the empire) and languages (the conquered nations with different first tongues). Not only is this further evidence that this was an empire-wide proclamation, but these high officials represented the rest of the empire. Their allegiance would demonstrate that they would carry the message to every corner of the Babylonian empire, thus ensuring a spirit of unity for Nebuchadnezzar through a state-imposed religion.

Archeologists have found a brick-making furnace that may have also been used for executions, as human bones were found within its chamber. It was a huge, sophisticated facility measuring a city block on each side. The bricks of Nebuchadnezzar's empire were so well made that even today they remain in excellent condition. For hundreds of years after the decline of the city of Babylon, they were recycled by locals for use as building materials. One of the reasons these construction materials held up so well is the sophisticated design of the firing furnaces.

The Aramaic refers to *instantly* or *immediately* which is a clear reference to the urgency of the punishment. The furnace was ready to go and there must have been some preparation already established in anticipation of any non-compliance.

DANIEL 3:7

7 **So as soon as they heard the sound of the horn, flute, zither, lyre, harp and all kinds of music, all the peoples, nations and men of every language fell down and worshiped the image of gold that King Nebuchadnezzar had set up. Therefore at that time, when all the people heard the sound of the horn, flute, zither, lyre, harp and all kinds of music, all the people, nations and languages fell down and worshipped the golden image that Nebuchadnezzar the king had set up.**

Exactly six instruments are mentioned by name. Six is the number of man, often used by Scripture to demonstrate incompleteness and imperfection or rebellion (some English translations do not include the final instrument in verses 5 and 10, which was *pipe*, possibly bagpipe or the Greek instrument known as "Pan's Pipe").

We see that there was immediate compliance by the crowd assembled before this huge statue. There is no doubt that they were expected to worship in synchronization, their heads touching the ground at the

THE SOUND OF MUSIC

Six musical instruments are specifically mentioned, though they don't exhaust the full range because of the reference to "all kinds of music." Above is a detail from an Assyrian relief showing a group of musicians with harps, flutes, and a dulcimer.

The six instruments mentioned by Daniel were:

▪ **Horn** or **Trumpet**. This may have been made from an animal horn.

▪ **Flute**.

▪ **Zither**, a name borrowed from the Greek "kitharis." This stringed instrument had been used in that region since Assyrian times.

▪ **Trigon** or **Triangular Lyre**.

▪ **Psaltery** or **Harp**. Probably sold by Greek merchants, as its use was common in Greece.

▪ **Pipes**, possibly **Bagpipe** or **Pan's pipes**, another instrument that came from Greece.

same time, a vast sea of people bowing in unison. To an egomaniacal king, it would have been an impressive sight.

Yet among this mass of compliance were three men who did not bow down. They refused to follow the pattern dictated by the world around them and stood their ground.

Scripture doesn't tell us where Daniel was, but it is often thought that he was on the dais with the king and was thus not required to bow down himself.

DANIEL 3:8

> 8 At that time certain Chaldeans came forward, and chewed out the Jews, accusing them.

The passage says that *certain* wise men came forward with accusations. They may have included the very ones whose lives Daniel had saved in chapter 2. These wise men, of whom Daniel was in charge, were essentially astrologers who related the position of the planets to earthly events, interpreting their movements as signs from the gods. Even though Daniel was their chief, it should not be assumed he practiced the same thing. Those who head up casino operations in state governments are not necessarily people who have ever practiced gambling.

THE THREE GREEKS

Critics of the authenticity of Daniel like to make a lot out of the fact that three Greek words are used in this chapter. They claim this is evidence that it was written much later than the sixth century BC.

The three Greek words are used to name three of the musical instruments mentioned here. These are the zither, the harp and the pipes. Greek merchants were common in that region, so it's perfectly natural to expect Greek names for some of these instruments, especially ones common in Greece. After all, we refer to the Ukelele by its Hawaiian name.

The fact that only three Greek words are used gives even more credibility to the original writing date of the book of Daniel, not less. If it had been written later, as critics claim, there would be many more Greek words.

It is most likely that these men came forward on the evening of the same day of the official dedication. As chief officials, the three men accused would have been present at the dedication ceremony.

DANIEL 3:9-12

> 9 They said to king Nebuchadnezzar, "O king, live forever.
>
> 10 You, O king, have issued a decree that everyone who hears the sound of the horn, flute, zither, lyre, harp, pipe and all kinds of music must fall down and worship the golden image,
>
> 11 and that whoever does not fall down and worship is to be cast into the midst of a burning fiery furnace.
>
> 12 There are certain Jews whom you have set over the affairs of the province of Babylon — Shadrach, Meshach, and Abednego — these men, O king, pay no attention to you. They neither serve your gods nor worship the golden image you set up."

The phrase *live forever* was an early version of our modern-day proclamation of *long live the king*.

Why repeat the proclamation? The whole thing looks like a legal proceeding designed to give the king no room to maneuver. They wanted to make sure these three men were punished exactly as the decree called for. Notice also the interesting wording in the accusation against the Jews. There was a clear tone of anti-Semitism.

Three accusations were made. First, that **they pay no attention to Nebuchadnezzar's commands** (this one specifically but the Aramaic covers a broader sense). This was, of course, patently false and he would know it. The second was that **they don't serve the gods of Babylon** (notice that they call them the king's gods). The third was that **they don't worship the image** (again it is referred to as the king's project). The last two accusations were true.

DANIEL 3:13

> 13 Then Nebuchadnezzar, furious with rage, commanded to bring Shadrach, Meshach, and Abednego. They brought these men before the king.

Nebuchadnezzar was 'furious with rage,' but it may have been directed at least partly to those who cornered him like this. He must have realized that he was being used as a pawn in their game. From what we've already seen of his ego, this would not sit well with him. If his fury were directed only to the three men, he would probably not have called them in for a second chance.

DANIEL 3:14-15

> 14 Nebuchadnezzar said to them, "Is it true, Shadrach, Meshach, and Abednego, that you do not serve my gods, nor worship the golden image which I have set up?
>
> 15 Now if you are ready to fall down and worship the image I have made when you hear the sound of the horn, flute, zither, lyre, horn, pipe and all kinds of music; well and good. But if you do not, you will be cast immediately into the midst of a burning fiery furnace. Then what God shall deliver you out of my hands?"

Nebuchadnezzar asked if these accusations are true. Notice that he ignores the first one made, because he knew it was ridiculously false. He deals only with the last two of the three claims.

The proclamation itself did not appear to give room for a second-chance interview with the king. This was an unusual move designed to give them a chance to put the whole incident behind them. They could comply now, in the presence of their accusers, or he would fulfil the punishment described.

Notice the interesting question posed by Nebuchadnezzar. He didn't argue with the religious beliefs of these three Jews, but cast doubt on their validity in an effort to get his way. He asked, "What God will deliver you out of my hands?"

This Babylonian king was a man who sought power and control in all situations. In his effort to have his way here, it seems that the king forgot all about the God of Daniel, the true God who had already proved Himself to the king earlier.

DANIEL 3:16-18

16 **Shadrach, Meshach, and Abednego answered the king, "O Nebuchadnezzar, we don't need to be careful to answer you in this matter.**

17 **If we are thrown into the burning fiery furnace, our God whom we serve is able to deliver us from it, and He will deliver us out of your hand, O king.**

18 **But even if He doesn't, be it known to you, O king, that we will not serve your gods, nor worship the golden image which you have set up."**

GETTING CHEWED OUT

In describing the slanderous accusations brought forward about Shadrach, Meshach and Abednego in verse 8, the Aramaic uses an interesting phrase that closely resembles our modern-day reference to being "chewed out" by someone. It literally says they accused the Jews by chewing them to bits and pieces.

This phrase was part of the common language in those days.

Even then there were slang expressions. Isn't it interesting that this phrase has made it into our modern language as well with nearly identical meaning?

What great faith is shown here! These men did not even attempt to defend their faith or their right to believe in God. The NIV offers perhaps the most accurate translation here: "we do not have to defend ourselves before you in this matter." They didn't argue with the king or offer some kind of life-saving explanation. They humbly gave the situation entirely to God. They are implying that He will deal with the king personally.

Note too that they don't push God into a corner. While they were confident that He will rescue them, they gave Him room to save them or not.

DANIEL 3:19-20

> 19 Then Nebuchadnezzar was furious, and his facial features were changed against Shadrach, Meshach, and Abednego. He ordered that the furnace be heated seven times hotter than normal.
>
> 20 And he commanded the most mighty men that were in his army to tie up Shadrach, Meshach, and Abednego, and to throw them into the burning fiery furnace.

Finally, the king snapped completely. He hated being powerless against these men, and their humility and trust in someone greater than Nebuchadnezzar was too much for him. He became so enraged that his facial features contorted and he flew completely out of control. A temper tantrum by a king.

Nebuchadnezzar ordered the fire made seven times hotter than normal — something quite impossible to do — and then commanded that the strongest and most valiant men in his military (probably from his personal guard) were to bind the three disobedient men and throw them into the furnace.

DANIEL 3:21-23

> 21 So these men were bound in their coats, pants, head gear and their other garments and were cast into the midst of the burning fiery furnace.
>
> 22 Because the king's commandment was urgent, and the furnace exceedingly hot, the flames of the fire killed the men who took up Shadrach, Meshach, and Abednego.
>
> 23 And these three men, Shadrach, Meshach, and Abednego, firmly bound, fell down into the midst of the burning fiery furnace.

The three men were tightly bound, clothes and all, when they were thrown into the fiery furnace. The mention of the clothing is important. The clothes were expected to burst into flame, creating a great spectacle.

The fire raged well above normal temperatures as slaves compressed huge bellows to create additional heat in a frantic attempt to appease the king.

A back draft hit the party as they opened a roof-top door, killing the soldiers. As a result, the three fell into the furnace.

DANIEL 3:24-26

24 Then Nebuchadnezzar the king leaped to his feet astonished, and said to his counsellors, "Did not we throw three men bound into the midst of the fire?" They answered and said to the king, "True, O king."

25 He answered, "Look! I see four men loose, walking in the midst of the fire, and they have no hurt; and the form of the fourth is like a son of the gods."

26 Then Nebuchadnezzar came near the mouth of the burning fiery furnace and shouted, "Shadrach, Meshach, and Abednego, servants of the most high God, come out, and come here!" Then Shadrach, Meshach, and Abednego came forth out of the midst of the fire.

SEVEN TIMES HOTTER? SERIOUSLY?

How do you heat a brick-firing furnace seven times hotter than usual?

The normal firing temperature is about 1,000 degrees Celsius. The most that could be achieved is 1,500° — which is only 50 percent hotter. Nobody argues with the tyrant about this impossible command. They pretend to follow his orders, terrified that they might join the condemned in a moment of royal outrage.

The fact that they had earlier been bound got Nebuchadnezzar's attention even more dramatically. The men were no longer tied up, but walking around. Imagine the scene: three men casually walking around in the fiery furnace, unharmed. In their midst was another man shining with supernatural light, one that even a pagan king understood to have divine qualities!

Obviously the fourth being is an angel, but some Bible teachers think it could be a **theophany**, an Old Testament appearance of Jesus Christ. That is a strong possibility, but we shouldn't make too much of the king's reference to one "like a son of the gods." Some try to turn his statement into "one like the Son of God" to give it special significance. It is unlikely that Nebuchadnezzar, the Gentile, pagan king of a nation that worshipped a plethora of gods, would have referenced the angel in a way that positioned him as *the* Messiah, the Son of the one and only God. The Aramaic is not specific to that usage, though it can mean the Almighty God if used in that context.

Nebuchadnezzar called for them to come out. It's interesting that he didn't call for the fourth one to come with them. The being with these men must have been so remarkable that no doubt was left in his mind. It was not a vision or mirage of light, but something very real and powerful beyond imagination. The fourth figure probably scared the wits out of the king.

DANIEL 3:27

> 27 And the satraps, prefects, governors and king's counsellors gathered together around these men. They saw that the fire had no power to harm their bodies, nor was a hair of their heads singed, neither were their coats scorched, nor any smell of fire upon them.

All these officials from across the kingdom — from all the captured cultures and nations of the empire — were still in Babylon, seeing with their own eyes something beyond human understanding, on the very day that the king proclaimed allegiance to false gods! What a contrast between the true God who acts, and the false, powerless gods the people had been ordered to worship. Ambassadors would take this story to every corner of the empire!

DANIEL 3:28

> 28 Then Nebuchadnezzar said, "Blessed be the God of Shadrach, Meshach, and Abednego, who has sent His angel and delivered His servants that trusted in Him. They have changed the king's word, and yielded their bodies, that they might not serve nor worship any god except their own God.

Nebuchadnezzar was not a man who fooled around or waffled when his preconceptions were tested. He quickly adapted and recognized that the God of the Hebrews was stronger than his own gods. One can't help but wonder if other tyrant leaders we are familiar with, like Ghengis Khan or Lenin, would have so quickly turned around and acknowledged God publicly the way Nebuchadnezzar did, had they been in this same situation.

The king was clearly aware of angels and their significance. Where did he learn this? From Daniel?

The king publicly acknowledged and even showed respect for the men's civil disobedience in light of their faith.

DANIEL 3:29

> 29 Therefore I make a decree, 'That the people of every nation and language which speak anything against the God of Shadrach, Meshach, and Abednego, shall be made into limbs, and their houses shall be made a dunghill; because there is no other God that can save in a way like this.'"

We laugh when we read this decree because we see the human weakness in the king that we can all identify with. He immediately resorted to old habits, applying his usual technique of brute strength to the situation.

Impulsive as ever, the king turned his attention to those who put him up to the whole charade. He was well aware it was a setup. He acted to put future efforts of this kind behind him by establishing severe punishment for any further accusations against the Jews.

Though some Bibles use the phrase *cut into pieces* when referring to the punishment bestowed on those who defied the decree, the Aramaic does not actually refer to cutting instruments. This phrase is the same used in chapter 2. The punishment was to be *torn limb from limb* or *made into limbs*, which may have referred to a form of punishment where the victim was tied hands and feet to four trees. When the binding holding the trees together was unloosed, the trees would fly apart, ripping the body into pieces.

The Babylonians had inherited many unimaginably cruel torture practices from the Assyrians, such as removing the skin from people's backs (known as *flaying*) and displaying them over the city walls, as well as the practice of impaling people on poles.[1] They boasted that they knew how to inflict these tortures in ways that would maximize the suffering. It was extremely dangerous to get on the wrong side of these barbarous ancient kings.

SON OF THE GODS?

The reference to "son of the gods" comes from Nebuchadnezzar's own lips. Many Bible teachers try to make a big deal out of this, as if Nebuchadnezzar was acknowledging the Son of the one and only God.

This is probably not what he was trying to say, so we should take care not distort his words to fit our perception of what we would like him to have meant. If he had meant the true God, he would not have referred to "gods" in plural. He was simply stating that the fourth figure looked like a divine being.

At the same time, we can certainly enjoy the Holy Spirit's detail. The word used by Daniel is the same word used in Genesis 1:1, the Aramaic form of **bar elohim**. This can be used as God (Trinity) or gods, depending on the context. Both are true.

The reference to turning the house into a dung heap or pile of rubble is actually quite crude: in the Aramaic it literally means turning their houses into outhouses, places where dung is gathered.

---

1 Albert Kirk Grayson, *Assyrian Royal Inscriptions, Pt 2: From Tiglath-pileser I to Ashur-nasir-apli II*

Centuries later, a group of wise men would mount camels and make the long journey from 'the east' (presumably Babylon) to Jerusalem, seeking a child whose birth was marked by a star. Archeological records show that two planets were aligned at that time and may have looked like a star moving towards the west. Wise men studied the movements of the planets and thought symbolic alignments to be signs from the gods. They knew the child had special significance as the promised Jewish 'King,' bringing to Him gifts of gold, frankincense and myrrh. How did they know? From Daniel? Just how far did his influence eventually extend?

DANIEL 3:30

> 30 **Then the king promoted Shadrach, Meshach and Abednego in the province of Babylon.**

These men were already high officials, so the promotions must have been quite significant. In their positions, these men would be even more influential in talking about the God of the Hebrews.

Nebuchadnezzar did not seem at all concerned about the impact they would have on his attempt to unify the nation in a religious sense. Yet we know from later events in Babylon, following Nebuchadnezzar's reign, that even the king's religious beliefs were not always respected. Historical records indicate that the priests of Babylon would be so upset by the religious emphasis on one particular goddess by a later king, Nabonidus, that they helped the Persians defeat the empire.[2]

Nobody knows what became of the statue. Presumably it was quickly abandoned, stripped of its gold covering, then left to decay on the Plain of Dura.

---

2 Herodotus, *The History,* Book 1: Clio

Application — My Notes & Bible Study Questions

07

DANIEL CHAPTER 4
THE INSANE KING

Chapter 4 of Daniel is one of the most remarkable chapters in the Bible. The venerated Jewish Scriptures, the Holy Word of God, the "Tanach" has been penned by the most holy, most godly men of the nation of Israel. Moses. David. Daniel. Isaiah and many other prophets. Now we come to a chapter in this holy Book of books written by a Gentile.

This chapter was written by not just any Gentile, but the king of a pagan nation. And not just any pagan nation, but the nation that conquered Jerusalem, took its people as exiles to an ungodly land and completely destroyed the Holy City and its temple.

What is it about this man that positioned him as one of the authors of the holy Scriptures?

In short, he received an object lesson on pride so dramatic it completely changed his heart. Chapter 4 is an affidavit that king Nebuchadnezzar published to the entire world as a testimony to the God of Israel. It is a description of the consequence of human pride and the power of God when we humble ourselves and acknowledge His authority over our lives.

GOD HATES PRIDE

Pride is just one sin, but in many ways it represents the root of all sin. Pride was the first sin experienced by man when Satan tempted Eve and Adam with the desire to be "like God."

> "For God knows that when you eat of it your eyes will be opened, and you will be like God, knowing good and evil."
> —Genesis 3:5 (NIV)

Pride was the very sin that caused Satan to be cast out of Heaven. This makes pride the original sin of Satan and of all the sins committed by mankind:

> "You were in Eden, the garden of God; every precious stone adorned you... You were anointed as a guardian cherub, for so I ordained you. You were on the holy mount of God; you walked among the fiery stones. You were blameless in your ways from the day you were created till wickedness was found in you... So I drove you in disgrace from the mount of God, and I expelled you, O guardian cherub... Your heart became proud on account of your beauty, and you corrupted your wisdom because of your splendor. So I threw you to the earth; I made a spectacle of you before kings."
> —Ezekiel 28:13-17 (NIV)

Pride lifts up the heart to place the holder of this sin into a position he doesn't own, forgetting his place and stealing respect and honor from the genuine holder of the position. There's a common saying, "a legend in one's own mind" which refers to how we are distorted by pride. The Bible says that Satan experienced this:

> "You said in your heart, I will ascend to heaven; I will raise my throne above the stars of God; I will sit enthroned on the mount of assembly, on the utmost heights of the sacred mountain. I will ascend above the tops of the clouds; I will make myself like the Most High."
> —Isaiah 14:13-14 (NIV)

The writer of the Proverbs assigns consequence to the sin of pride:

> "The LORD detests all the proud of heart. Be sure of this: They will not go unpunished. Pride goes before destruction, a haughty spirit before a fall." —Proverbs 16:5,18 (NIV)

Daniel's fourth chapter is specifically about the pride of one man, but we see in him a lesson for us all.

Although Nebuchadnezzar's punishment for his pride was severe, it serves to tell us that we will all be brought down a notch according to our own position.

DANIEL 4:1

> 1 Nebuchadnezzar the king, to all people, nations, and languages that live in all the earth; Peace and prosperity be multiplied to you.

Nebuchadnezzar writes an affidavit to the world. His memorandum includes the entire Chaldean Empire; this is not restricted to the province of Babylon.

There is some disagreement over when this edict was written. Many scholars believe it was issued shortly before the king's death, putting the likely date at 564-563BC.

DANIEL 4:2-3

> 2 I thought it good to tell you about the signs and wonders that the Most High God has demonstrated toward me.
>
> 3 How great are His signs! How mighty are His wonders! His kingdom is an everlasting kingdom, and His dominion is from generation to generation.

Unlike the king we saw earlier, the Nebuchadnezzar we see here does not try to force people to serve and honor the God of Israel. He merely tells his story and allows them to take it and use this information as they see fit. Nebuchadnezzar has mellowed in the one or two decades that have passed since the incident with the golden image.

The reference to God's great and mighty signs and wonders is an understated translation of the actual words used. His language implies that they are not just great as we usually use that term, but **stupendous** or **awesome**. He is offering a sense of awed wonderment at the miracles of God.

He describes God's kingdom as everlasting and His dominion as unchanging, quite different from the kingdoms of men that change dramatically from one year to the next (as we will see in the next chapter). Nebuchadnezzar's kingdom didn't change dramatically during his reign, so this is a powerful picture of the contrast between God and Nebuchadnezzar.

DANIEL 4:4-5

> 4 I Nebuchadnezzar was at rest in my house, and flourishing in my palace:
>
> 5 I saw a dream which made me afraid, and the thoughts upon my bed and the visions of my head troubled me.

Having completed a number of successful military conquests, Nebuchadnezzar was quite content. Yet his dream made him afraid. We've seen this before, in chapter 2, but this time we see a king willing to admit his weaknesses. A remarkable change for this arrogant tyrant who craved power so much.

In that part of the world, dreams are thought to come from the gods (even today), so people see a great deal of meaning in dreams. Something about this dream in particular made Nebuchadnezzar deeply concerned about his future. He probably understood part of it, giving him a sense of foreboding.

DANIEL 4:6-7

> 6 Therefore I made a decree to bring all the wise men of Babylon before me, that they might tell me the meaning of the dream.
>
> 7 The magicians, astrologers, Chaldeans and diviners came before me. I told them the dream; but they did not make known to me its meaning.

This is familiar territory for those reading the Daniel account. The wise men were brought in because they are supposed to understand these messages from the gods.

The Bible doesn't say that they *can't* interpret the dream, as is sometimes implied. It just says they *didn't* interpret the dream.

We are about to see a dream that is quite negative about the king and his position of power. If you were a wise man in the kingdom of Babylon, and you had to tell this hot-headed king really bad news with the risk that he would fly into a rage, would you willingly tell him? It is possible that these wise men didn't know the meaning of the dream, but even Nebuchadnezzar appears to have had some understanding of its meaning so it seems doubtful that they were clueless about it. Chances are they knew some of what it meant but were too terrified to tell him.

DANIEL 4:8-9

> 8 **But at the end Daniel came in before me, whose name was Belteshazzar, according to the name of my god, and in whom is the spirit of the holy gods. Before I told him the dream, I said,**
>
> 9 **"O Belteshazzar, chief of the magicians, because I know that the spirit of the holy gods is in you, and no secret troubles you, tell me the visions of my dream that I have seen, and its interpretation.**

It is a remarkable sign of respect that the king referred to Daniel by his Hebrew name. When he was first deported to Babylon, Daniel was given a Babylonian name and it would be customary for the king to refer to him that way alone. However, here he refers to Daniel and then his Babylonian name, so that everyone familiar with that name knows who he's talking about.

💡 Insight

THE PURPOSE OF DREAMS

With our modern scientific knowledge, we often don't give much thought to dreams as having a spiritual element. The book of Job provides an interesting perspective on how God sometimes uses dreams to keep us from falling into pride.

Job's fourth friend, Elihu, offers some wise counsel that has an eerie resemblance to the account of Nebuchadnezzar recorded centuries later in Daniel. Notice the reason he gives for God's purpose in dealing with man through dreams and warnings:

"For God does speak – now one way, now another – though man may not perceive it. In a dream, in a vision of the night, when deep sleep falls on men as they slumber in their beds, he may speak in their ears and terrify them with warnings, to turn man from wrongdoing and keep him from pride, to preserve his soul from the pit, his life from perishing by the sword." —Job 33:14-18 (NIV)

Elihu says that God's specific purpose in dreams such as the one given to Nebuchadnezzar is to turn us away from sin and especially pride, in order to bring us to salvation.

The king said that Daniel is chief of the magicians. The word *magicians*, or *magi*, comes from the root word **stylus** referring to the instrument used to inscribe the complex Cuneiform letters. It doesn't mean magicians in the sense we use today, but essentially just acknowledged that they were wise men. Daniel was the head of the entire body of wise men. Although they did practice astrology and pagan arts, Daniel did not have to engage in those practices to be in charge of the division.

Nebuchadnezzar says he knows that the Holy Spirit is in Daniel. Clearly Daniel has established a ministry in his position. He has walked the talk during the entire term of his service to the king, establishing himself as someone different from the pack. How much impact is your life making on those around you?

Though the king's statement at first seems to be just a message of confidence in Daniel's ability, there appears to be a challenge implied. The king knew the dream was bad news and may have been trying to box Daniel in so he wouldn't bail on him as his other wise men did.

DANIEL 4:10-12

> 10 **These were the visions of my head while I lay in my bed: I saw, and beheld a tree in the midst of the earth, and the height of it was great.**
>
> 11 **The tree grew and was strong, and its height reached to the sky, and it was visible to the end of all the earth.**
>
> 12 **The leaves of the tree were fair, and it had much fruit, and in it was food for all. The beasts of the field had shade under it, and the birds of the air lived in its branches, and all flesh was fed from it.**

Trees and plants are common metaphors in the Bible for kingdoms. They grow, or wither, or suffer from drought.

In the dream, this tree grows to cover the earth with *food for all*.

In just a few verses, we'll see that one of Daniel's admonitions to the king is to regard the plight of the poor. There is a clear implication that Nebuchadnezzar was no longer using his kingdom's wealth to look after the needs of the empire.

Saddam Hussein, who saw himself as the reincarnation of Nebuchadnezzar, also took riches from the country while his people went hungry. Just the day before American bombs began to fall, he and his son took $1 billion in cash from the bank.[1] Many of the Iraqi people were starving during Saddam's reign. Most tyrant kings throughout history have similarly lived in luxury while people throughout their kingdoms starved to death.

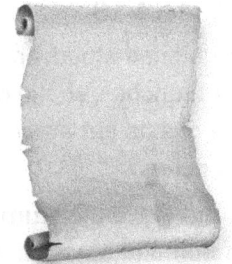

POLITICALLY DANGEROUS EDICT

In a nation that was very devoutly committed to a large number of gods with Marduk above them all, it was politically incorrect, quite dramatically so, for the king to put one god, especially the God of a conquered nation, above Marduk and the others.

An edict like this had no benefit to the king, and was politically quite risky, especially in light of the story he tells.

Clearly his statements were representative of a genuinely changed life.

DANIEL 4:13

> 13 **In the visions of my head as I lay upon my bed, I saw a watcher, a holy one came down from heaven;**

The term used to describe the angel is **watchman**. One other reference has been found among the scrolls of the Dead Sea caves using the phrase "watchman angel"[2] implying that this may be a special class of angelic messenger.

---

1   CNN, May 6, 2003 (*www.cnn.com/2003/WORLD/meast/05/06/sprj.irq.main/index.html*)
2   Henning Reventlow, *Eschatology in the Bible and in Jewish and Christian tradition*

DANIEL 4:14-18

> 14 He cried aloud, and said, 'Chop down the tree, and cut off his branches, shake off his leaves, and scatter his fruit. Let the beasts get away from under it, and the birds from his branches.
>
> 15 But leave the stump of his roots in the earth, with a band of iron and brass, in the tender grass of the field; and let it be wet with the dew of heaven, and let his portion be with the beasts in the grass of the earth.
>
> 16 Let his heart be changed from a man's and let a beast's heart be given to him until seven times pass over him.

The stump of the tree's roots is left in the ground, with a protective band around it, providing a way to regrow in time.

Note the reference to the tree being called a man. Nebuchadnezzar probably understood the kingdom metaphor and understood that this was a reference to himself. No wonder the dream terrified him with its talk of cutting him down and turning his mind to that of an animal!

Seven times mean seven years. The Jews use references like these frequently, just like we might use the word *decade* to refer to a period of 10 years.

DANIEL 4:17-18

> 17 This matter is by the decree of the watchers, and the verdict by the word of the holy ones so that the living may know that the most High rules in the kingdom of men, and gives it to whomever He will, and sets up over it the lowest of men.'
>
> 18 This is the dream that I, king Nebuchadnezzar, have seen. Now you, O Belteshazzar, tell me what it means. None of the wise men of my kingdom are able to tell me its meaning. But you can for the spirit of the holy gods is in you."

Why is the verdict declared about this fall from greatness? To tell the world that God is sovereign. The watchman angel explains that this edict is the fulfilment of the entire purpose of the events described in the dream!

Does Daniel 4:17 contain a Messianic prophecy? Is it possible that the dream given to the Gentile king of a pagan nation could include a reference to the coming Messiah?

There's an interesting reference in verse 17 which says that God sets up over the entire body of the kingdoms of men "the **lowest** of men." What exactly does this mean?

The King James Bible interprets this as **basest** while other translations refer to *lowest* or *lowliest*. Could this be a reference to Jesus Christ as the One — indeed the servant of all, the "lowest" of men — whom God will set up over all the kingdoms of earth after the great and glorious Day of the Lord? While Daniel contains a number of Messianic prophecies, what makes this situation interesting is that it was actually given by an angel to Nebuchadnezzar, a Gentile king.

Let's take a closer look at Daniel 4:17:

> This matter is by the decree of the watchers, and the verdict by the word of the holy ones so that the living may know that the most High rules in the kingdom of men, and gives it to whomever He will, and sets up over it the lowest of men.' —Daniel 4:17

The word used here is the Chaldean/Aramaic word **Shphal**. The exact same word is also used in Daniel 4:37, 5:19, 5:22 and 7:24. Except for its use in Daniel 4:17, the word always means "lowest" in the sense of being humbled or lowly in position or esteem. This would fit with a Messianic prophecy, while an interpretation of "basest," meaning crude, would not.

The King James Bible interprets the identical word differently in 4:17, claiming that it means *basest* of men, a term that means low in the sense of crudeness or inability to perform the duties involved. This would mean the angelic watchman is implying that God gives kingdoms to men who don't deserve to be king, perhaps even representing a put-down of Nebuchadnezzar himself.

ENTER STRONG'S DICTIONARY

Because of the King James Authorized English interpretation, James Strong's Hebrew Chaldean Dictionary, used as a primary source for much translation work, applies a new entry to this word (*8215* vs *8214*) for Daniel 4:17, even though the spelling and context are identical to the other uses of the word. Why would the KJV apply a different meaning here? Was it because of the bias of King James himself, as a member of the team working on that translation, who may have taken an interest in this particular story? Was it a negative view of the tyrant king which caused him to see the referencing word differently?

There appears to be no obvious reason, other than perhaps a sensitivity to verse 32 (still to come), as to why the KJV would interpret **Shphal** differently here than its meaning everywhere else. All other translations use a consistent interpretation.

If the watchman really did mean Nebuchadnezzar was one of the "basest" of men, this would seem to conflict with Daniel 5, where Daniel himself praises King Nebuchadnezzar's reign as being a reasonably good one overall (in a human sense) except for the unfortunate time when he filled himself with pride and God humbled him through seven years of madness. He doesn't put down the former king here as being unfit for leadership.

SINGULAR, NOT PLURAL

The plural of the Chaldean word **malkuw** ends with a *thawv* character (**malkuth**). That's not the case here. The Chaldean/Aramaic text used by Daniel does not actually refer to the **kingdoms** of men in the plural, but to the **kingdom** in the singular, to *it*, not *them*. While this may refer to Nebuchadnezzar as the "king of the world" (the empire covered most of the known world of that time), it seems plausible that it might mean the ultimate worldwide kingdom that will be ruled by the Messiah.

An exact translation of the passage says *the Most High (is Master) in the kingdom of men; and to whomever He wishes He gives it, and the lowest of men He sets up over it.*

The angelic messenger in the dream says that God sets up over all the kingdoms on earth (as a whole) the *lowest* of men. We cannot know for certain if the Chaldean word used includes in its meaning a Messianic prophecy, but it appears that the KJV translation of **basest** is certainly an inconsistent rendering of **Shphal**.

The Chaldean word may mean nothing more than God demonstrating His control over the world of men by setting up as kings men who don't necessarily deserve to be kings. Yet, there's a strong

שׁפל

WHEN BIBLES DISAGREE

The Chaldean (or Aramaic) word "Shphal" is always interpreted as meaning "lower" in the sense of being humbled or reduced in position or esteem. This is indeed how the word is used in Daniel 4:37; 5:19; 5:22 and 7:24. Each time its meaning in all Bibles is consistent.

However, in the King James version a different interpretation is applied to the same word in Daniel 4:17, referring to God's kingdoms being given to the "lowest" of men. The KJV says in this case only, it means the "basest" (crudest) of men, while all other Bibles refer to lowest.

Why the difference? There appears to be no reason for this discrepancy except perhaps the world view of King James and his translation team.

possibility that this is also a double reference, including the concept of the Servant King — the lowest of men — who will ultimately be set up over all the kingdoms on earth, the one and only kingdom that will then exist. Jesus Christ, the servant of all, born in a manger, beaten and crucified, is the humblest of men in this sense. How remarkable that the king of a pagan empire, writing a chapter in the Hebrew *Tanach*, may have been given a Messianic prophecy!

Daniel has just heard a deeply disturbing dream described to him. Even the king appears to have understood that its meaning was not good news. No wonder none of the wise men were interested in interpreting this dream for the king!

DANIEL 4:19

> 19 Then Daniel, who was also called Belteshazzar, was puzzled for one hour, and his thoughts troubled him. The king said, "Belteshazzar, do not let not the dream or the meaning of it trouble you." Belteshazzar answered, "My lord, if only the dream applied to those who hate you, and its meaning to your enemies!

Daniel is not perplexed because he doesn't understand the dream. He's upset and troubled because he *does*. He doesn't know how to tell the king this ominous, deeply disturbing news. He doesn't know what impact this will have on his people, the Jews. Will this event usher in civil or political unrest that will affect the Jewish captives? And how can he even begin to tell this hotheaded tyrant such news?

It is obvious that Daniel was very transparent about his troubled heart. How else would the king know how he was feeling? It takes an open, transparent heart to transmit feelings of fear or concern to others. While these two know each other well, there's a sense that Daniel's response was dramatic, and we see a snapshot of his integrity and character.

Nebuchadnezzar knew the message is bad news. But notice the nature of the relationship. We see a strong bond here between these two men. The king loved Daniel and was willing to accept the message because he knew that Daniel cared for him from the heart, unlike the pretense from other advisors.

DANIEL 4:20-26

> 20 The tree you saw, which grew and was strong, whose height reached to the sky, visible to all the earth;
>
> 21 Whose leaves were fair and the fruit plentiful, providing food for all; under which the beasts of the field lived, and upon whose branches the birds of the air had their nests,
>
> 22 that tree is you, O king! You have grown and become strong; for your greatness has grown to reach the sky, and your dominion to the end of the earth.
>
> 23 You, O king saw a watcher, a holy one, coming down from heaven saying, 'Chop the tree down and destroy it; yet leave the stump of the roots of it in the earth, with a band of iron and brass, in the tender grass of the field. Let him be wet with the dew of heaven and let his portion be with the beasts of the field, till seven times pass over him.'
>
> 24 This is the interpretation, O king, and this is the decree of the Most High that He has issued against my lord the king:
>
> 25 That you will be driven from men, and you will live with the beasts of the field, and you will eat grass as oxen, and you will be wet with the dew of heaven. Seven times shall pass over you, until you acknowledge that the Most High rules in the kingdom of men and gives it to whomever He will.

> 26 Whereas they commanded to leave the stump of the tree roots; this means your kingdom will be restored to you after you recognize that Heaven rules over you.

Daniel cut to the chase fairly quickly. The bad news was that the king will go insane for a period of seven years. The good news was that God is gracious enough that He will restore the kingdom when the king understands who is really in charge.

The message is conditional. When Nebuchadnezzar recognizes the authority and dominion of God over his kingdom, then and only then will his sanity and his kingdom be restored to him.

DANIEL 4:27

> 27 Therefore, O king, let my advice be acceptable to you: Break off your sins by doing what is right and by showing mercy to the poor. It may lead to a lengthening of your peace."

A TEST OF CHARACTER

How would it feel to stand in the court of the king of one of the greatest empires on earth and tell him that he will be driven from people to live as a wild animal?

How would it feel to tell this tyrant that until he acknowledges the Hebrew God, he would be set lower than the lowest slave in his kingdom?

It should come as no surprise that God chose Daniel to be the messenger of such disturbing news. Only a person of genuine integrity and inner strength of character could convey such a thing to this king and not be condemned to immediate execution.

What great things would Christians today attempt if they could only stand before others with such a spotless character as Daniel did?

Daniel asked the king to look after the poor (some Bibles use the word **oppressed**, but the Chaldean word actually refers to poverty more than oppression). This suggests that one of the wicked things Nebuchadnezzar was about to be punished for is his insensitivity to the poor.

There is scriptural precedent for a king's repentance overturning a prophetic judgement. This happened a number of times to Hebrew kings, and to the king of Nineveh as described in the account of Jonah. But Daniel wasn't implying that the prophecy won't come true. He knew better than that. He was merely trying to hold off the sentence. If Nebuchadnezzar changes his ways, God might wait a little longer. He did spare the Assyrian city of Nineveh for its repentance after declaring that it would be destroyed because of sin, but eventually it did lay in ruins.

DANIEL 4:28-30

> 28 All this came upon the king Nebuchadnezzar.
>
> 29 At the end of twelve months, as he walked in the palace of the kingdom of Babylon,
>
> 30 the king spoke and said, "Is not this the great Babylon that I have built as the royal residence by the might of my power, and for the glory of my majesty?"

We don't know if 12 months was early or late. Did the king perhaps make an effort to change some of his ways, staving off sentencing for a year? There are no records that shed light on this, but the watchman angel was ready for the exact moment that Nebuchadnezzar's heart would be puffed up with pride.

Although the king had reason to be proud of this great city, he gave all the credit to himself. Through his earlier vision 35 years before, God has already told him that his mighty powers were a gift from God. In the vision he refers to, given just one year earlier, the angels told him that God sets up whomever He wishes as king.

DANIEL 4:31-33

> ₃₁ While the words were still in the king's mouth, there fell a voice from heaven saying, "O king Nebuchadnezzar, to you it is decreed; The kingdom is taken from you.
>
> ₃₂ And you will be driven from people, and will live with the beasts of the field. You will eat grass as oxen. Seven times will pass over you until you know that the Most High rules in the kingdom of men, and gives it to whomever He wishes."
>
> ₃₃ That very hour what had been said about Nebuchadnezzar was fulfilled. He was driven from men and ate grass as oxen. His body was wet with the dew of heaven, till his hair had grown like eagles' feathers and his nails like birds' claws.

Imagine the scene: a majestic king filled with pride as he surveys his kingdom, then a voice from heaven reciting very familiar words. Was there dread? Was there fear and trembling? How much time did he have to ponder the words that came from the air before the madness set in?

THE DISEASE

The specific mental derangement that hit Nebuchadnezzar is called **Lacanthropy** and refers to a belief that the person is actually an animal. Though Lacanthropy generally refers to a wolf (we get our werewolf legends from this disease) it can mean any kind of animal. Some would say this particular form experienced by Nebuchadnezzar should more accurately be called **Boanthropy**, which is a belief that the victim is an ox. There was a documented case of Boanthropy in England in the late 1920's.

There is a tradition in the Jewish *Talmud* that during this seven-year period of madness, Nebuchadnezzar was cared for by Daniel. From what we know of him, that would certainly be in character for this man of God, especially given his knowledge that the disease would eventually be lifted.

There is a seven-year period in the life of Nebuchadnezzar when nothing is said about him historically.

DANIEL 4:34-35

> 34 At the end of the days, I Nebuchadnezzar, lifted up my eyes to heaven, and my sanity returned unto me, and I praised the Most High, and I glorified and honored Him who lives forever, whose dominion is an everlasting dominion; His kingdom endures from generation to generation:
>
> 35 All the people of the earth are reputed as nothing. He does according to His will in the army of heaven, and among the people of the earth. Nobody can hold back His hand or say to Him, "What are you doing?"

CHRONICLE OF NEBUCHADNEZZAR
This clay tablet, now in the British Museum, chronicles the highlights of Nebuchadnezzar's reign using the complex Chaldean "cuneiform" language.

First, Nebuchadnezzar recognized God as being in charge. That's the first step to salvation for all of us.

Then he praised and glorified God for two unique qualities: His eternal existence (the **I AM**) and His unchanging nature. Unlike the kingdoms of men that change 180 degrees in a day (we'll see just how fast in Daniel 5), the kingdom of God remains unchanging forever. What a great source of comfort for us all!

Note that the Aramaic text includes a reference to **the army of heaven** (some Bibles do not make this clear). Nebuchadnezzar has gained a deep understanding of the reality of spiritual warfare.

DANIEL 4:36

> 36 At the same time my reason returned to me. For the glory of my kingdom, my honor and splendor returned to me. My advisors and nobles sought me out, and I was restored to my throne and became even greater than before.

How humble Nebuchadnezzar has become since lifting his eyes to Jehovah! What transparency! He is clearly a changed man. He recognized that his honor and splendor weren't his doing but given to him by God, saying that his throne was *restored* to him. This is only possible if someone else controls these things.

Note how he now refers to his magicians, astrologers, diviners, and other wise men as his *advisers and nobles*. He views them now as people, not merely as tools for wielding power over others.

He was restored to his throne and **became even greater than before**. This is remarkable. A king going insane for years, then regaining his previous status is possible only through God's intervention. Nebuchadnezzar's political enemies would have worked furiously to take over the power vacuum.

Even the most rapid kingdom restoration process would take months. This testimony was not written a day or two after his sanity was restored, but many months, and possibly even years later, because it was after the restoration was complete. The changes in Nebuchadnezzar were not short-term changes but lasting ones.

DANIEL 4:37

> 37 Now I Nebuchadnezzar praise and lift up and honor the King of heaven, whose works are truth, and His ways just. And those that walk in pride He is able to humble.

This last line is a powerful conclusion to this remarkable chapter in the book of Daniel, the personal testimony of a king.

Nebuchadnezzar no longer tries to force his faith on others with brute strength, as we saw in the last chapter, but acts as a witness and tells people that he has decided to praise, lift up and glorify God. He has also grasped the purpose of his ordeal. This appears to have been a true conversion. We can expect to see Nebuchadnezzar when we get to Heaven, possibly at Daniel's side.

We often look at acts of judgement by God as punishment. In fact, they are really a form of discipline, designed to bring us closer to Him. A careful study of the Bible shows that discipline is a sign of God's love. He must have loved Nebuchadnezzar deeply and seen within him a man worthy of salvation to put such effort into his life and redemption.

WHAT'S YOUR TESTIMONY?

We all have a story. God uses our stories in powerful ways to impact those around us. Yours may not be as dramatic as that of king Nebuchadnezzar of Babylon. But don't think it won't or can't have an impact! Many people can relate to your life, no matter how much or how little struggle you've been through. Have you ever written down your testimony? Years ago, while serving with Campus Crusade for Christ, I was taught to write down my testimony in a form that could be told aloud in two minutes or so. It was a great exercise and has served me well.

If you haven't yet done so, start today. Write down your story in one or two pages, using the following three parts:

- What your life was like before you met Christ
- How you came to make a decision to follow Him
- How your life has changed as a result

When you've finished, practice reading it aloud to friends or family members. Memorize your story. Then ask God to give you opportunities to share it.

Application — My Notes & Bible Study Questions

08

DANIEL CHAPTER 5
THE KINGDOM FALLS

After a reign of 43 years, Nebuchadnezzar died in 562BC. His son Evil-Merodach (in Akkadian "Amel-Marduk") took over the kingdom.

Evil-Merodach immediately released Jehoiachin, the captured Jewish king, from prison, giving him an honorable place at the court (see 2 Kings 25:27-30). It's interesting that he would have been so kind to the former Jewish king. Jehoiachin was the king so evil God had declared him "childless." Why the change of heart in Babylon?

Josephus records that Evil-Merodach even lavished gifts on him because "his father, Nebuchadnezzar, had not kept faith with Jehoiachin when he had surrendered himself and his family to spare Jerusalem."[1] In other words, he was now being painted as the *good guy* who surrendered Jerusalem instead of having been conquered by the Babylonians, while Nebuchadnezzar was made to look like the bad guy!

NERIGLISSAR TAKES CHARGE

Two years later the new king was assassinated by his brother-in-law, General Neriglissar[2] (or Nergal-Sharezer, whose name means "Nergal, protect the king"). He had served under Nebuchadnezzar when Jerusalem was destroyed (see Jeremiah 39:3,13). His high military spending led to inflation that rose to staggering levels.

CIVIL REVOLT AND A NEW KING

Neriglissar died four years later in 556BC and was succeeded by his son Labashi-Marduk, who lasted only nine months. He was murdered by Nabonidus, the leader of a massive civil revolt.

1　Josephus, *Antiquities of the Jews*
2　*Easton's Bible Dictionary*

To legitimize his place on the throne, Nabonidus later married a daughter of Nebuchadnezzar. His mother was the high priestess of a cult that followed the moon god Sin. His religious views deeply offended Babylonian priests. The priests are said to have eventually assisted the Persian king Cyrus in his efforts to seize Babylon.

Nabonidus was a weak king, and unpopular at home. He devoted most of his attention to Northern Arabia and Edom, which he conquered in 552.

He made his home the city of Teima (also called Tema) in Arabia, putting Belshazzar, his son, in charge as co-regent responsible for the province of Babylon and possibly the entire empire.

CYRUS MAKES HIS MOVE
Around this time, Nabonidus had supported a revolt over Astyages, king of the Medes to the north. This revolt was led by the king's Persian son-in-law, Cyrus (some say Cyrus was Astyages' nephew).

Cyrus had also asked for assistance from Lydia but when Lydia's king Croesus turned him down he simply conquered Lydia, then turned his attention on the Chaldean empire. He swept into the nation from the east and north, quickly subduing cities grown weak under the inept leadership of Nabonidus and his son Belshazzar. He destroyed the city of Opis just north of Babylon with considerable destruction and loss of life. A few days later he seized Sippar without a battle.

It was now the beginning of September, the month of *Tishri*. The heat of the desert gave way to icy cold nights. By now, Nabonidus had retreated south to the city of Teima, while Belshazzar shut himself up inside the impressive walled city of Babylon, a city considered militarily unconquerable. Archeological records show that the Babylonians had stockpiled many provisions and brought their idols inside the city walls, a sign that they were preparing for a lengthy siege.

On the 15th of Tishri, Cyrus and his army gathered around Babylon like a dark cloud, while nobles and officials throughout the city dressed in their finest clothing to attend a gala party organized by the king. That fateful day begins our narrative of Daniel chapter 5.

DANIEL 5:1

> 1 **Belshazzar the king gave a great banquet for a thousand of his nobles and drank wine before the thousand.**

A feast for 1,000 nobles is a significant event. It was a sign of defiance against the situation in which the city found itself, facing a hostile army outside its gates. But it was much more than just snubbing their noses against Cyrus.

DANIEL 5:2-4

> 2 **While Belshazzar was drinking the wine, he commanded to bring in the golden and silver vessels which his father Nebuchadnezzar had taken out of the temple in Jerusalem; so that the king, and his officials, his wives and his concubines might drink from them.**
>
> 3 **So they brought the golden vessels that were taken out of the temple of the house of God at Jerusalem; and the king and his officials, his wives, and his concubines, drank from them.**
>
> 4 **As they drank wine, they praised the gods of gold and of silver, of brass, iron, wood and stone.**

Of all the vessels available from all the nations Babylon had conquered — many of them quite impressive compared to the small nation of Judah — why did Belshazzar choose to pick on the Jews? Those vessels had sat in the museum for 47 years.

These were not merely ordinary drinking cups taken from the city of Jerusalem. These were from the "temple of the house of God." They were holy instruments previously used only by priests. Josephus records that they were "the vessels of God."[3]

Note the contrast: they're drinking from vessels taken from the temple in Jerusalem, but praising the gods of gold, silver, brass, iron, wood and stone. There was something much deeper going on behind this action. It was a public defiance against the God of the Hebrews and the predictions from 150 years earlier that Babylon would be given to Cyrus.

RECORD OF BELSHAZZAR
For many years, critics of the book of Daniel claimed that his account of Belshazzar was in error because no archeological record of that name had been found. All that changed with the discovery of the cylinder of Nabonidus, shown above, which mentions Belshazzar by name.

Isaiah 45 and 46 predicted Cyrus by name, indicating that God would use him to conquer Babylon. Tens of thousands of Jews living in various parts of the empire had certainly been discussing these passages for weeks or months with an attitude of eager expectation. There is no doubt that these prophecies had been the subject of much political discomfort and discussion among the leaders of Babylon. Belshazzar wanted to make a highly visible statement to regain confidence in his leadership. One way to do that would be to publicly humiliate the God of the Jews. So he drank from God's holy vessels while publicly praising his gods.

---

3   Josephus, *Antiquities of the Jews*

DANIEL 5:5-9

> 5 In the same hour the fingers of a man's hand suddenly appeared and wrote on the plaster of the wall of the king's palace near the lamp stand. The king watched the part of the hand that wrote.
>
> 6 Then the king's face became pale, and he became so frightened that the joints of his loins shook and his knees knocked together.
>
> 7 The king cried out to bring in the astrologers, Chaldeans and diviners. And the king said to the wise men of Babylon, "Whoever reads this writing, and shows me its meaning, shall be clothed in purple and have a chain of gold placed around his neck, and will be made the third highest ruler in the kingdom.
>
> 8 Then all the king's wise men came in, but they could not read the writing, nor tell the king what it meant.
>
> 9 So king Belshazzar became even more afraid, and all the color drained from his face, and his nobles were baffled.

Remember Nebuchadnezzar's "voice from heaven," timed precisely to the second that he lifted up his voice in pride? It seems that the hand writing on the wall appeared with uncanny timing ("in the same hour"), possibly even at the very moment of an announcement against or joke about the God of Israel.

The Aramaic text describing Belshazzar's reaction is perhaps best translated by the quaint language of the King James version:

> **"the joints of his loins were loosed and his knees smote one against the other"** —Daniel 5:6 (KJV)

You've probably encountered situations that made you afraid. But chances are, you've never been so scared your knees actually banged together. The king was not merely shocked. He was terrified beyond ordinary fear. The God he had just mocked suddenly

Persian Empire, 330BC

THE PERSIAN EMPIRE
The forerunner of modern-day Iran, the Persian empire was originally smaller than that of Babylonia or of the Medes to the north. Cyrus used shrewd political maneuvering, along with a carefully timed murder of Astyages, king of the Medes, to take over the entire empire, then extend his reach to Babylon. By the time Alexander the Great unleashed his fury against the Persians in 330BC, it had grown to enormous proportions.

made His presence known before the king and his guests in a dramatic, powerful way.

A lamp stand is mentioned as being *the* lamp stand. There were actually many lamp stands in the banquet hall, so this reference may mean something significant, such as a Jewish menorah taken from the temple along with the other artifacts.

Notice the reference to the hand writing on the **plaster** of the wall. We know from recent archeology that all the walls of this room except one were covered in glazed blue bricks. One wall was white plaster, confirming that Daniel was an eyewitness to these events. It also suggests that the hand wrote into charcoal dust that would have gathered on this white wall from the flames of the lamp stand. Picture the scene: a mysterious hand appears in thin air and carves letters out of the blackened area of the wall, or marking the white plaster with charcoal dust. It would have been a disturbing and extremely frightful event for the audience.

WHICH LAMP STAND?
The text gives unexpected importance to a lamp stand, saying that the hand wrote on the plaster "near *the* lamp stand" (verse 5). Since there would have been many lamps in the room and especially near the white wall, why was this one given such prominence? It is quite possible that a Jewish menorah was brought with the other vessels from the temple treasures and placed near the head table. The menorah was a symbol of God's plan for Israel.

Belshazzar could offer no rank higher than *third highest ruler* because he himself was just second in command, after his father Nabonidus.

The king called for his wise men, but Daniel was not among them. He would have been well over 80 years of age by this time. He was semi-retired by now, though he would serve the next king for a short time after Babylon changes hands.

After the wise men fail to interpret the words on the wall, Belshazzar's face becomes as white as a sheet. He is really terrified and deeply concerned, quite sober by now.

DANIEL 5:10

> 10 Now the queen, hearing the commotion of the king and his nobles, came into the banquet house. The queen said, "O king, live forever! Do not let your thoughts trouble you, and don't look so pale.

The queen is a daughter of Nebuchadnezzar, and Belshazzar's grandmother. Obviously she wasn't at the party. She came into the banquet room only after hearing the commotion.

She admonishes her grandson to not look "so pale." Only a grandmother could speak to the king in that way and get away with it! He was clearly showing signs of stress, and she was attempting to help him regain his composure and fulfill his leadership responsibilities. This banquet was given in front of 1,000 of the empire's top leaders. It wasn't good for them to see him fall apart like this.

DANIEL 5:11-12

> 11 There is a man in your kingdom who has the spirit of the holy gods in him. In the days of your father, insight and understanding and wisdom, like the wisdom of the gods, was found in him. King Nebuchadnezzar your father — your father the king, I say — made him chief over the magicians, astrologers, Chaldeans, and diviners;

> **12** This man Daniel, whom the king named Belteshazzar, was found to have an excellent spirit and knowledge and understanding, and also the ability to interpret dreams, explain hard riddles and solve difficult problems. Now let Daniel be called, and he will show the meaning."

The term "father" simply means "ancestral relative" which can include "father-in-law" and even "grandfather."

The queen, as the daughter of Nebuchadnezzar, would have grown up with Daniel's influence a major part of her childhood years. She is very respectful of Daniel. Her words indicate that she does not support her grandson's cavalier attitude about the state of the empire. They also showed great faith in Daniel.

DANIEL 5:13-14

> **13** Then Daniel was brought in before the king. The king said to Daniel, "Are you that Daniel, of the exiles brought by my father out of Judah?
>
> **14** I have even heard of you, that the spirit of the gods is in you, and that intelligence and insight and excellent wisdom is found in you.

Belshazzar meets Daniel face-to-face for the first time. Isn't it interesting that Belshazzar had never previously bothered to meet the guy who had been in charge of all the wise men of Babylon? The king tells Daniel that he had "even heard of" him. It's not clear whether he was referring to the queen's mention and simply trying to save face, or if he had actually recalled the reputation and past stories about Daniel from his youth.

DANIEL 5:15-16

> 15 Now the wise men, the astrologers, were brought before me to read this writing and make known to me the meaning of it. But they could not explain it.
>
> 16 I have heard that you can interpret such things, and solve difficult problems. Now if you can read the writing and make known to me the meaning of it, you shall be clothed with purple and have a chain of gold placed around your neck, and you will be made the third highest ruler in the kingdom."

He explains that the wise men could not read the writing. They were experts in Cuneiform script and Chaldean, so the letters on the wall were either written in another language or put in a structure that required wisdom to understand.

Some Bible teachers suggest that the words were placed in an unusual configuration, possibly in a grid or code structure. They did not have vowels, making interpretation more challenging than what we're used to in modern times. We will examine the words momentarily.

It is possible that the wise men could read the text yet didn't understand what the words actually meant.

DANIEL 5:17

> 17 Then Daniel answered the king, "Let your gifts be to yourself, and give your rewards to another. Even so I will read the writing to the king, and tell him what it means.

Daniel doesn't care for the trappings offered by the king. But he agrees to interpret the words because their appearance had a purpose beyond simply scaring the king. They are a message from God, meant to be understood, meant to demonstrate the sovereignty of God.

DANIEL 5:18-21

18 O king, the most high God gave Nebuchadnezzar your father a kingdom and majesty and glory and honor.

19 Because of the high position that He gave him, all people, nations and languages trembled before him and feared him. Those he wanted to kill, he killed. Those he wanted kept alive would live. He promoted whomever he wished to promote, and he humbled those he wanted to humble.

20 But when his heart was lifted up and his mind hardened in pride, he was deposed from his kingly throne, and his glory was taken from him.

21 And he was driven from people. His heart was made like that of an animal, and he lived with the wild beasts. They fed him with grass like oxen, and his body was wet with the dew of heaven; until he knew that the most high God ruled over the kingdom of men and set up over it whomever He wanted.

Before he goes into the explanation, Daniel reminds Belshazzar of the experience that Nebuchadnezzar went through as a result of his pride.

Except for the mention of Nebuchadnezzar's prideful heart getting him in trouble, Daniel gives what can be understood as a positive description of the former king. He says God gave him "majesty and glory and honor." He explains that he was an absolute monarch who was given his power and authority as a gift from God.

Again we see the reference to *the kingdom of men* and the emphasis that God will "set up over it whomever He wanted."

DANIEL 5:22-24

> 22 But you his son, O Belshazzar, have not humbled your heart, though you knew all this;
>
> 23 Instead, you have lifted yourself up against the Lord of heaven. You had the vessels of his house brought before you, and you and your nobles, your wives, and your concubines, drank wine from them. And you praised the gods of silver and gold, of brass, iron, wood and stone, which cannot see nor hear, nor know. And you have not glorified the God who holds your breath in His hand, and who has power over all the things you do.
>
> 24 Therefore he sent the part of the hand that wrote this inscription.

Daniel points out that Belshazzar is not like his father. Even though he grew up with full knowledge of the wondrous accounts of Nebuchadnezzar's encounters with God, his heart was proud. He claims that Belshazzar was well aware of this lesson, another suggestion that Nebuchadnezzar's conversion, described in Daniel chapter 4, had been very real.

DANIEL 5:25-28

> 25 This is the inscription that was written: MENE, MENE, TEKEL, UPHARSIN
>
> 26 This is what these words mean:
>
>   { Mene } : God has numbered the days of your kingdom and brought it to an end.
>
> 27 { Tekel } : You have been weighed on the scales and found wanting.
>
> 28 { Peres } : Your kingdom is divided and given to the Medes and Persians.

The inscription was **Mene Mene Tekel Peres**. There were no vowels in the language of that time; these were implied. This means that only consonants were visible on the wall by the lamp stand. Depending on how you placed vowels, the words could have been viewed in a variety of ways that would mean different things. Some Bible scholars also suggest that the words may have been placed vertically or backwards, either of which would have been even more cryptic.

You may be confused by the use of "Upharsin" or "Parsin" used in verse 25 as compared to "Peres" used in verse 28. This is simply the plural form of Peres. Daniel was referring to its double meaning as he explained the writing, including both references in the single word.

Mene
Mene means "numbered." God had numbered Belshazzar's reign and today was the end of it. Other word variations of the same consonants that could have confused the wise men earlier include mena, mina, maneh.

Tekel
Tekel means "weighed." Other variations using the same consonants include teqal, teqil, teqel (Hebrew shekel).

Peres
Peres means "to divide" though Daniel used the passive participle "peris" which means "divided." If you use the "a" instead of the "e" it means "Persia," so this was meant as a double reference to both division and the Medes and Persians. Upharsin is simply the plural form.

DANIEL 5:29-31

29 **Then at Belshazzar's command, Daniel was clothed in purple, and a gold chain was placed around his neck, and he was proclaimed the third highest ruler in the kingdom.**

30 **That very night Belshazzar, king of the Chaldeans, was slain.**

31 **And Darius the Mede took over the kingdom, being about sixty-two years old.**

Daniel's interpretation must have troubled Belshazzar greatly, but the king followed through with his promise of honor and position. Perhaps he thought that God would relent if he treated him well. But it was too late for repentance.

CYRUS ENTERS THE CITY

It is now past midnight in the early hours of 16th Tishri. At the very time that all these events were taking place, Cyrus' general Ugbaru, with the help of Babylonian priests wanting to overthrow Nabonidus, had diverted the Euphrates river into a channel dug about eighty years earlier. This caused the moat around Babylon to drop to a level halfway up a man's thigh. Cyrus' men slipped quietly into Babylon underneath the many huge gates, and took the city by surprise.[4]

Cyrus would boast for years that he had conquered Babylon — the world's strongest fortress city — without a battle. Taking over this spectacular city, the center of the great empire of Babylon, had gone so smoothly the inhabitants of the central part of the giant city didn't even know they had been conquered for some time.[5]

CYRUS RELEASES THE JEWISH EXILES

The prophet Isaiah had prophesied some 150 years earlier that God would call Cyrus to victory against Babylon, free the Jews, and rebuild the city of Jerusalem. Shown above is a cylinder where Cyrus describes his release of the Jewish exiles, as had been foretold by Isaiah some 150 years earlier.

"This is what the Lord says to his anointed, to Cyrus, whose right hand I take hold of to subdue nations before him and to strip kings of their armor, to open doors before him so that gates will not be shut"
—Isaiah 45:1 (NIV)

"I will raise up Cyrus in my righteousness: I will make all his ways straight. He will rebuild my city and set my exiles free, but not for a price or reward, says the LORD Almighty."
—Isaiah 45:13 (NIV)

---

4   Herodotus, *The History, Book 1: Clio*
5   ibid.

General Ugbaru died just a month or so later. Cyrus appointed a man named Gubaru as governor over Babylon. The names are similar and thus cause much confusion. Though there is some disagreement about Darius, it appears most likely that this was the name given to governor Gubaru. It was common practice for Cyrus to appoint Medes to important positions,[6] including that of a Viceroy, with royal powers — essentially a king. A Babylonian tablet from 535BC says Gubaru was appointed a Satrap to Babylon and another contains an inscription that reads, in part:

> **"the guilt of a sin against Gubaru, the Governor of Babylon and the district beyond the river... (the area west of the Euphrates)."**[7]

The name Darius is actually a title meaning *the royal one*. Some argue that a Viceroy would not have issued a decree such as the one we'll see in Daniel 6:25, but the Aramaic used in that decree does not mean the whole *earth*, but the whole *land*, the part under his authority.

In just a few hours, an empire has changed hands and a new king now sits on the throne of Babylon, the world's mightiest city, the pride of the Chaldeans. Babylon has fallen, and Persia now controls the world.

---

6   R. Ghirshman, *Iran*
7   Inscriptions in the Collection of James B. Nies, *pt. 2, 1918, nos. 69 and 114*

Application My Notes & Bible Study Questions

09

DANIEL CHAPTER 5
POLITICALLY INCORRECT

What does faith look like? Can you see it? Lots of people refer to themselves as Christians or adherents of a faith, but how do you know if someone truly believes what they claim? Daniel gives an example of what true faith looks like to those peering in from the outside. Even centuries later, it's crystal clear.

Earlier, in Daniel chapter 2, we saw Shadrach, Meshach and Abed-nego being persecuted for not bowing down to the idol set up by king Nebuchadnezzar. But Daniel was not included in the political attacks on those men. In this chapter, we see Daniel himself put to the test and persecuted for bowing down before the living God.

DANIEL 6:1-2

> 1 It pleased Darius to appoint 120 satraps, which should rule throughout the whole kingdom;
>
> 2 And over these three presidents, of whom Daniel was first. The satraps were made accountable to them so that the king should suffer no loss.

DARIUS THE MEDE

Who exactly was Darius? Josephus records that Darius the Mede (see Daniel 5:31) was "the son of Astyages, who ended Babylonian rule along with his relative, Cyrus."[1]

Some higher critics suggest that Darius is actually Cyrus. But this is impossible if you believe Scripture. The final verse of this chapter lists the two as different figures. This Darius (the term actually means "Royal One") is not the same Persian king Darius

---

1 Josephus, *Antiquities of the Jews*

who served during the time of Ezra, interacting with Zerrubbabel to issue a decree that would rebuild the temple.²

Many Bible scholars believe the Darius mentioned here in Daniel was Gubaru. Though Gubaru was technically called a governor in archeological records, it is also apparent that he was given powers equal to that of a king, so it's quite acceptable that official records assign him as king.

Darius was organizationally creative. He understood a need to restructure the empire. This act suggests that there was great civil disobedience following Belshazzar's rule and the fall of Babylon, which Darius was attempting to clean up.

Satraps are high-level civil administrators. These 120 were of lesser rank than a group of 20 mentioned by the historian Herodotus.³ Above those 20 were three commissioners of whom Daniel was one. It is likely that most of the others were either Medes or Persians. Because the Persian empire had been born from a partnership between the Medes and Persians, there was great effort to give both groups equal opportunities in positions of power, to avoid civil strife and establish peace within the empire.

EXAMPLES OF FAITH

Hebrews 11:17-40, the great chapter of faith, gives us a wonderful review of the entire purpose of the story described here in Daniel 6.

The passage describes many great people of God and how their strength of character in various circumstances has stood the test of time and sets an example for all generations. Included in the list is a reference to God "shutting the mouths of lions," alluding to Daniel's experience here.

---

2   Josephus, *Antiquities of the Jews*
3   Herodotus, *The History, Book 1: Clio*

DANIEL 6:3

> 3 **Then Daniel was preferred above the presidents and satraps, because an excellent spirit was in him; and the king planned to set him over the whole realm.**

Obviously some additional time has passed for Daniel's reputation to be so well established with Darius that the king planned to promote him to such a high level of authority. It's easy to forget that Daniel was by now a very old man, in his 80's. He was clearly still very healthy and both mentally and physically active to be considered for the role of Prime Minister of the empire.

DANIEL 6:4-5

> 4 **Then the presidents and satraps looked for grounds against Daniel in his conduct over the kingdom, but they could find no occasion nor fault; because he was trustworthy, neither was there any negligence or corruption found in him.**
>
> 5 **Then these men said, We will not find any grounds for charges against this Daniel, unless we find something that has to do with the law of his God.**

Imagine being of such principled character that people can't even find a weakness that they might eventually be able to use against you! Daniel's character was above reproach in every way, without even a hint of anything that might give way in the future.

The New Living Translation, though a paraphrase, has what seems to be the clearest translation of verse 5, pointing out that the only charges these men are likely to find has to do with *the requirements* of Daniel's faith. They will use the requirements of his faith against him, the things he must do as he serves God and practices his faith.

DANIEL 6:6-7

> **6** Then these presidents and satraps assembled together before the king and said to him, "King Darius, live forever!
>
> **7** All the presidents of the kingdom, the governors and the satraps, advisors and captains have agreed together to establish a royal edict, and to make a firm decree, that whoever prays to any God or man for thirty days, except to you, O king, shall be cast into the den of lions.

It's not necessary to assume that the entire body of 120 satraps went to see the king. It may well have been a contingent representing them and those under them. The group would have been large enough to be impressive.

Notice how they announce that this was unanimous ("**all** the presidents, governors, satraps, advisors and captains"), implying that the entire body of government had agreed to this course of action. They have hatched a plan in secret and now, in an effort to avoid resistance from the king, they attempt to claim that every leader in the kingdom is behind it. This lie, which implies that Daniel and his friends also supported the plan, will prove to be their undoing later.

How many weeks of planning had it taken to come up with this bold plan? In those days, there were no E-mails or telephone conference calls. To organize a plan of this magnitude, they would have sent secret letters and held private meetings over many months.

Timing was critical, as they had to be certain that the king would not discuss this plan with Daniel, who may have been out of Babylon while all of this was taking place.

The plan they proposed was presented to the king as a way to solve what was apparently a problem with civil unrest throughout the empire.

The lions' den was a large pit in the ground, but not very deep. An opening in the top, possibly for viewing, could be covered with a large stone. Yet they did not use the pit for sport, as the Romans would later, but for administering capital punishment. Lions were released into the pit from doors in the side that would be pulled up or lowered from above. Access was from above or from tunnels in the sides of the pit.

DANIEL 6:8-9

> **8 Now, O king, issue the decree and sign the writing so that it cannot be changed, according to the law of the Medes and Persians."**
>
> **9 So king Darius signed the writing and the decree.**

There appeared to be pressure on the king to do this immediately. They could not take a chance that he would wait and discuss it with Daniel, who was being groomed for the position of Prime Minister and was no doubt close to the king.

It is possible that Daniel was out of the country on official business, or at least in some other part of the empire. As it would take some time for this large group representing large portions of the empire — Phoenicia, Palestine, Syria, Cypress — to make the trip here and hold this conference, we have to assume that they knew Daniel would be unavailable to the king.

The Medes and the Persians (this was now the Persian empire) had long been very sensitive to political issues. It was the practice of Cyrus to appoint evenly balanced numbers of Medes and Persians into high positions to gain the support of both racial groups. It should not be assumed that the king's quick acceptance of this plan was a sign of weakness or gullibility. It quite likely followed a standard political procedure and took into account many cultural sensitivities.

 Insight

STORIES OF TRUE FAITH

Throughout history, Christians have suffered greatly for their faith in Christ, yet remained strong. Their stories are a great source of encouragement.

Plinius Secundus, known as "Pliny the Younger," was a Roman governor ordered to persecute Christians in AD112. It's apparent that he had great respect for their love of truth. He wrote to emperor Trajan, stating that Christians are "people who love the truth at any cost." He described their vows not to do any evil deed, not to cheat anyone, and never to steal or lie.[1] He told Trajan that true Christians would refuse to denounce their leader Jesus Christ, even under extreme torture. He expressed contempt for those who did recant their faith in Christ even though it was his job to bring about such declarations.

During the 1500's, a young female servant in Roneses, Flanders proudly told the Inquisitors who had discovered her forbidden Bible that "This book is mine. I am reading from it, and it is more precious to me than anything." She was then suffocated by being bricked in behind a wall.[2]

Evangelist Richard Wurmbrand, who spent many years during the 1950's in a Soviet prison for his faith in Christ, reported that Christians would be tortured with red-hot iron pokers, with truncheons, and with sticks, but instead of fear they responded by looking upon those who tortured them with love and pity.

In 1992, Muslims in Kaduna, Nigeria went on a rampage against Christians, killing over 300. They severed the right hand of a pastor. When it fell, he raised the other one and sang, "He is Lord, He is Lord! He is risen from the dead, and He is Lord. Every knee shall bow and every tongue confess that Jesus Christ is Lord." [3]

A young Muslim man named Asif, living in Pakistan, turned from Islam to Christianity in 2001. He was severely beaten on many occasions, including once in a police station. When asked how he could endure this and not be discouraged, he quoted Philippians 1:29, "For to you it has been granted for Christ's sake, not only to believe in Him, but also to suffer for His sake." [4]

---

1 Pliny the Younger, *The Letters of Pliny the Younger; Correspondence with the Emperor Trajan*
2 DC Talk and the Voice of the Martyrs, *Jesus Freaks*
3 Ibid.
3 DC Talk and the Voice of the Martyrs, *Jesus Freaks, Volume II*

In Daniel's absence, a decree has now been published that forms the ultimate test for any person of faith.

When staring certain death in the face, would you fudge a bit with the rules? Even under less severe moments of discomfort, do you soften your public actions in relation to your faith? In a case like this, would you apply tests of reasoning to justify your actions on the grounds that they weren't technically required, or that God will forgive you? How would you respond?

DANIEL 6:10

> **10 Now when Daniel learned that the decree was signed, he went into his house where his windows opened in his room toward Jerusalem. Three times a day he kneeled and prayed, and gave thanks before his God, as was his custom.**

Daniel heard about this decree after it was established. His response was to change nothing in his spiritual habits. It would have been very easy for him to 'hide' his continuing worship of God behind shuttered windows, or to pray silently. After all, it was a mere 30-day decree. How many of us, in a setting where we

OUR RESPONSE TO A FAITH UNDER ATTACK

In today's world, any example of firm commitment to a faith is under attack. Those who hold fast to Scriptural truth are often ridiculed, whether on campuses, in the workplace, in the media, or in politics.

Schools are denying the use of rooms for prayer meetings, while those same spaces are often granted to other religious groups. Students may write or talk about many spiritual topics, but not about Jesus.

Faced with this onslaught of pressure, many Christians are retreating behind closed doors. Bibles are disappearing from sight. Prayer is not as visible in restaurants when meals are placed before patrons. Where Christians used to gather publicly to practice their faith, they are increasingly doing so only in private.

How about you? How firm is your faith?

might be conspicuous, take the easy way out and change our usual habits! Daniel is the example of how we should behave at all times.

Windows in those days were not made of glass. They were solid shutters. Yet, even knowing he would be watched, he kept them open, aware that his accusers would be relentless in trapping him.

As Christians, we are not required to be public about our prayer time. Indeed, Jesus said that we should go behind closed doors to make our petitions in private.[4] How do we reconcile Jesus' teaching with the example of Daniel? There are two key points here:

1 **Daniel did pray in private.** He simply had the practice of keeping his windows open to Jerusalem in honor of that city's significance as the place where the holy temple had once stood.

2 **Daniel did not change his habits.** Whatever your prayer habits are, they shouldn't change under the pressure of persecution. God will honor your continued strength of commitment. Daniel did not defiantly react with a new, bold way of praying in public. Neither did he shy away from his pattern of prayer. He just continued to do what he had always done.

DANIEL 6:11-12

> 11 Then these men went as a group and found Daniel praying and making requests of his God.
>
> 12 So they came and spoke before the king concerning the king's decree: "Have you not signed a decree, that every man that prays to any God or man within thirty days, except to you, O king, shall be cast into the den of lions?" The king answered, "The thing is true, according to the law of the Medes and Persians, which cannot be changed.

The men knew how Daniel would respond. Do those who know you have a clear idea how you would respond in a situation like this? Do they even know you're a Christian?

---

4   Matthew 6:4-6

The decree was about *who* was prayed to, not the act of prayer itself. So the investigating group was listening to Daniel's prayer. This means they must have been close enough to hear the actual content of his prayers clearly. They weren't just observing from a distance. Daniel could have chosen to pray silently, but didn't.

Daniel's opponents first ask the king to confirm his authority. They don't mention Daniel just yet. It's interesting when you see his answer, because it suggests that they accused him of some kind of trickery or false behavior. He affirms that he signed the document and that the law cannot be changed. The empire had this decree to assure allegiance by these two diverse racial and cultural groups.

DANIEL 6:13

> 13 **Then they answered the king, "That Daniel, one of those exiles of Judah, pays no attention to you, O king, nor to the decree that you signed, but prays to his God three times a day."**

GETTING DOWN ON OUR KNEES

Notice that Daniel gets down on his knees to pray. In our modern culture, we tend to increasingly ignore this position of prayer.

It isn't required, of course, but it is a position honoring to God and was modelled by Christ. For thousands of years, people got down on one knee before a king or queen. Getting down on two of them identifies the proper attitude towards God as the King of kings.

See Luke 22:41, where Christ prays on his knees. Stephen kneels to pray as he is stoned to death in Acts 7:59-60. Paul kneels in Acts 9:40. Acts 20:36 shows the humility of a group on their knees before God. The apostles are shown to kneel again in Acts 21:5.

Yet isn't it amazing that we can come before the King of kings without needing to adopt this position of subservience or even an appointment!

Note the anti-Semitism in their accusation, "**that** Daniel," and "one of **those** exiles." The Jews had not yet been released from captivity, but they had been in the kingdom nearly 70 years, yet the bigotry towards them is unmistakable.

DANIEL 6:14-15

> 14 When he heard these words, the king was deeply displeased with himself, and set his heart on Daniel to rescue him. He made every effort until sundown to save him.
>
> 15 Then these men assembled before the king and said to him, "Remember, O king, that the law of the Medes and Persians is that no decree nor statute which the king sets up may be changed."

The king's response is remarkable. He was distressed at himself (this is accurately translated in the King James Version, but sometimes lost in other versions). It dawned on him that he's been had.

Contrast his actions to those of Nebuchadnezzar, who simply flew into a rage when things went against him. This guy sprang into motion and tried legal means to change the situation.

Darius made every effort until sundown to save Daniel. He didn't just throw up his hands and say, "Oh well." Besides showing a character of great personal integrity, this also demonstrates that he had a strong relationship with Daniel.

The men who put the king up to this now hear about his attempts to save Daniel and remind him that keeping Daniel away from the required punishment would be illegal.

John 19 contains a detailed account of another innocent man charged with a capital crime, and another governing leader attempting (though not with much conviction) to ensure that justice prevails rather than letting the innocent man fall to the clutches of a nasty mob. Take a few moments to read John 19 and study both the differences and similarities between the two accounts.

DANIEL 6:16-18

> ₁₆ Then the king gave the order, and they brought Daniel and threw him into the den of lions. Now the king said to Daniel, "May your God, whom you serve continually, rescue you."
>
> ₁₇ A stone was brought and laid over the mouth of the den, and the king sealed it with his own signet ring and with the signet rings of his nobles; that the purpose might not be changed concerning Daniel.
>
> ₁₈ Then the king went to his palace, and passed the night fasting and without musical entertainment being brought before him. He was unable to sleep.

The Persians were polytheistic, believing in a number of gods with no basis for the reality of their faith. But in Daniel's Jewish culture, there were many examples of genuine miraculous intervention. Darius shows enormous faith in Daniel's God when he says that God may be able to save his life. Although he goes back home, he wonders all night if Daniel's God will save him.

A stone has been sealed over the opening to keep people out, just as another stone would eventually be sealed against another opening nearly 600 years later. Against the power of the one and only true God, no seal of a mortal king can stand.

King Darius spent a sleepless night considering Daniel's situation and his commitment to his faith. What an impact his life has made! What a great opportunity for us to reflect on the impact of our lives to those around us. Is your character of such value that others who don't share your beliefs would try to spare your life under persecution?

Daniel had no doubt his God *could* save him. But neither Darius nor Daniel could be sure that He *would* spare the man of faith. As the hours ticked by, Darius struggled with this question.

DANIEL 6:19-22

₁₉ **Then the king got up very early in the morning, and hurried to the den of lions.**

₂₀ **When he came close to the den, he cried with an anguished voice to Daniel, "O Daniel, servant of the living God, was your God, whom you serve continually, able to save you from the lions?"**

₂₁ **Then Daniel answered the king, "O king, live forever!**

₂₂ **My God sent his angel, and has shut the lions' mouths. They have not hurt me. I was found innocent before him. Also, before you, O king, I have done nothing wrong."**

The stone may have been removed as Darius arrived, but some critics make too much of his ability to speak clearly with Daniel as he approached. Remember that the stone had been sealed with wax. Any effort to open it without the king's express command would have led to severe consequences.

If the stone had been removed without the presence of key congressional leaders, it could have led to accusations that Darius had interfered. So it's likely that the covering stone was still in place. It would be normal for the king to call out, since he might be unable to see clearly into the den.

Imagine the joy on Darius' face when he heard Daniel's voice! He would have been thrilled, yet surprised. He showed remarkable faith in God, a testament to the witness Daniel had been to the reality of his faith. As a Gentile, Darius would have been deeply impressed by this answer to Daniel's prayer.

Daniel reminds the king that he was innocent of doing anything that would harm the kingdom. This appears to be a subtle admonition to Darius that he should be more balanced in the decisions he makes: his focus should be on dealing with wrongdoing, not managing religious affiliations.

DANIEL 6:23-24

> 23 The king was extremely pleased, and commanded that they take Daniel up out of the den. So Daniel was lifted up out of the den, and no wound was found upon him, because he trusted in his God.
>
> 24 At the king's command they brought those men that had accused Daniel, and they threw them into the den of lions along with their children and their wives. And the lions overpowered them and broke all their bones in pieces before they even reached the bottom of the den.

Now the tables are turned on the evildoers who put the king up to this trickery. It was common practice in those days to put entire families to death to ensure that some vengeful family member wouldn't try to take out the king or cause political trouble later on. An example of this is found in the book of Esther. Even today, family revenge is a big part of middle eastern culture, carrying on for generations.

DANIEL 6:25-27

> 25 Then king Darius wrote to all the people, nations and languages that lived throughout the land: "Peace be multiplied to you.
>
> 26 I issue a decree, That in every part of my kingdom men tremble before and fear the God of Daniel. For He is the living God, and steadfast forever, His kingdom will not be destroyed, and His dominion shall be even unto the end.
>
> 27 He rescues and saves, and He works signs and wonders in heaven and in earth, and has saved Daniel from the power of the lions."

This decree is remarkable considering Persia's polytheistic culture. Darius, like Nebuchadnezzar had before him, now issues a decree declaring the God of the Jews the "living God." What a contrast to the lifeless god of metal the earlier king had ordered the people to worship. After Daniel's friends were saved from the fiery furnace, Nebuchadnezzar had issued a public empire-wide decree claiming that "there is no other God that can save in a way like this."[5]

It should be noted that Darius, although he had the royal powers of a king, was a Viceroy put in charge of Babylon by Persian king Cyrus. The Aramaic in his decree refers to the whole *land*, not the whole *earth* as some Bibles translate. It covers only the territory Darius is in charge of.

DANIEL 6:28

> 28 **So Daniel prospered in the reign of Darius and the reign of Cyrus the Persian.**

There is much confusion about Darius and Cyrus. Some liberal critics even claim that both men are one and the same. That is impossible given this verse. Archeological records show that Cyrus appointed Medes to powerful positions. He put Darius the Mede in charge of Babylon while he continued his conquests of the prior Babylonian empire, before taking the throne of the Persian empire.

PERSECUTION FROM TWO DIRECTIONS

Depending on where we live, we may not have to worry about being thrown to physical lions, but Christians continually face persecution from two aspects:

1. **For not following the world's patterns.**

2. **For believing what we specifically believe, that the Bible is the Word of God.**

The two are very different. We can face persecution for not believing in the politically correct philosophies of the world. And we can face persecution for believing in the truth of the Bible.

It is never comfortable to face unpopularity or difficulties because of our faith. But too often we make compromises in an effort to fit in rather than standing strongly for what we believe regardless of the consequences.

---

5   Daniel 3:29 (see chapter 6)

In Daniel chapter 1 we saw that Daniel remained in the city of Babylon until the first year of Cyrus, when he left the city. An old man by the time of the release of the Jewish captives (well into his eighties), it is unlikely that Daniel made the trip to Judah.

His final prophetic vision was given to him on the shores of the Tigris river (Babylon is on the Euphrates) in the third year of Cyrus. When we put that together with Daniel Chapter 1 we can assume that he left Babylon after the first year of Cyrus but continued to live in that part of the world.

Application
My Notes & Bible Study Questions

PART 3
The Prophecies

10

DANIEL CHAPTER 7
THE FOUR WILD BEASTS

From the beginning of chapter 2 through the end of chapter 7, Daniel has switched from Hebrew to write in the Gentile language of the day, Aramaic (also known as Chaldean). The Aramaic language uses the same letters as Hebrew, but in different order, just as Spanish and English use the same Roman letters, but differently. Why the change in language?

Most of Scripture deals with history as seen through the lens of Israel, with the Jews and the nation of Israel as the "center point" of the story. The first few chapters we've read from the book of Daniel deal primarily with Gentile history. So it makes sense that Daniel would write them in the common Gentile language to make the distinction obvious. At the end of this chapter, as he moves again to focus on the future of the Jewish people, Daniel switches back to Hebrew.

This vision in chapter 7 is the same one given to Nebuchadnezzar in chapter 2, but with different idioms used. It is appropriate that Daniel chose to start and end the use of Aramaic language with the account of these visions, since they represent the same history.

What makes this chapter particularly interesting is that while Nebuchadnezzar was shown a vision reflecting man's view of these kingdoms, Daniel was shown God's view.

In Nebuchadnezzar's vision, a man of precious metal was seen, a story of impressive wealth and superiority. His vision was about man's push for power and riches, ultimately overcome by Christ.

Human beings tend to think of empire building as a way to bring order and unity to the world. Daniel's view of the same history shows these kingdoms from God's point of view, as a series of voracious beasts causing pain and turmoil in their rebellion against God. They are chaotic, not unified. They are ugly and disturbing. Rather than the shining beauty of accomplishment represented by precious metals, there is only destruction.

DANIEL 7:1-2

> 1 In the first year of Belshazzar king of Babylon Daniel had a dream and visions while he lay upon his bed. He wrote down the dream, and told the sum of the matters.
>
> 2 Daniel said, "I saw in my vision by night, and, behold, the four winds of heaven moved upon the great sea.

This vision was given to Daniel in the first year of the co-regency of Belshazzar. We don't know exactly when Nabonidus began to share the kingdom with his son. Most historians believe it was about 3 or 4 years after Nabonidus became king. So when Daniel interpreted the writing on the wall the night Belshazzar is killed, he would have already had the perspective of this vision in his mind.

The Great Sea was a common term for the Mediterranean Sea, but is used in several places of the Bible to describe the "sea" of humanity in its Gentile sense. For other references, see Isaiah 17:12-13; 57:20; Jeremiah 6:23; 46:7-9; 47:2; Revelation 13:1; 17:1,15.

The *four winds of heaven* is another common term in Scripture. We see it used to describe spiritual forces, both good and evil. The term is used 90 times in the Old Testament, 30 times in the New.

DANIEL 7:3-4

> 3 Four great beasts, each different from one another, came up from the sea.
>
> 4 The first was like a lion, and had eagle's wings. As I looked, its wings were torn off, and it was lifted up from the ground and made to stand upon its feet as a man, and a man's heart was given to it.

From God's perspective, the empires of man are not pleasant but represent different forms of rebellion against God. No wonder He shows them to Daniel as wild beasts.

The first beast was *something like* a regal lion, the king of beasts, with wings of an eagle, the king of birds. It wasn't actually a lion but that was the closest metaphor Daniel could find to describe what he saw.

Although a lion with eagle's wings was one of the key symbols of the Babylonian empire, we shouldn't make the mistake of assuming God was using the commonly known human symbolism for this empire. In any case, it clearly represents the Babylonian empire under Nebuchadnezzar. Note the interesting reference to the "heart of a man" given to it, apparently representing Nebuchadnezzar's conversion as described in Daniel 4. At the point he acknowledged God's authority over him, he was no longer a beast in the spiritual sense but a human being with a "man's heart."

DANIEL 7:5

> 5 And before me was a second beast, like a bear, and it raised itself up on one side, and it had three ribs between its teeth. It was told, "Arise, devour much flesh."

The second beast is like a powerful bear. This was the Medo-Persian empire that would follow the Babylonian empire.

Whenever a prophet says he saw what looked *like* something, it means this was not exactly what he saw, but that he is finding a common analogy he can use to describe what he saw as clearly as possible. In this case, he didn't see a bear, but it was the closest idiom he could find to the beast he saw. Daniel repeatedly says that the empires seen in his vision look "like" certain wild beasts. The apostle John does the same thing in the book of Revelation, when he describes "something *like* a burning mountain was thrown into the sea."[1] He didn't see a mountain but it was the closest thing he could find to describe what he saw. Likewise, Daniel uses wild beasts but can find no suitable idiom for the fourth beast.

THE PERSIAN GIANT
Daniel saw Persia as "something like a bear" with three ribs in its mouth. Scholars are unsure what the ribs represent, but history has left much evidence about the massive size of the Persian army under king Xerxes.

Scholars are divided on the meaning of the three ribs. They may represent the unsuccessful alliance of the Urartians, Manneans and Scythians who tried to stop the Persians, but they are much more likely to represent Lydia, Babylon and Egypt, which were the three major conquests of the Persian empire.

The Persians under Xerxes would later boast an enormous army numbering two million men. During a period known as the "Persian wars" they waged brutal military conquests, committing many atrocities, especially against the Greeks. The graphic motion picture "300" illustrates some of the brutality of those battles. They certainly "devoured much flesh" in this sense.

---

1   Revelation 8:8

DANIEL 7:6

> 6 After this I saw another beast, like a leopard, which had on its back four wings. The beast also had four heads, and authority to rule was given to it.

The third beast was like a leopard, a fast-moving, agile cat. Under the leadership of young Alexander the Great, the Greeks swept from the west into the east and south, decimating the massive military might of the Persians and Egyptians all the way to India. Alexander had four key generals. After he died at the age of 32, these generals fought over the empire, killing both his sons during the next 13 years. After 22 years of power struggles, this once-great world empire was broken up into four parts:

Cassander took over Greece and Macedonia.

Lysimachus took Thrace and Bithynia (modern-day Turkey).

Seleucus took Syria, Babylonia, Persia and all the way to India.

Ptolemy took Egypt, Palestine and Arabia.

These were the four wings and four heads of that empire. The struggles for domination between Seleucus and Ptolemy and their descendents fills Daniel chapter 11 in the most incredible detail.

DANIEL 7:7

> 7 After this I saw in the night visions a fourth beast, dreadful and terrible, and very strong. It had great iron teeth; it devoured and broke its victims in pieces, and trampled the residue with its feet. It was different from all the beasts that were before it, and it had ten horns.

The fourth beast is so terrible it leaves Daniel without an adequate metaphor to describe it.

Note that it has iron teeth, like the iron of the similar vision that had been given to Nebuchadnezzar.

Rome's style was very different from that of previous empires.

While all were brutal in military terms, ancient empires prior to the Romans had appreciated the cultures and assets of the nations they conquered. They were generally respectful of the people's cultural practices and capabilities. Rome, on the other hand, crushed everything it took, trampling the history, culture, people and religions into oblivion in an attempt to enforce the Roman might on these conquered peoples. The Romans felt that any other system these cultures had lived under was inferior. Tacitus even said they were "too simple to see that what they called civilization was really a form of slavery."[2]

THE GRANDEUR THAT IS ROME

Rome began with the occupation of Sicily in 241BC. Spain was conquered, then Carthage at the battle of Zama in North Africa, 202BC. The Mediterranean became a Roman lake by the beginning of the Second Century. They subjugated areas north of Italy then moved east to conquer Macedonia, Greece and Asia Minor (the name given by that time to the area we now call Turkey). Pompey swept into Jerusalem in 63BC after destroying what was left of the Seleucid Empire in Syria. The empire eventually con-

FAST AS A LEOPARD

The third empire shown in Daniel's vision looked something like a leopard, a fast and agile cat.

In another vision, Daniel saw that this empire moved so fast the animal's feet didn't even touch the ground. Alexander the Great moved through the world more rapidly than any military leader before or since to this day. In just 11 years after the battle of Marathon, Alexander conquered the known world all the way to India.

Just a young man of 20 when he began his rule using a small, determined army and unique military tactics, he was said to have fallen on his bed in tears at the age of 29 because there were no more empires left to conquer.

---

2   Cornelius Tacitus, *Agricola XXI*

trolled Britain, France, Belgium, Switzerland, and Germany west of the Rhine. After peaking in AD117, it began to decline slowly. The empire left Britain in 407 and the city of Rome was sacked by the Visigoths in 410.

Rome, unlike all the previous empires, was never conquered by another culture. Though it did suffer many defeats, most were from within. Its ideals continue to exist, virtually unchanged.

The *Republic* style of government, in which congressional representatives are elected to make decisions on behalf of the people (in contrast to Greek's style of pure democracy), is in place throughout the modern world. Rome introduced the idea of a Senate as a protective body of sober second thought to confirm that new laws being introduced were fair. A formal constitution gave the people citizenship rights, designed to protect them from tyranny.

Rome introduced the concept of a census office to track immigration and to record population, a structure which continues today.

Roman military structure still forms the foundation of today's modern armies, with platoons and companies and battalions. Even many military strategies are virtually unchanged.

Our modern views on many aspects of life, including education and marriage, come from Rome.

The structured legal system, using courts of law with lawyers, judges and juries, was begun under the Romans. Magistrates were given veto powers to stop irresponsible actions by others. There were even rules in place to put term limits on key positions so that men would not abuse their power.[3]

Compare the style of empire building used in the later period of Rome to the approach we use today to convince foreign nations to

---

3 J.C. Stobart, *The Grandeur That Was Rome*

embrace a western style of democracy. Tacitus wrote of an effort to convert barbarians in Britain to Romans in AD79:

> "To make a people which was scattered and barbarous, and therefore prone to warfare, grow accustomed by comfort to peace and quietness, Agricola urged them by private exhortations and public assistance to build temples, forums and houses, with praise for the eager and admonitions for the lazy... The next step was towards the attractions of our vices, lounging in colonnades, baths, and stylish dinner parties."[4]

Pax Romana, or the Peace of Rome, was such an important concept that the Romans made "disturbing the peace" a criminal offense. This remains a foundational concept of our modern rule of law throughout the world.

We may not wear togas today, but not much has changed beyond mere fashion styles and architecture. In God's eyes, we are still very much living in the Roman empire.

It is fascinating to see how recent developments in Europe have begun the process of reviving the Roman empire. When the new currency of the European Union was introduced, it featured an image of Europa riding Zeus, eerily similar to the description of a woman sitting on a scarlet beast as described by the apostle John in Revelation.[5] This symbol has also been put forth as the "quality mark" for suppliers of the European Standards Committee.

The Club of Rome, formed in 1968 as a European think tank, offers studies into problems of the New World Order and suggests that the only useful solution is a world government. Interestingly, the Club of Rome and similar organizations like the Trilateral

---

4 Cornelius Tacitus, *Agricola XXI*
5 Revelation 17:3

Commission and the Council on Foreign Relations each use a *ten kingdom* administrative model in their plans for the coming world government.[6]

DANIEL 7:8

> 8 As I thought about the horns, there came up among them another little horn, before whom three of the first horns were plucked up by the roots. In this horn were eyes like the eyes of man, and a mouth speaking boastfully.

The *boastful mouth* is one of the primary descriptions applied to the coming world leader, the one generally referred to as the Antichrist. He is described in several places as uprooting three of 10 future rulers or nations of a revived Roman empire. Note that this is *another* horn, not one of the first ten.

For other references to the coming ten kingdoms, see Daniel 2:31-35; 40-45; 7:19-24; Revelation 13:1-2; 17:3,7,12-18.

The reference to *plucking up by the roots* indicates a slow and deep process. It isn't a rapid, sudden forceful event. This implies a political process rather than a military one.

Now Daniel's attention is moved to a higher level, from the earth to Heaven.

DANIEL 7:9

> 9 As I looked thrones were set up, and the Ancient of days sat down, whose garment was white as snow, and the hair of His head like pure wool. His throne was like the fiery flame, and its wheels like burning fire.

There are other places where Jesus Christ and God the Father are described in similar terms. See Revelation 4 and 5. In this particular case, *the Ancient of Days* refers to God the Father.

---

6   Grant R. Jeffrey, *Prince of Darkness*

Insight

ROMANS STILL?

We tend to think of empires in relation to the tangible things we identify them with, like the architecture they used, their clothing or other details. From that point of view, the Roman empire seems long past. After all, nobody wears togas anymore except college students at wild parties.

God looks at empires differently and from His point of view the Roman empire is still very much alive. It was never actually conquered by any other empire but collapsed politically and militarily from within.

The Roman Catholic church was founded during that empire and has continued its religious structure virtually unchanged to this day.

The political system developed by Rome, of government representatives elected by the people, is still in use in most of the western world. Rome's legal system of courts with lawyers, judges and juries has survived, as have the census office and many of the military strategies we still use in modern warfare.

Rome's policy of "Pax Romana," or the Peace of Rome, made "disturbing the peace" a crime, a policy still in place throughout the world today.

The last Roman ruler wasn't actually killed until 1453 at the fall of Constantinople!

In the eyes of God, we are still living in the Roman empire. Much of Daniel's vision (and others given to him later) describes the future state of a revived form of this Roman empire.

Daniel sees that a number of thrones are set up, but only one figure, the *Ancient of Days*, is seated at this point. Because the church does not yet exist, Daniel is not shown who will occupy the remaining thrones. The apostle John is later shown that there are 24 additional thrones, and he sees that the elders are seated upon them.

The *blazing wheels* of the throne of God are also described by Ezekiel. It's hard to fully understand their appearance, but fire is a common metaphor for judgement. We see its use in many other places in Scripture, including 1 Corinthians 5:13-15.

DANIEL 7:10

> 10 **A fiery stream flowed from before Him. Millions ministered to Him, and ten thousand times ten thousand stood before Him. The court of judgement was set, and the books were opened.**

Note the reference to more than one book.

We know of the **Lamb's Book of Life** in which are recorded the names of those who follow Christ,[7] but there are several others mentioned in the Bible:

The **Book of Evil Deeds** is mentioned in Isaiah 65:6.

PLUCKED BY THE ROOTS

The reference to being plucked up by the roots in verse 8 indicates a slow and deep political process rather than sudden military conquests.

Daniel uses the term to describe how the coming world leader will remove three kings or rulers from power or take over control of their nations. The same word is used again in chapter 12.

To be uprooted, in the sense of the word used here, represents a gradual process, as you might gently but firmly pry a weed out of the ground to ensure that you get all the roots. Pulling quickly would leave the roots behind.

---

7   Psalm 69:28, Philippians 4:3, Revelation 3:5, 13:8, 17:8, 20:12, 20:15, 21:27

The **Book of Remembrance** is mentioned in Malachi 3:16. This reference suggests that every time you think about God, or do something as a result of your love for God, an entry is made. Could this be a source of the reward talked about by Jesus Christ?

There is an **unnamed book** mentioned in Exodus 32:32,33 and the **Book of Truth** is mentioned later in Daniel.

DANIEL 7:11-12

> 11 I continued to watch because of the voice of the boastful words which the horn spoke. As I looked the beast was slain and his body destroyed and thrown into the burning flame.
>
> 12 The rest of the beasts had their authority taken away, yet their lives were prolonged for a season and time.

The other beasts, representing the former kingdoms, continue to survive in some form. Note that virtually all of the nations making up those ancient empires have been revived in recent decades:

- **Greece** was absorbed by Rome in 146BC, but re-emerged as a nation (though not an empire) in 1830.
- **Lysimachus' kingdom** was taken by Rome in 133BC, yet Medea re-emerged as Turkey in 1924.
- **Seleucus' kingdom** was made up of Syria, Jordan, Lebanon, Cyprus, Babylonia (Iraq), Persia (Iran), Afghanistan and Pakistan. These were absorbed by Rome in 64BC but have emerged again: Afghanistan in 1921; Iran, 1925; Lebanon, 1930; Jordan, 1946; Pakistan, 1947; and Israel, 1948.
- **Ptolemy's Egypt** was taken by Rome in 31BC, yet re-emerged as a nation in 1922.
- **Nebuchadnezzar's Babylonia** re-emerged as Saddam Hussein's Iraq with even the same symbolism of a lion with the wings of an eagle! Saddam even saw himself as the reincarnation of Nebuchadnezzar.

Insight

WHO WILL SIT ON THE HEAVENLY THRONES?

Daniel sees that there are many thrones set up in heaven, but only God, "the Ancient of Days," is seated at this point (Daniel 7:9).

Later in Revelation 4 we see 24 additional thrones occupied by the 24 elders, a reference to the raptured church (12 elders) and the 12 tribes of Israel. The disciples of Jesus also seemed to understand that the thrones in heaven were to be occupied by saints like themselves, and even argued about the seating arrangements.

Scripture sets up a clear distinction between priests and kings. Besides Jesus Christ and the priest-king named Melchizedek, only we (those who follow Christ) are described as being kings and priests simultaneously.

The church is hidden in the Old Testament according to Matthew 13:34,35 and Ephesians 3:5,9 so it wasn't revealed to Daniel. Thus, when the vision was given to Daniel nobody was yet seated on the other thrones.

In Revelation chapter 5, the elders on these thrones in heaven refer to their salvation. Salvation in the New Testament context comes only through faith in Christ, so the thrones were still empty in Daniel's vision.

Depending on the Bible translation you use, this may not be clear, so it is helpful to read other translations for greater insight.

DANIEL 7:13-14

> 13 **I saw in the night visions, and, behold, One like the Son of man came with the clouds of heaven. He came to the Ancient of days, and they brought Him near before Him.**
>
> 14 **And there was given to Him authority to rule and glory and a kingdom, that all people, nations and languages should serve Him. His dominion is an everlasting dominion, which shall not pass away, and His kingdom is one that will never be destroyed.**

Daniel saw these visions *in the night*. The reference to night is singular, suggesting that the visions all happened in a single night. But here he refers to visions in plural, while in verse 2 it was a single vision. It isn't entirely clear whether he saw himself, within the main vision, having more visions, or if these were new visions he saw later in the night, added to the one mentioned so far. Verse 16, which we'll look at shortly, shows him, within the vision, asking an angel about these visions. So it can be interpreted that the new visions and the discussion with the angel are all happening within the one main vision he started with.

Daniel was first to use the term "Son of man" in reference to the Messiah.

Note the reference to *coming with the clouds of Heaven*. There are many references to Jesus coming with the clouds of heaven at the time of His return.[8]

Jesus Christ receives the Father's gift as described by the Psalmist.[9] He will rule over all nations.[10] This description is remarkably similar to the vision given by the watchmen angels to Nebuchadnezzar before his years of madness.

---

8   Matt 17:5; 24:30; 26:64; Mark 14:61,62; Luke 21:27; Acts 1:9,11; 2 Thess 2:6-10; Rev 19, 20:1-4
9   Psalm 2:6-9
10   Psalm 72:11; Revelation 19:15-16

DANIEL 7:15-19

> 15 I, Daniel, was grieved in my spirit in the midst of my body, and the visions of my head troubled me.
>
> 16 I came near one of those that stood by, and asked him to explain all this. So he told me the interpretation of the things I had seen.
>
> 17 'The four great beasts are four kingdoms which shall arise out of the earth.
>
> 18 But the saints of the most High will receive the kingdom, and possess the kingdom for ever — yes, for ever and ever.'
>
> 19 Then I asked about the fourth beast, which was so different from all the others and exceedingly dreadful, with its iron teeth and claws of brass; which devoured, crushed its victims, and trampled the residue with his feet;

Daniel is stunned by what he has seen. But he isn't frozen in fear. He takes the initiative and asks one of the angels there in the vision to please help him understand the terrible and glorious things that have been shown to him.

Daniel was deeply troubled by the fourth beast. He had already been told that it was a metaphor for an empire, but he was having difficulty getting his head around the reason why any kingdom would be so destructive. Until the Romans came along (which wouldn't happen for more than 200 years), kings became powerful by using the resources that were already established. Daniel could not understand a strategy so dramatically different.

Note the reference to the saints inheriting and ruling over the kingdom forever. What comfort, knowing this promise from God! We will rule with Christ for eternity. We are called "children of God,"[11] and will inherit the kingdom of God[12] through faith in Christ.

---

11   Romans 8:16, 9:8; Philippians 2:15; 1 John 3:1-2, 10, 5:19
12   Ephesians 1:18; Colossians 1:12, 3:24; Hebrews 6:12, 9:15; James 2:5; 1 Peter 1:4

DANIEL 7:20-22

20 I also wanted to know about the ten horns on his head, and of the other horn that came up, and before whom three fell — this horn that had eyes, and a mouth that spoke very boastful things and whose look was more stern than the others.

21 I watched, and the same horn made war with the saints, and prevailed against them;

22 until the Ancient of days came, and judgment was given in favor of the saints of the most High; and the time came that the saints possessed the kingdom.

CITY OF REFUGE?
There is reason to believe that during the "war against the saints" mentioned in Daniel 7:21, Jewish believers will find refuge in Jordan's rock city of Petra. Daniel is told in Chapter 11 that the territories of Edom and Moab would be safe from the murderous attacks of the coming world leader.

The horn that represents the coming world leader is waging war against the saints and appears to be winning until interrupted by the return of the Messiah. The Bible tells us that two-thirds of believers will fall.[13] Zechariah 14:1-2 also tells us that Jerusalem will fall, and we are told that it will be trampled by the Gentiles.

Some scholars say that this reference to *overcoming* or *prevailing against* the saints in verse 21 is evidence that this happens after the rapture of the church, since Jesus promised that the gates of Hell would not "overcome" or prevail against the church.[14] The believers at that time are thought to find refuge in the ancient rock city of Petra, located in the area once occupied by Edom and Moab, which is today the kingdom of Jordan.

---

13   Zechariah 13:8,9
14   Matthew 16:18; Revelation 2, 3

The Roman empire does not end in God's sight until after the great and glorious "Day of the Lord" when Jesus returns and judges all mankind.

DANIEL 7:23-26

> 23 He answered, "The fourth beast will be the fourth kingdom upon earth, which shall be different from all other kingdoms, and shall devour the whole earth, and will trample it down and crush it.
>
> 24 And the ten horns out of this kingdom are ten kings that will arise. After them another will rise, and he will be different from the earlier ones, and he will subdue three kings.
>
> 25 And he will speak boastful words against the most High, and will oppress the saints of the most High, and try to change times and laws. The saints will be given into his hand for a time, times and the dividing of time.
>
> 26 But the court of judgment will sit, and his authority will be taken away from him, and he will be destroyed forever.

The time of persecution will last 3-1/2 years. There are many references to this time period in Scripture to ensure that we don't allegorize it (like turning days into years) or try to modify how much time is meant for the assault against the saints. It's a literal time period, with minor differences to reflect various events which take place within that time (they'll be discussed later):

- **Time, times and the dividing of time** (Daniel 7:25)
- **Half a week of years** (Daniel 9:27)
- **42 months** (Revelation 11:2; 13:5)
- **1,260 days** (Revelation 11:3, 12:6,)
- **Time, times and half a time** (Daniel 12:7, Revelation 12:14)
- **1,290 days** (Daniel 12:11)
- **1,335 days** (Daniel 12:12)

💡 Insight

THE DESTRUCTIVE EMPIRE

The fourth empire terrified Daniel. He asked for more information about this empire because he could not understand how any people group could be so destructive.

Previous empires respected the cultures they dominated, using the people, tools and techniques to their advantage. Rome would bring a different style. The Romans in their first two centuries of conquest simply ran over everything like a bulldozer, with no regard for prior value.

They looked with disdain upon those they conquered, considering their knowledge inferior and their ways barbaric.

The final Roman leader who will rule during the last days will also use terror and massive destruction in an effort to force his will upon the world.

The Bible first referred to the "iron teeth" of Rome hundreds of years before the empire even took shape. Yet that term came into common use during the Roman period as a description of its military might.

Throughout the Bible, God uses the lunar calendar of 360-day years: 12 months of 30 days each.

DANIEL 7:27

> 27 **And the kingdom and authority, and the greatness of the kingdom under the whole heaven, will be given to the people of the saints of the most High, whose kingdom is an everlasting kingdom, and all rulers will serve and obey Him.**

The everlasting kingdom is mentioned in too many places to make the effort of listing them all here. For a few of them, see Deuteronomy 28:1-44; Isaiah 65:17-25; 2 Timothy 2:12; Revelation 5:10; 20:6

DANIEL 7:28

> 28 **"This is the end of the matter." As for me Daniel, my visions troubled me deeply, and my face became pale. But I kept the matter in my heart.**

The first sentence of verse 28 is actually the last statement by the angel begun in verse 23. It really should have been attached to the end of verse 27. Verse numbers were applied to Scripture centuries later. The angel is saying that after Jesus is set on the throne, it ends the entire story of human history as we are meant to know it in the present age.

Here Daniel changes from the common Gentile language of Aramaic back to Hebrew. The rest of the book views events specifically through the lens of Israel, with the Jews as the center point of the story.

Application — My Notes & Bible Study Questions

11

DANIEL CHAPTER 8
THE PERSIAN WARS

In 330BC, Jaddua the high priest showed Alexander the Great the eighth chapter of Daniel. Alexander was so impressed as he saw his military conquest of Persia laid out before him in a 200-year-old account that he not only spared the city but granted the Jews many concessions.

Daniel's eighth chapter is an account of how an angry Greek empire, not yet in existence when Daniel wrote his book, would violently attack and defeat the Persians. It also tells how the empire will break apart into four distinct pieces, then goes on to describe a ruler who will come out of that division to wreak havoc on the Jewish people.

DANIEL 8:1-2

> 1 In the third year of the reign of king Belshazzar, a vision appeared to me, Daniel, after the one that appeared to me earlier.
>
> 2 And it happened that, when I saw, I was in the palace at Susa, which is in the province of Elam; and I saw in the vision that I was beside the Ulai Canal.

This vision was given to Daniel in the third year of Belshazzar, who was co-regent of the Babylonian empire under Nabonidus. The earlier vision described in chapter 7 was given two years earlier, in Belshazzar's first year.

Scripture is not clear about whether Daniel was physically in the palace at Susa (also called *Shusan*) when he saw himself beside the canal, or if he saw himself projected both into the palace *and* near the canal, the whole thing a vision. There are valid arguments for both points of view, though Bible translations may present one or the other as a definitive statement. The NIV, for example, assumes the whole thing was seen in his vision.

The view that Daniel saw the entire thing as a vision seems less likely than the view that he was physically there, because the passage puts him both inside the palace of Susa and beside the canal. How could he be inside and outside the palace at the same time? It makes more sense to assume that Daniel was in the palace, and given a vision that saw him outside, beside the canal.

The reason scholars doubt his presence there is that while Susa eventually became the capital of the Persian empire, at the time of Daniel's writing it was not significant. They see no reason why he would be there.

THE BOY WHO RULED THE WORLD
Alexander the Great proved himself to be a tremendous leader, conquering the world from Greece to India in just 11 years. He was brutal in his aggression, and reveled in his power. He was one of the first Greeks to be worshipped as a god in his own lifetime.

The palace at Susa referred to in the book of Esther was not even built until the time of Darius, decades from the time of this vision.

However, on closer inspection there may be very good reasons for Daniel to be physically present in Susa. Just a few years earlier Nabonidus had granted Cyrus help in taking control of the Medes. It is certainly possible that Daniel was on some kind of political mission for Nabonidus (not for his son Belshazzar, as Daniel 5 makes it obvious they had never met). The last verse of this chapter says he went back about the king's business. Cyrus may have been headquartered in Susa, and there could easily have been a palace prior to the one built by Darius the Great. If Daniel was on a mission for Nabonidus, the whole scenario makes perfect sense.

DANIEL 8:3-4

> ₃ **Then I lifted up my eyes and saw that there stood before the canal a ram with two horns on its head. The two horns were high; but one was higher than the other, and the higher one came up last.**
>
> ₄ **I saw the ram charging westward and northward and southward. No beasts could stand against him, nor were any able to rescue from his power. He did according to his will, and became great.**

The ram represents the Medo-Persian empire. The longer horn that grew up later was the Persian side. The Medes were originally the dominant force but Cyrus quickly turned things around so that the Persians overwhelmed the Medes and claimed the empire through shrewd political maneuvering.

DANIEL 8:5-8

> ₅ **And as I was thinking about this, a male goat came from the west across the face of the whole earth without touching the ground: and the goat had a prominent horn between his eyes.**
>
> ₆ **And he came to the two-horned ram that I had seen standing before the canal, and charged at him in great fury and power.**
>
> ₇ **And I saw him come close to the ram, and he was moved with rage against him, and battered the ram, shattering his two horns. The ram was powerless against him; the goat knocked him down to the ground and trampled him. Nobody could rescue the ram from his attack.**

Most goats have two horns on top of their heads. This one had a single horn between its eyes.

It's not surprising that Daniel was shown the goat as moving so fast it didn't touch the ground. The goat, representing the Greek (or Macedonian) Empire under Alexander, moved so fast it flew eastward. Alexander conquered the known world in just 11 years.

The Persian king Xerxes had built a huge army numbering two million men whom he had trained for four years. Yet Alexander's small army decimated the powerful Persian might with ferocity and innovative military tactics. The Persians were powerless to stand against the Greeks.

DANIEL 8:8

> 8 **The male goat became very great. And when he was mighty, the great horn was broken. In its place four notable ones came up toward the four winds of heaven.**

THE RAM AND THE PERSIAN EMPIRE

Persia was long associated with the image of the ram. The king of Persia, when leading his army into battle, did not wear a crown but instead wore a ram's head with horns as his headpiece.

The sign of the zodiac associated with Persia is Aries the Ram. While God does not deal in human metaphors, it is interesting that the image shown to Daniel representing the Persian empire was the image of a ram.

Alexander died at the height of his power, of a sudden fever following a drunken party in Babylon at the age of 32. There were rumors that he was actually poisoned by Cassander, one of his generals.

He was eventually succeeded by his four key generals who divided the kingdom among them after 22 years of infighting, murder, bribery and political chicanery.

Daniel had been shown the rise of Persia while the dominant empire was still Babylonia. He then saw the rise of the Greek empire which wouldn't take place for another 200 years.

After Alexander's kingdom broke up, two of the four generals, Seleucus and Ptolemy, would begin generations of conflict, and Daniel was given insight to these wars in a later vision.

DANIEL 8:9

> 9 **And out of one of them came up a little horn, which grew to great power, toward the south and the east and toward the beautiful land.**

Now Daniel is shown a future king who rises out of the remains of the Greek empire — specifically out of the Seleucid portion of Syria just north of Palestine.

Horns are biblical metaphors for kings or rulers because they often represent the power of animals.

Out of the Seleucid empire would rise Antiochus IV Epiphanes (*the manifest one* or *the coming one*). Though he had no claim to the throne, he usurped the throne from his nephew by having his brother killed and his nephew kept as a hostage in Rome. He expelled Onias III from his office as high priest, installing Onias' brother Jason as the result of a bribe. Onias was murdered in the fall of 171.

Antiochus moved south to invade Egypt in 170BC. He succeeded in eastern invasions into Parthia and Armenia. Offered a larger bribe by Jason's brother Menelaus, he deposed Jason and installed Menelaus as high priest, but Jason laid siege to Jerusalem while Antiochus was fighting Ptolemy VII in Egypt. Antiochus reinstalled Menelaus.

In December 168BC, Antiochus was turned back from Alexandria by Roman commander Popilius Laenas in a humiliating incident on the beach. Outraged, he began to attack the Jews, militarily a weaker group.

DANIEL 8:10

> 10 And it became great, reaching to the host of heaven; and it threw some of the starry host down to the earth and trampled on them.

This reference to *starry host* should not be interpreted as heavenly beings. It simply means the Israelites. There are biblical references to the starry host as meaning the Israelites, who are to become as the stars in number (Genesis 15:5). In Exodus 12:41 they are referred to as *the hosts of Yahweh*.

Antiochus IV saw himself as divine, though he wanted to make the worship of Zeus the official state religion of the Jews. Surprisingly, his Hellenistic efforts were actually supported by some Jews, though most were deeply offended.

A ONE-HORNED GOAT?
Goats have two horns, one on each side of the head. Yet Daniel is shown a goat with a single horn between its eyes, representing Alexander the Great's furious attack against the Persians who had so badly abused the Greeks during the Persian wars.

The sign of the zodiac associated with the Macedonian empire of Alexander the Great was Capricorn the Goat, though that seems to have come later and possibly as the result of Daniel's prophecy.

After he was turned away from Alexandria by the Romans, Antiochus IV sent his general Apollonius with 20,000 troops to Jerusalem, supposedly on a peace mission. But when they arrived on a Sabbath day, they mercilessly slaughtered thousands of men, women and children. From there, things went from bad to worse.

DANIEL 8:11-12

> 11 He set himself up to be above even the Prince of the host, took away the daily sacrifice, and cast down the place of the holy sanctuary.
>
> 12 And the host of the saints and the daily sacrifice were given over to him because of rebellion, and truth was thrown to the ground. And it succeeded in its efforts and prospered.

Antiochus had a swine sacrificed on the altar of the Jewish temple, desecrating the sanctuary by bringing it low to human relevance. He cancelled the daily morning and evening sacrifice and made it illegal, upon penalty of death, to read the Scriptures (truth thrown to the ground).

He then set up an idol of Zeus in the Holy of Holies on December 25, 167BC, an event called "the abomination that causes desolation" because it represents the worst form of idolatry possible (the reference that he would cast down the place of the holy sanctuary).

Judas Maccabeas and his brothers sprang into action, eventually overthrowing him and rededicated the temple exactly three years later on December 25, 164BC, an event commemorated to this day in the Jewish celebration of Hanukkah.

DANIEL 8:13-14

> 13 Then I heard a holy one speaking, and another holy one said to the one that spoke, "How long will it be for the vision to be completed concerning the daily sacrifice, the rebellion that causes desolation, and for both the sanctuary and the saints to be trampled under foot?"
>
> 14 And he said to me, "It will be 2,300 evenings and mornings; then the sanctuary will be cleansed."

There are major disagreements over this passage. Some have tried to interpret the 2,300 days as "years" assuming it was some kind of coded reference and gotten themselves into big trouble by pinpointing dates in the 19th century as the year Christ would return. Others say that it refers to "days" while still others say it means "evening mornings." They see it as a sacrifice in the evening, followed by another the next morning (2 per day), which would come out as about three years and two months.

Jewish days start at sundown, explaining why the evening is mentioned first. With so many views, can we make any conclusions?

2,300 WHAT?

Under no circumstances can this mean "years." It means either days or total sacrifices. If it means days, then the period from the ending of the daily sacrifice to the cleansing of the temple would add up to nearly 6-1/2 years. Onias III, the rightful priest, was murdered about that length of time before the cleansing of the temple took place (I haven't been able to find an exact date to confirm). This appears to be the view that has the closest link to an actual event of significance.

The term *evening mornings* can refer to the two daily sacrifices. Given that perspective, it would represent about 3 years and 55 days. However, according to the best information available, that time period doesn't match up to anything meaningful if you work backwards from the rededication of the temple under the Maccabees December 25, 164BC.

A FORESHADOWING?

This reference may relate exclusively to the second occasion that these events will take place. Jesus made it clear that the events under Antiochus IV were only a foreshadowing and that Daniel was really referring to a future event that had not yet happened when Jesus walked in Jerusalem. Still, while foreshadowing is common in Scripture, the view that this reference to 2,300 days or sacrifices is *only* intended for the final version of these events is not generally accepted.

There are many examples in Scripture where a promised event was "foreshadowed" or presented in a form very similar to the prophecy but years ahead of time. The effect is like a spiritual preview of the actual event that was prophesied so that we know what to expect. It brings prophecy closer. The coming world leader will behave very similar to how Antiochus behaved. The prophecy lets us know how to recognize the actions and impact of the Antichrist when he does appear.

DANIEL 8:15-17

> 15 And it came to pass, when I, Daniel, had seen the vision, and tried to understand it, there stood before me one with the appearance of a man.
>
> 16 And I heard a man's voice between the banks of the Ulai calling, "Gabriel, tell this man the meaning of the vision."
>
> 17 So he came near where I was standing. When he came, I was afraid, and fell upon my face. But he said to me, "Understand, son of man, that the vision deals with the time of the end."

This is the first place we see Gabriel's name in the Bible. Only four angels are revealed by name: **Gabriel, Michael, Apollyon** and **Lucifer**. Every time Gabriel is mentioned, he is shown as a Messianic messenger.

Later, in chapter 9, Daniel immediately recognizes Gabriel when he sees him. This shows that angels have distinct physical characteristics just like people.

Another heavenly being who isn't identified gives Gabriel the authority to tell Daniel the vision.

DANIEL 8:18-22

> 18 As he was speaking with me, I was in a deep sleep on my face toward the ground, but he touched me, and brought me to my feet.
>
> 19 He said, "I will explain what will happen at the end of the time of wrath, for the vision concerns the appointed time of the end.
>
> 20 The two-horned ram you saw represents the kings of Media and Persia.
>
> 21 And the shaggy goat is the king of Greece. And the large horn between his eyes is the first king.
>
> 22 After that is broken, the four others which come up in its place are four kingdoms that will rise up out of his nation, but not with his level of power.

The angel touches Daniel and helps him to his feet. Then he explains that the vision refers to the time of the end. This is interesting, because identical events were clearly fulfilled in the life of Antiochus IV. Yet we know that Antiochus was only a foreshadowing of the coming Antichrist, because Jesus himself said so! He identified the *abomination that causes desolation* (an idol placed in the Holy of Holies) as an event that is yet to come, placing that event long after Antiochus IV had died.

DANIEL 8:23-25

23 **In the later time of their kingdom, when rebels are fully wicked, a king of fierce countenance, and skilled at intrigue, will arise.**

24 **He will become mighty, but not by his own power. He will cause incredible destruction, and will prosper, and will accomplish things, and will destroy the mighty and the holy people.**

25 **Through his strategies he will cause deceit to prosper. He will magnify himself in his heart, and through assurances of peace will destroy many and will stand up against the Prince of princes. Yet he will be broken, but not by human power.**

ANTIOCHUS IV "GOD MANIFEST"

Coins have been found showing Antiochus IV with a stylistic treatment designed to make him look like the god Zeus. The words "Antiochus IV" and "God Manifest" were on the back of the coins. He saw himself as divine, yet worshipped Zeus and forbid the Jews from the requirements of their faith, desecrating the altar and setting up an idol of Zeus in the Holy of Holies. He called himself Antiochus IV Epiphanes (the "Manifest One" or the "Coming One"). The Jews called him Antiochus Epimanes ("the madman").

Daniel is now given a specific message about the coming world leader, the one we often refer to as the Antichrist.

He will be stern-faced yet smooth, charming and politically clever. He will not be revealed until after the "hinderer" is removed (generally thought to be a reference to the Holy Spirit). Although he won't be revealed until the last seven years before Armageddon, he may already be alive today.

Even this passage applies well to Antiochus IV. He died shortly after hearing of the Maccabean victory over Jerusalem, with sudden severe abdominal pains accompanied by a report that he was being consumed by worms. Josephus wrote that he confessed on his deathbed that he was suffering for having desecrated the Jewish temple.[1]

DANIEL 8:26

> 26 The vision of the evenings and mornings which was told is true, but seal up the vision, for it will not take place until much time has passed.

Daniel was told to seal up the vision. There is some disagreement over what is meant by this command. Some scholars believe it means that some parts of his vision are hidden and will be revealed at the proper time. Others think it means simply to close the book by writing down what he saw. Still others believe it refers to people being unable to fully understand it until much later in history.

There is precedence for believing that additional documents by Daniel may have been sealed, or hidden, for a future time. When the magi came to Bethlehem after the birth of the Christ child seeking the "one who was born King of the Jews" they were guided by prophetic knowledge, which may have originated with Daniel. Such things are pure conjecture, and must never form doctrine nor any firmly held belief. If any additional documents ever come to light, they will never represent Scripture. In fact, among the Dead Sea Scrolls are documents claiming to be additional prophecies of Daniel, but we do not know much about their authenticity.

We must be very careful with opinions of such things, diligently defending the Bible as the only reliable source of scriptural truth. It is complete in its current form, and nothing will be added.

---

1 Josephus, *Antiquities of the Jews: The Maccabees*

DANIEL 8:27

27 I, Daniel, fainted and was sick for several days. Afterwards I got up and went about the king's business. I was astonished by the vision, but could not understand it.

The vision was so disturbing that it made Daniel not only faint, but become sick for several days. There is no doubt that he knew the significance of the images he had been shown of the Great Tribulation and the death and destruction it would bring.

Daniel went about the king's business. Yet we know from Chapter 5 that he had never met Belshazzar. As a result, we have to assume that he was working directly for Nabonidus, not Belshazzar. This suggests that he may well have been physically in the city of Susa on a diplomatic mission.

Application — My Notes & Bible Study Questions

12

DANIEL CHAPTER 9
TIME OF THE MESSIAH

Daniel's beloved city of Jerusalem lay in ruins far to the west. Its once glorious holy temple was now merely a pile of rubble. The fertile fields of Israel and Judah had remained neglected and unplowed for decades, sifted by desolate winds.

Daniel, just a teen when he was taken prisoner by the Babylonians, was now an old man. He had endured persecution for his faith, and witnessed countless examples of anti-Semitism, including attacks against himself by those he managed.

Now, after almost 70 years of bondage in a foreign land, we find Daniel reading Scripture. No doubt he did so on a daily basis. In this case, he's reading a prophecy by Jeremiah, who had foretold Israel's captivity in Babylon, and had specified an exact time period of 70 years.

There are two places where Jeremiah makes this reference. Daniel may have been reading the scroll, or book which Jeremiah had written *before* the captivity took place. This contained a specific reference to serving Babylon for 70 years:

> "This whole country will become a desolate wasteland, and these nations will serve the king of Babylon seventy years."
> —Jeremiah 25:11 (NIV)

An even more detailed reference is the letter Jeremiah wrote to the Jews in Babylon, which eventually became part of the book of Jeremiah. In this prophecy, Jeremiah quotes God saying He will come back to the Jewish people at the end of 70 years to rescue them from their exile, with a promise to restore hope and a future to the nation:

> "This is what the LORD says: 'When seventy years are completed for Babylon, I will come to you and fulfill my gracious promise to bring you back to this place. For I know the plans I have for you,' declares the LORD, 'plans to prosper you and not to harm you, plans to give you hope and a future.'" —Jeremiah 29:10-14 (NIV)

Daniel realized that Israel's time of judgement was almost over! This discovery caused him to confess his sins and those of his people. He began to pray and worship God with an unusually deep intensity. Towards the end of the day, during a lengthy prayer which probably lasted most of the day, the angel Gabriel came to him with a message. What followed was one of the most astonishing promises in the entire Bible.

DANIEL 9:1-2

> 1 In the first year of Darius the son of Ahasuerus [or Xerxes], a Mede by descent, who was made king over the kingdom of the Chaldeans —
>
> 2 in the first year of his reign, I, Daniel, understood from books the number of years given by the word of the LORD to Jeremiah the prophet, that the desolation of Jerusalem would last seventy years.

Daniel records that this took place during the first year that Darius was made ruler by Cyrus over Babylon. Cyrus had not yet taken the throne, so the Jews were still in captivity.

The Babylonians counted only from the first *full* year of a king's reign, and Daniel has consistently used this Babylonian reckoning, so this would most likely have happened in the second year of Darius by our modern-day form of measurement.

Daniel mentions *books* as a plural, so he may very well have been referring to both of Jeremiah's prophecies.

DANIEL 9:3

> ³ So I turned to the Lord God, pleading with Him by prayer and petition, with fasting, in sackcloth and ashes.

Daniel goes into intercessory prayer with fasting. This occupied at least the entire day. The reference to fasting suggests that it covered a long period of time, possibly days. His prayer is rich and beautiful in its scope, humility and emotion. To help you see how the intensity increases as he shares his heart, I will let you read the entire prayer before making further comments. Notice how Daniel's pace quickens and his urgency and passion grows:

DANIEL 9:4-19

> ⁴ And I prayed to the LORD my God, and confessed, and said, "O Lord, the great and awesome God, who keeps His covenant of loving mercy to all who love Him and keep His commandments;
>
> ⁵ We have sinned, and have done wrong and have been wicked and have rebelled, even by turning away from Your commands and laws.
>
> ⁶ Neither have we listened to Your servants the prophets, who spoke in Your name to our kings, our princes, and our fathers, and to all the people of the land.
>
> ⁷ O Lord, righteousness belongs to You, but our faces are covered with shame as on this day; to the men of Judah and the people of Jerusalem and to all Israel, near and far, through all the countries where You scattered them, because of their unfaithfulness to You.
>
> ⁸ O Lord, the shame of our faces belongs to us, to our kings, to our rulers, and to our fathers, because we have sinned against You.
>
> ⁹ The Lord our God is merciful and forgiving even though we have rebelled against Him;

₁₀ We have not obeyed the voice of the LORD our God; we have not walked in His laws, which he gave us through His servants the prophets.

₁₁ Yes, all Israel has transgressed Your law and turned away from it, refusing to obey Your voice. Therefore the curse and the sworn judgment that is written in the law of Moses, the servant of God, are poured onto us, because we have sinned against Him.

₁₂ And he has confirmed His words spoken against us, and against our rulers that ruled over us, by bringing disaster upon us. Under the whole heaven nothing has ever been done as has been done to Jerusalem.

₁₃ Just as it is written in the law of Moses, all this trouble has come upon us, yet we have not come in prayer before the LORD our God, that we might turn from our perversions and focus on knowing Your truth.

₁₄ Therefore the LORD looked on this evil, and brought it onto us. For the LORD our God is righteous in everything he does, yet we did not obey His voice.

₁₅ Now, O Lord our God, who brought Your people out of Egypt with a mighty hand, and made for yourself a name that extends to this day; we have sinned, we have done wickedly.

₁₆ O Lord, in keeping with all Your righteousness, I beg of You, let Your anger and Your fury be turned away from Your city Jerusalem, Your holy mountain. Our sins and the sins of our fathers have made Jerusalem and Your people an object of scorn to all that are around us.

₁₇ Now, our God, hear the prayer of Your servant, and his petitions. Look with favor on Your desolate sanctuary, for the Lord's sake.

₁₈ O my God, incline Your ear and hear; open Your eyes and see the desolation of the city called by Your name.

> We do not present our requests before You because of our righteousnesses, but because of Your great mercies.
>
> 19 O Lord, hear! O Lord, forgive! O Lord, listen and act! For Your own sake, O my God, do not delay, for Your city and Your people are called by Your name."

Even though God Himself has described Daniel as one of the three most righteous men ever, Daniel takes upon himself the sins of his people. He includes his own sinfulness in this prayer. How humble of this man of God!

Daniel's prayer puts the blame entirely on the sinful actions of God's people. They failed to obey the commandments, including the command to obey the "Sabbath of the land" by giving it the required periods of rest. This was the reason for the exile.

In his prayer, he recognizes that the sovereign and holy God had every right to impose disciplinary action on the nation. He refers to God's forgiving nature, recognizing in that discipline a God of love and graciousness, who is slow to anger and merciful in response to genuine confession and repentance. Daniel pleads with the Lord to bring that mercy to bear quickly.

DANIEL 9:20-21

> 20 While I was speaking and praying, confessing my sin and the sin of my people Israel, and presenting my requests before the LORD my God for His holy mountain —
>
> 21 Yes, while I was speaking in prayer, Gabriel, the man I had seen in the vision at the beginning, flying swiftly, came and touched me about the time of the evening sacrifice.

The *holy mountain* is a reference to the temple mount of Jerusalem, on which the temple stood.

Gabriel comes in *swift flight* (some Bibles leave out this reference but it is implied in the Hebrew text). Notice that Daniel immediately recognizes Gabriel. This is evidence that angels have physical characteristics just like people have. They are not "clones."

Daniel records that the angel Gabriel appeared to him *about the time of the evening sacrifice*. How remarkable! Seven decades after he was removed from the observance of the daily sacrifices — one every evening and one every morning, he still records time by those events.

What a contrast to our modern weakness in honoring our commitment to church. How many Christians go on a two week vacation and forget what time church service starts!

Each time Gabriel is mentioned in Scripture, he is shown as a messenger angel.

DANIEL 9:22-23

> 22 **And he informed me and talked with me, and said, "O Daniel, I have now come to give you insight and understanding.**
> 23 **As soon as you began to pray, the answer came forth which I have come to show you; for you are greatly loved. Therefore, understand the message, and carefully consider the vision.**

Gabriel was sent as soon as Daniel began to pray. An answer was assigned to Daniel through Gabriel immediately. In a later chapter we'll see the spiritual forces at work which can hinder the deliverance of answers to prayer. Gabriel may have been tied up in a spiritual battle of that kind, causing him to be delayed and thus in "swift flight" when arriving.

Notice the reference to Daniel being *greatly loved*. Another prophet was referred to as *the one whom Jesus loved,* and he too was given prophetic insight into God's plans for the future.

DANIEL 9:24

> 24 **Seventy weeks [or 'sevens'] are decreed for your people and upon your holy city, to finish the transgression, to put an end to sins, to atone for wickedness, to bring in everlasting righteousness, to seal up the vision and prophecy and to anoint the Most Holy.**

This prophecy relates specifically to the Jewish people. The seventy weeks of years (in Hebrew **shabuim**) represent a period of 490 years decreed for Israel and Jerusalem. It does *not* refer to the Gentile world.

Throughout the Bible, years are referenced as exactly 360 days in length: 12 months of 30 lunar days. This lunar calendar was used in most of the surrounding cultures. Our modern calendar of 365.25 days wasn't invented until after Christ. Even in the book of Revelation, God continues to use 360-day references.

God has a comprehensive plan for Israel. The vision clearly referred to the Jews (*your people*) and the city of Jerusalem (*your holy city*). Seventy weeks of years are 490 years. It is not a Gentile reference. It does not refer to the church.

Note that the message goes on to say that those seventy weeks of years involve an *end to sin* and other conditions which are not yet fulfilled. We see the following items which must be fulfilled before the seventy years are complete:

- **To finish the transgression**, or the sins of the Jews (Daniel's people). In one sense, this happened when Cyrus released the Jews, as promised by God, after 70 years of captivity. However, the exile was punishment for only one transgression, that of not keeping the Sabbath of the land. This may well refer to all the transgressions of the Jewish people, which will only be finished at the final return of Christ.

- **Put an end to sins.** The Hebrew refers to putting it out of sight. We all know that sin continues to this day, so in a literal sense this hasn't yet been fulfilled. Revelation 21:22 points out that there will be no temple in the New Jerusalem because the Lord God and the Lamb (Christ) are its temple. Sin continues to exist until the final Day of Judgement. This reference to the end of sin may be pointing to the intercession of Christ, through whom all our sins are washed away, or ended. But while this is true, it's not likely as the meaning of the phrase in the overall context of the passage.

- **To atone for wickedness.** The Old Testament understanding of atonement was *propitiation*, which was a turning away of God's punishment for sin by making an offering. The New Testament understanding is, of course, that of Jesus the Messiah atoning for sin on our behalf. In this context, the condition may refer to the work of Christ making Himself an offering for our sin. This is supported by the Hebrew used, which says to *cover*, or *overlay*, as one would cover a surface with something new.

WHY 'WEEKS OF YEARS'?

In our current culture we use a number of common terms to describe increments of years. We immediately know what people mean when they say millennium, century, or decade.

The Jewish culture has a number of common ways to describe weeks, since seven is a significant number to the Jews. There are weeks of days, weeks of months, and weeks of years.

Daniel's vision involved the Hebrew word 'shabuim' which means 'sevens' or specifically weeks of years. Thus, the phrase refers to a seven-year period.

- **To bring in everlasting righteousness.** This refers to the final part of God's plan for Israel (and all of humanity), which has not yet been completed. It portrays the ideal relationship between God and man, as He intended. Scripture tells us:

  "there shall be no more night; they have no need for lamplight or sunlight, for the Lord God will illuminate them and be their light, and they shall reign [as kings] forever and ever [through the eternities of the eternities]"
  —Revelation 22:5 (AMP)

- **To seal up the vision and prophecy.** This refers to the vision and prophecy now being shared. It talks about being *sealed up*, not being *unsealed*. John MacArthur feels that this simply means no more revelation of God's plan will be needed and that "God will bring these anticipations to completion by their fulfillment in Israel's blessing as a nation."[1] In that sense, it's a reference to the vision being complete.

- **To anoint the Most Holy.** Throughout Scripture, persons and things were anointed to signify holiness or separation unto God. The Most Holy is generally a reference to the Most Holy Place, the inner sanctum of the temple where God dwelt. As a result, some believe this refers to the anointing of a temple. But given the entire context of the passage, this almost certainly means the anointing of the Messiah. He is the ultimate representation of the Most Holy Place and, as we know from the Gospel accounts, was anointed by the Holy Spirit, which he confirmed in Luke 4:18-21.

Regardless of how one interprets the conditions in this reference to 70 weeks of years, only some have been completed. Some remain unfulfilled and will not be finished until the final return of Christ.

---

1 John MacArthur, *MacArthur Study Bible*

DANIEL 9:25

25 Know therefore and understand, that from the issuing of the decree to restore and to rebuild Jerusalem to Messiah the king, there will be seven weeks and sixty-two weeks. The street shall be rebuilt, and the wall, but in times of trouble.

The prophecy concerns the coming of Christ, *Messiah the king*. Note the wording which refers to Christ as a "ruler" or king. Some English Bibles translate this as "prince," but the Hebrew phrase **Maschiach nagid** really means "Messiah the king." The word **nagid** is used repeatedly throughout the books of Samuel, Kings, and Chronicles to refer to various kings of Israel and Judah. This means that the Messiah would be recognized as a king at this time.

MESSIAH THE KING

There were times in the life of Jesus that he was about to be made a king by force, but rejected it or slipped away.[2] Then, one remarkable day, he *arranged* it. He rode over the brow of the Mount of Olives on the foal of a donkey, as had been predicted in Zechariah 9:9, and people threw coats and palm branches on the road as they declared Him both Messiah and King.

> "When he came near the place where the road goes down the Mount of Olives, the whole crowd of disciples began joyfully to praise God in loud voices for all the miracles they had seen: 'Blessed is the king who comes in the name of the Lord! Peace in heaven and glory in the highest!'"
> —Luke 19:37-38 (NIV)

When asked by the pharisees to rebuke the people for blasphemy, Jesus responded that if the people didn't declare Him king then the very stones along the road would cry out that proclamation.

---

2 John 6:15

God had decreed at the time of the Exodus from Egypt that the Passover celebration was to be held every year on the 14th day of the Jewish month of Nisan. The Bible tells us that Jesus rode into Jerusalem *four days* before the Passover, establishing this event as happening on the 10th day of Nisan.

The Emperor Tiberius took office in AD14, and Scripture tells us that Jesus began His ministry in the 15th year of the reign of Tiberius.[3] This means he began His ministry in AD29. According to detailed calculations by Sir Robert Anderson,[4] which have been confirmed by many Bible teachers, the exact date of the triumphal entry was Nisan 10, AD32. That date corresponds to April 6, AD32 (or 32BCE) on our modern calendar. This was 69 *weeks of years* to the day from the decree to rebuild the city.

The triumphal entry took place exactly 483 biblical years after the decree. The time period measures 173,880 days, which is 69 weeks of years in length. Remember that the Bible always refers to the lunar calendar of 12 months of 30 days each.

It is interesting to study the response of Jesus as he viewed the city during that moment of earthly glory. He wept for Jerusalem and declared great sadness that she did not recognize the hour of His appearing.

> "If you, even you, had only known on this day what would bring you peace—but now it is hidden from your eyes. The days will come upon you when your enemies will build an embankment against you and encircle you and hem you in on every side. They will dash you to the ground, you and the children within your walls. They will not leave one stone on another, because you did not recognize the time of God's coming to you.'" —Luke 19:42-44 (NIV)

---

3   Luke 3:1
4   Sir Robert Anderson, *The Coming Prince*

YOU DO THE MATH

You can calculate the dates of Daniel's prophecy for yourself. Here's a handy guide. The starting point is the date of the decree to rebuild Jerusalem given to Nehemiah.

STARTING POINT: MARCH 14, 445BC

62 + 7 = 69 weeks of years.

69 x 7 = 483 **biblical** years of 360 days each.

483 x 360 days = 173,880 days in Daniel's prophecy.

445(BC) + (AD)31 = 476 **modern** years between March 14, 445BC and March 14, AD32. Note that there is only 1 year between 1BC and 1AD. There is no "year zero," so you need to account for that distinction.

476 x 365 = 173,740 days. We'll allow for leap years next.

173,740 + 116 leap days = 173,856 total days between March 14, 445BC and March 14, AD32.

173,856 + 24 (March 14 to April 6) = 173,880 days.

ENDING POINT: APRIL 6, AD32

This is the 10th day of the Jewish month of Nisan in AD32, four days prior to Passover that year. Scripture decrees that Passover must take place on the 14th day of Nisan regardless of the day of week involved.

Scripture indicates that Jesus rode into Jerusalem on a donkey while people declared Him "Messiah the King" exactly four days before Passover. In AD32, the Passover happened on April 10, marking the day we celebrate as Palm Sunday on April 6 that year. That date is exactly 173,880 days after the decree issued by Artaxerxes to Nehemiah.

He was holding the Jewish people accountable for something they should have known! Daniel's prophecy had been available to the Jews for centuries. Anyone could have made a simple calculation. Jesus was holding them accountable for *not* knowing this exact date, for not being prepared that Messiah the king had come.

At the time Daniel was given this prophecy, the city of Jerusalem lay in ruins, its walls completely destroyed by King Nebuchadnezzar's attack of 586BC. Gabriel told Daniel that a decree would be issued to rebuild the walls of Jerusalem. A time period of seven plus sixty-two weeks of years (69 weeks of years) begins with a proclamation that the city of Jerusalem will be restored and rebuilt.

THE ROYAL DECREE

Only one decree is possible here. Although there were a total of four decrees regarding the Jewish people, three of these referred specifically to the rebuilding of the temple, not the city. One decree by Artaxerxes did make an obscure reference to the walls, but was really about the temple. The decree to rebuild Jerusalem came in the month of Nisan in King Artaxerxes' twentieth year.

> "In the month of Nisan in the twentieth year of King Artaxerxes... I answered the king, 'If it pleases the king and if your servant has found favor in his sight, let him send me to the city in Judah where my fathers are buried so that I can rebuild it...' And because the gracious hand of my God was upon me, the king granted my requests."
> —Nehemiah 2:1,5,8 (NIV)

The Royal Observatory in Greenwich, England has calculated that this decree was issued on the first day of the Jewish month of Nisan (the spiritual new year). In our modern calendar, that date is March 14, 445 BC. Note that Daniel was given this prophecy about 100 years before that decree would come.

Daniel describes a rebuilt city and troublesome times. Times would indeed be troublesome under Roman occupation.

It's not clear why the 69 weeks are broken into two time periods. Some say it refers to 49 years taken to rebuild the city of Jerusalem, others say it refers to the time required to rebuild the temple. There are difficulties with both views.

DANIEL 9:26

> 26 After the sixty-two weeks, Messiah will be cut off, but not for Himself. And the people of the prince that shall come will destroy the city and the sanctuary. The end of it will be with a flood. War will continue to the end, and desolations have been decreed.

The events referred to now will take place *after* the 69 weeks of years. But the 70th week has not yet started!

We know from many other prophecies, including later ones given to Daniel, that the final *week of years* refers to a seven year period under the rule of the coming Antichrist, who will make a covenant of peace with the Jewish people, then after 3-1/2 years will turn on them, ushering in 3-1/2 years of tribulation.

This demonstrates that God has stopped the clock for an undetermined length. The church takes place during this time. Christ's death and resurrection begin the age of the church. When the church is taken out of the way by the event we call the *Rapture* then God will restart the clock, ushering in the final week of years decreed for the Jewish people.

The crucifixion of Jesus of Nazareth in AD32 allows for the fulfillment of the prophecy in the prescribed time.

Less than one week after he rode into Jerusalem, with a great crowd lining the street waving palm branches and declaring Him the King of the Jews, Jesus was *cut off* on a Roman cross. He died

💡 Insight

A FRESH VIEW OF TIME

How hard it is for us to visualize time as anything but the steady march of seconds, hours and years! Yet Scripture makes it clear that time was invented for our benefit. It has a specific beginning:

"This grace was given us in Christ Jesus before the beginning of time" —2 Timothy 1:9

God exists outside the restrictions of time and space that we must live within. Time is past, present and future all at the same instant to God and the heavenly hosts:

"But do not forget this one thing, dear friends: With the Lord a day is like a thousand years , and a thousand years are like a day."
—2 Peter 3:8

We won't sit around playing harps for endless hours, as is commonly suggested!

God doesn't treat the foretelling of future events casually. He gives prophecies only to accomplish specific purposes, and carefully structures them to ensure that we don't abuse them. Daniel's 9th chapter is remarkable as a mathematical prophecy that could easily be tracked by ordinary people to a specific day in history.

not for Himself, but that God's plan would be fulfilled. Christ gave Himself up to save mankind, so that anyone who would turn to Him would be saved.

> "I tell you the truth, whoever hears my word and believes Him who sent me has eternal life and will not be condemned; he has crossed over from death to life."
> —John 5:24 (NIV)

His resurrection enabled Him to atone for our sins as our living Redeemer, the Lord and Savior of all who call upon His name.

70 WEEKS AND THE CHURCH

There is much misunderstanding about the 70 years of Daniel because of earlier teachings by some before the restoration of Israel in 1948.

It was inconceivable to many in the late 19th and early 20th century that Israel could ever again become a nation. A number of teachers contorted Galatians 6:16 to turn the Christian church into the *new Israel*, claiming that the Jews had now forfeited their right to the promises God had made and these were now passed on to the church.

> "And as many as walk according to this rule, peace be on them, and mercy, and upon the Israel of God."
> —Galatians 6:16 (KJV)

God did not replace His plan for Israel with the church, he merely interrupted His plan for a time, and will return to it following the end of the *times of the Gentiles*.

> "Jerusalem will be trampled on by the Gentiles until the times of the Gentiles are fulfilled." —Luke 21:24b (NIV)

A gap of unknown length exists between the end of the 69th week and the start of the 70th week. Within that gap the Messiah would be "cut off" or crucified, and the city of Jerusalem along with the still-to-be-built temple would be destroyed. The final week of years still hasn't started, so that gap has lasted almost 2,000 years so far.

Some Bible teachers have interpreted the 70 weeks as being 70 *consecutive* weeks of years. In their view, it is inconceivable that any kind of a time gap of indeterminate length could be placed in Scripture. It's an understandable concern, but leads to many incorrect conclusions.

Using the model of 70 continuous weeks, these theologians have assigned the start of the *times of the Gentiles* mentioned by Jesus to such events as the stoning of Stephen (described in Acts 7:59). They place the biblical account of the Antichrist receiving his fatal head wound on Pope Pius IV in 1798, and claim that the beginning of judgement in Daniel 8:14 took place in 1844!

The many biblical references to a final earthly temple, the restoration and ending of the daily sacrifice, and other aspects of Daniel's prophecies are ignored or brushed off as mere allegories when using this model.

There is nothing allegorical about Daniel's prophecies, nor any prophecies in Scripture.

THE PRINCE WHO IS TO COME

The people of the ruler or prince who is to come is a remarkable double reference. It refers both to Titus who would enter Jerusalem after a siege in AD70, and to the coming one-world leader we often refer to as the Antichrist.

Note the astounding accuracy: the temple was destroyed not by an order of Titus, but by the random act of one soldier.

It is a reference to the *people of* that prince. If someone refers to the people of Daniel, you would understand it to mean the Jewish exiles. Likewise, this reference refers not directly to the prince himself but to his people, the Romans.

Jewish historian Josephus points out in his account of the Roman invasion that the destruction of the temple took place against the orders of General Titus. His soldiers ("the people of the prince who is to come") went berserk as they entered Jerusalem after a long siege and committed countless atrocities, slaughtering thousands of men, women and children.

One soldier threw a burning torch into the temple, causing the dry cedar to catch fire. When Titus was told that the temple was on fire, he reportedly raced to the scene and fell to his knees proclaiming, "I did not order this!" He tried to have the fire extinguished but it was too late.[5]

> "Do you see all these great buildings?" replied Jesus. "Not one stone here will be left on another; every one will be thrown down." —Mark 13:2 (NIV)

Titus ordered the temple torn down to get at the gold that had melted within. Not one stone was left upon another, just as Jesus had told His disciples in the Olivet sermon.

DANIEL 9:27

> 27 **And he will confirm a covenant with the many for one week. In the middle of the week he will put an end to sacrifice and offering, and on a corner of the altar [or wing of the temple] he will set up an abomination that causes desolation, until the end that has been decreed is poured out upon him.**

We see here a reference to a complete week of years. The first 69 weeks ended with "Messiah the king." Then a number of things

---

5   Josephus, *The Jewish Wars*

were described as taking place, such as the Messiah being cut off and the city and sanctuary being destroyed, and now we see a reference to a full week, with the ending of the daily sacrifice in the middle of that seven year period.

Naturally, a temple will have to exist in Jerusalem before this seven year time period can begin. Since the temple was destroyed in the previous statement, this refers to a yet-unbuilt temple.

The final ruler will first be peaceful and will 'confirm,' or enforce some kind of treaty to give the Jews the right to carry on their sacrificial requirements. It appears that a peace treaty with Israel may already exist but has fallen into disarray, and this world ruler achieves political victory through a worldwide agreement to support the treaty. Suddenly, after 3-1/2 years, he will turn on the Jews, stop the sacrifice, end any allowance of religious observance except to him or his god, and will desecrate the temple by placing his idol in a sacred place.

Centuries after this was written, and almost 200 years after Antiochus IV placed an image of Zeus in the Holy of Holies, Jesus made reference to "the abomination that causes desolation spoken of by the prophet Daniel."[6] Since the similar event by Antiochus IV had already happened, this refers to something yet in the future. Thus, Antiochus was merely a foreshadowing of an even more terrible time which still lies in the future.

---

6   Matthew 24:15; Mark 13:14

Application — My Notes & Bible Study Questions

13

DANIEL CHAPTER 10
SPIRITUAL FORCES AT WAR

We tend to think of the tangible things we can see and feel as the real world we live in. Although Christians are well aware that a spiritual dimension exists, it seems far away and removed from the "genuine" world that affects us throughout the events of our lives.

We get promoted, and our spirits soar. We lose our jobs and sink into deep concern and fear, forgetting that God really is in control. Babies are born and we rejoice. People we love get hurt, sick, or are taken from this world and we grieve. It often seems that these circumstances happen merely because of things we do or that other people do to us. Yet the Bible tells us that the real issues of life don't take place on levels we can physically experience. Scripture says that the real battle is not one of flesh and blood but of spiritual warfare.[1]

During the reign of king Hezekiah of Judah, Assyrian king Sennacherib taunted the God of the Jews, saying that He was powerless against the Assyrians. Sennacherib called for the Jews to find even 2,000 soldiers and he would equip them with horses to ride, a taunt designed to show his numerical superiority. That night a single angel put to death 185,000 Assyrian warriors! Sennacherib retreated to Nineveh in shame.[2]

Another example from 2 Kings 6 shows how God is on our side in huge numbers, though we are usually unaware of it. The king of Aram sent troops to find and arrest the prophet Elisha after learning that he was telling Hezekiah his most secret plans. When Elisha's servant opened the door of the house and cried in dis-

---

1 Ephesians 6:12
2 2 Kings 19:9-36

may upon seeing the Aramean army covering the hillsides, Elisha prayed that his eyes might be opened to see the spiritual dimension. Suddenly the servant saw vast numbers of spiritual warriors scattered throughout those same hills.

> And Elisha prayed, "O LORD, open his eyes so he may see." Then the LORD opened the servant's eyes, and he looked and saw the hills full of horses and chariots of fire all around Elisha. —2 Kings 6:17 (NIV)

In his book *God's Secret Agents*, Billy Graham tells a similar story about missionary John Paton and his wife in the New Hebrides. One night they were surrounded by hostile natives. Sensing that the natives wanted to kill them, Paton and his wife prayed through the night. Years later the chief of the tribe was asked about the event. He explained that they never attacked the missionary couple because there were a great number of men with drawn swords surrounding and protecting the home.[3]

Ephesians tells us that we are at a constant state of war with spiritual forces attacking us from the heavenly realms. This is the true source of all the events, human interactions and physical things that affect our lives.

> "For our struggle is not against flesh and blood, but against the rulers, against the authorities, against the powers of this dark world and against the spiritual forces of evil in the heavenly realms." —Ephesians 6:12 (NASB)

Romans 8:38 shows that these evil forces are highly organized into "principalities." Daniel makes it clear they have a structure associated directly with power structures on the earth, including demonic forces in charge of specific empires and countries.

---

3   Billy Graham, *God's Secret Agents*

We often have an attitude that is much too cavalier about the spiritual world, as if we don't fully believe this state of war exists. Even some church songs make light of the powers wielded by the side of evil. The apostle Jude made it clear that we must show a great deal of respect even to the forces of evil:

> Yet in the same manner these men, also by dreaming, defile the flesh, and reject authority, and revile angelic majesties. But Michael the archangel, when he disputed with the devil and argued about the body of Moses, did not dare pronounce against him a railing judgment, but said, "The Lord rebuke you." —Jude 8-9 (NASB)

Jude refers to an incident in which Michael the great warrior angel *did not dare* speak in a negative tone to Satan. Instead, he recognized that only God has the authority to rebuke spiritual beings. After this, he goes on to identify other sins related to speaking against the spiritual forces.

Angels can reveal themselves with physical bodies. They can eat with us and be entertained by us, looking like ordinary people. Abraham met three angels (one of them the Lord Jesus) and ate with them. The writer of Hebrews suggests this may be common!

> "Do not forget to entertain strangers, for by so doing some people have entertained angels without knowing it."
> —Hebrews 13:2 (NIV)

ANGELS IN SCRIPTURE

- Angels were present when God created the world, and shouted for joy (Job 38:4-7).
- They were present at the birth of Christ (Luke 2:8-14).
- Angels strengthened Jesus during His temptation in the wilderness (Matthew 4:1-11).
- Angels were there during the transfiguration.

- Angels provided encouragement during the night of agony in Gethsemene (Luke 22:43).
- They talked to the women near the tomb at the resurrection (Luke 24:1-7).
- They spoke to the apostles at the ascension (Acts 1:10-11).
- Angels will accompany Jesus' return (Matthew 13:39; 24:31).

Yet despite all the references to angels throughout the Scripture, Daniel's account introducing his final vision is certainly the most graphic description of how angels are constantly at war in the heavenly realms.

DANIEL 10:1

> 1 In the third year of Cyrus king of Persia a message was revealed to Daniel, (who was called Belteshazzar). And the message was true, but the time appointed was long and filled with strife. He understood the message through a vision.

This vision was given to Daniel in the third year of the reign of Cyrus, which was the fourth year after he officially took the throne and released the Jews from captivity. This was after the fall of Babylon as described in Daniel chapter 5.

DANIEL 10:2-4

> 2 At that time I, Daniel, was in mourning for three full weeks.
>
> 3 I ate no pleasant bread, nor allowed meat or wine in my mouth. I used no lotions on my body at all, until the whole three weeks were completed.
>
> 4 On the twenty-fourth day of the first month, as I was by the side of the great river, the Tigris [also called Hiddekel],

Daniel has been in mourning for three weeks. It was now the 24th day of the first month.

WHICH MONTH DID DANIEL MEAN?

The Jewish year was changed by God at the time of the Exodus to begin in the month Nisan. He had said that the *seventh* month (at that time Nisan) would become the *first* month. This created an interesting challenge, as the Jews now celebrated a calendar that was vastly different from that of the surrounding nations. Imagine if any one country suddenly changed its calendar so that July became the first month of the year!

The secular calendar remained unchanged, with Tishri as the first month. This traditional month order applied to the calendars of all the surrounding cultures and even the Jewish secular calendar.

To maintain commerce and some sense of order, business and non-religious affairs were still conducted according to the secular calendar. That's why the Jews, even today, celebrate their new year on the first two days of Tishri.

One could say the "first" month and still be correct whether he meant Nisan or Tishri. In fact, at the time of this prophecy, the Jews had lived for over seven decades in a culture in which the first month would consistently be Tishri.

We are not certain whether Daniel meant *Nisan* or *Tishri*. It's not critically important either way. But we can draw some inferences to help us reach an intelligent conclusion.

First, it would normally seem odd that he began his fast on the third day of the month. Daniel was very organized and punctual, an excellent administrator. A thorough planner, he was extremely specific about the three weeks. So why begin on the third day of the month? If he meant Tishri, it would make perfect sense because **Rosh Hashana** (*the New Year celebration*) took place on 1-2 Tishri, making the third day of the new year, immediately after the holiday, a wonderful time to begin a fast as an act of spiritual dedication at the start of the new year.

Second, such a long fast during the month of Nisan would mean fasting right through Passover, the holiest celebration in Judaism. Knowing Daniel's character and reverence for God, why would he wish to fast through this extremely important once-a-year event when the eating of the Passover Lamb held such religious significance and he had so many other opportunities to avoid missing it? Again it would seem completely out of character for Daniel.

Third, he ends his fast on the evening of the 23rd day. This would make perfect sense if the fast ended on the evening of **Simhat Torah** (the *Feast of Rejoicing*), in which case he could feast with everyone else and start a new day as that celebration of God's law came to a close. This celebration happens 21 days after Rosh Hashana.

The Jewish *Feast of Rejoicing* (called Simhat Torah) takes place on 23 Tishri. This is a celebration of the completion of the annual reading of the Torah, or Law of God.

It appears most likely that Daniel's three-week fasting period had begun right after Rosh Hashana and had just concluded on the Feast of Rejoicing when he had this vision.

This was not a complete fast. We often think that only complete fasts are "holy" but any fast is acceptable to God, as it represents a sacrifice on our part of something that we enjoy. Daniel was avoiding wine, meat, delicacies and lotions commonly used for hygiene.

Immediately after the Jewish New Year, Daniel went into three weeks of deep mourning with intense prayer and fasting. Why was he grieving? The first verse of Daniel 10 suggests that he had received a message from God, one that was so disturbing he mourned. Now he looks up and sees a vision that will interpret what he had previously told or been shown.

DANIEL 10:5-6

> 5 Then I looked up and saw a certain man dressed in linen, who wore a belt of the fine gold of Uphaz.
>
> 6 His body also was like beryl [or chrysolite], his face looked like lightning, his eyes like flaming torches, his arms and feet were the color of polished brass, and his voice was like the sound of a multitude.

The description of this angel is almost identical to that of Jesus' appearance to the apostle John in Revelation 1:13-16. White robe, gold belt, face shining impossibly bright, eyes like fire, flesh like glowing bronze, voice like rushing water, rain or white noise (**qol hamon**). There are scholars who believe this is Jesus, for many reasons, including the sense of dread described in the next verse. It also describes him as a *certain* man, and that phrase usually assigns significance. Others say this could not be, because verse 13 says he was *held back* by a demon. Yet there are good explanations for the potential of evil forces holding back even Jesus for a time in this context. The result is an inconclusive argument. This angel is most likely Jesus, but may be just an angel.

DANIEL 10:7-8

> 7 I, Daniel, was the only one who saw the vision, for the men with me didn't see it, but such terror fell upon them that they fled to hide themselves.
>
> 8 So I was left alone, and saw this great vision. There remained no strength left in me, for my color turned deathly pale and I became helplessly weak.

Daniel was evidently with companions at the Tigris river. But like the experience of Saul hundreds of years later, the men don't see the vision but know something spiritual is happening, which affected them in a powerful way.

> "The men traveling with Saul stood there speechless; they heard the sound but did not see anyone." —Acts 9:7 (NIV)

Daniel's companions fled with an overwhelming sense of dread. Only he was left. We flee from such a presence because spiritual forces connect us with a deep awareness of our fallen nature. The fear comes from knowing that we are filled with sin and evil.

Daniel had no strength left. Though he didn't feel the terror his companions experienced, the impact of this close interaction with the spiritual dimension left him trembling and weak, unable to move. That he didn't feel the same weakness when meeting Gabriel earlier is a strong argument that this must be Jesus.

DANIEL 10:9-11

> 9 Then I heard him speaking. As I listened to the voice of his words, I fell into a deep sleep with my face toward the ground.
>
> 10 A hand touched me, which set me upon my hands and knees.
>
> 11 And he said to me, "O Daniel, a man greatly loved, understand the words that I speak to you, and stand up, for I am now sent to you." And when he had said this to me, I stood trembling.

DANIEL'S VISION
- Dressed in linen (assumed white)
- Belt of fine polished gold
- Body like chrysolite
- Face bright as lightning
- Eyes like flaming torches
- Flesh like gleaming bronze
- Voice like falling rain or many voices speaking (equivalent to white noise)

JOHN'S VISION
- Long robe (assumed white)
- Golden sash/belt
- Head white as snow
- Eyes like blazing fire
- Flesh like glowing bronze
- Voice like rushing water
- Face shining like the sun

The angel seen by Daniel has many similarities to the vision of Jesus shown to John as described in Rev 1:13-16.

Some believe the angel is an Old Testament appearance of Jesus Christ (a "Theophany") but this is not certain and the subject of much debate.

Daniel is called *highly esteemed* or *beloved of God*. In the New Testament gospel accounts, the apostle John is called *the one Jesus loves* and he is the one who receives the apocalyptic vision. Here in the Old Testament, it is also the one loved by God who receives the incredibly detailed apocalyptic vision.

DANIEL 10:12-13

12 Then said he to me, "Don't be afraid, Daniel. From the first day that you set your heart to understand, and to humble yourself before your God, your words were heard and I have now come in response to them.

13 But the ruler of the kingdom of Persia resisted me twenty-one days. Then Michael, one of the chief princes, came to help me, because I remained there with the kings of Persia.

This angel was held back from his attempt to reach Daniel by the spiritual forces of darkness. For 21 earthly days he battled the spiritual *king of Persia*, a demon king in charge of the empire. This is the key reason why some scholars don't feel that this angel is Jesus, though there are strong rebuttals to this argument.

Note that in the second sentence related to this battle, the angel refers to these demon *kings* in the plural. It wasn't just one demon king giving the Persian empire its blood lust!

Here we see a very real example of the structure of spiritual forces, both good and evil. The statement shows that demonic forces are organized into structural hierarchies. There are "ranks" of both angels and demons. Some are put in charge of groups, some in charge of cities, some in charge of countries and even of empires.

This passage also highlights a unique perspective on time. The angel indicates that he was held back for 21 days battling the demon kings of Persia. God did not allow him to merely go back in time 21 days so that he appeared at Daniel's side the moment Daniel began to pray.

Though God created time and has dominion over it, God does not apparently permit the spiritual forces to travel backwards in time. As with all of His perfect rules, this would make sense as a way to protect us. If spiritual forces could travel back in time they could potentially change history, so it would make sense that God does not allow this. Scripture always moves forward in time, never backwards.

Scripture *looks* back in order to show us through examples of history our sinful condition or God's infinite love and grace. But Scripture never *moves* back in time. When king Hezekiah saw the shadow move backwards on the steps (2 Kings 20:9-11), it was not an example of time going backwards but the shadow of the sun moving backwards.

Hebrews 1:14 asks, "are not all angels ministering spirits sent to serve those who will inherit salvation?" The archangel Michael helped this angel so he could be free from barriers in order to help Daniel.

Sometimes when we pray we struggle with patience, because we fail to understand the depth of the battle raging in the spiritual realm that causes delays even when an answer is immediately on its way. This chapter of Daniel is an excellent picture of how God is continually at work on our behalf even when we don't see the results of our prayers. The answers are already on their way. It is up to us to trust God.

DANIEL 10:14

> 14 Now I have come to make you understand what will happen to your people in the distant future, for the vision concerns a time many days away."

The vision will be an explanation of what Daniel already knows. He was in mourning because of a message about the future that concerned Israel and the Jewish people. Now he will receive the explanation so he can understand it.

DANIEL 10:15

> 15 When he had said these words to me, I set my face toward the ground and became speechless.

Some Bibles say that Daniel *bowed* with his face to the ground, suggesting that Daniel was worshipping the angel, and one of the arguments in favor of considering that this was Jesus. However, that isn't entirely clear from the passage so we can't draw conclusions from it.

DANIEL 10:16-18

> 16 Then one in the form of a man touched my lips, and I opened my mouth and spoke. I said to him who stood before me, "O my lord, because of the vision I am filled with sorrow, and I have no strength left.
>
> 17 For how can I, your servant, talk with you, my lord? I have no strength left in me and I can hardly breathe."
>
> 18 Again one who looked like a man touched me and strengthened me,

The prophet Isaiah also had a vision in which he became speechless until an angel held a coal to his lips.

Angels are sometimes used to strengthen us when we are fatigued or weakened by spiritual warfare. When Jesus prayed in agony in the Garden of Gesthemene, an angel came to give him strength.

💡 Insight

FASCINATION WITH ANGELS

There are many false ideas about angels. Popular television shows like "Touched by an Angel," while admirable as family fare, actually continue to create false perceptions about the spiritual warfare around us.

A few facts about angels from Scripture:

Spiritual warfare is real and furiously rages around us at all times. We can see and feel the effects as both righteousness and evil flow through history in waves, but we cannot see the battles taking place.

Most historical images of angels are of female beings. Yet only male angels are ever revealed in the pages of Scripture. Though there is a possibility that female angels exist, we shouldn't make assumptions just because of how we would imagine things to be. Angels are created beings and God may just as well have chosen to make them all male.

Angels don't know everything. They ask questions. They are eager to learn.

The only angels that are named in Scripture are Gabriel and Michael as well as two from the side of rebellion: Lucifer and Apollyon.

The word "angel" comes from the Greek word "angelos" which means "messenger."

Angels seem to have free will to choose between right and wrong, just as people have. References in Scripture suggest that a third of the angels were evicted from heaven after the fall of Lucifer, apparently because their loyalties lay with him.

Cherubim are usually depicted in art as chubby little babies. In fact, they are fierce warriors with huge wings.

DANIEL 10:19-20

> 19 and said, "O man greatly loved, don't be afraid. Be filled with peace! Be strong now, be strong." When he spoke to me, I was strengthened and said, "Speak lord, for you have given me strength."
>
> 20 Then he said, "Do you know why I have come to you? Shortly I will return to fight against the prince of Persia. When I have gone forth, the prince of Greece will come.

Spiritual battles continue to rage at all times, and this being, whether Jesus or an angel, will have to return to the fight. Notice the references to the demon princes of the kingdoms of Persia and Greece. The Greek empire would not rise to prominence for another 200 years! When it does, it would usher in bloodthirsty war against Persia, with almost unimaginable loss of life.

DANIEL 10:21-11:1

> 21 But I will show you that what is written in the Book of Truth. No one supports me in these things except Michael your prince.
>
> 11:1 And in the first year of Darius the Mede, I took my stand to support and strengthen him.

There is a reference to *the Book of Truth*. We previously explored the various books mentioned in Scripture, in chapter 10.

The spiritual being before Daniel explains that only Michael the Archangel supported him in his efforts. What does this mean?

We should not assume that the angel's words about support mean that no one *bothered* to help him. It may just as easily mean that nobody was available to help him because they were assigned to other tasks.

Don't assume he meant "I was helpless except for Michael's assistance." He actually meant "Only Michael was assigned to assist me." So this reference to amount of support doesn't invalidate the view that this angel is the Messiah. Michael is the greatest warrior angel described in Scripture. If this being is Jesus, it would make sense that only Michael is assigned as his personal guard, so to speak.

Revelation 12:7 tells us that there was war in heaven and that Michael the archangel and his army fought against the dragon, and his angels fought back.

Currently Satan has been granted limited authority as the ruler of the space we live in.[4] When Jesus was tempted in the wilderness, one of the temptations Satan used was to promise him all the kingdoms of earth. It would not have been a temptation if Satan didn't have the right to make such an offer!

At this point, I've included the first verse of Daniel chapter 11. The reason is that it deserves special comment because of how some scholars see the passage.

The first verse of chapter 11 is actually the end of the angel's statement in chapter 10. Chapter and verse numbers were not part of the original Scripture writings, but added centuries later.

A HISTORY OF ANTI-SEMITISM

The Jewish people have many times in their history faced attempts to wipe them out of existence. Satan continually tries to block God's long published plan for Israel.

In this chapter of Daniel, the angel's reference to the battle with the spiritual king of Persia may be related to the attempt by Haman (still about 100 years away when this vision is given) to eliminate the Jews through the decree by Xerxes, the one thwarted with the help of Esther.

Another attempt to destroy the Jews would come from Antiochus IV Epiphanes. Later would come orders to expel the Jews from the Roman empire and during the Spanish inquisition, from Russia in 1914, and then of course the well-documented holocaust under Hitler. In recent years we've seen Iran's public declarations of hatred.

It is clear that this continued attempt to eliminate the Jewish people means God's plan for the Jews is far from complete.

---

4   Ephesians 2:2

Speculation is that the passage was broken this way because the preceding verses have to do with the angel's alliance with Michael and the next (Daniel 11:1) with the angel's involvement in the life of the human king Darius the Mede.

Remember that this vision took place in the "third year of Cyrus," which was actually the fourth year since Cyrus took the throne, based on traditional Babylonian reckoning of a king's reign. The Jews had been restored to their land under Cyrus, an event that would pave the way for the ultimate appearance of the Son of God as the Messiah for God's redeemed. As a result, it's no surprise to learn that Satan and all his hosts had been engaged in an all-out battle to hinder the release of the Jews and their return to the promised land. We can only imagine some of the things that may have been going on, both politically and culturally, at that time.

For the angel here to specifically point out that he was involved in supporting Darius the Mede, we must assume there was great spiritual oppression during his three years of reign leading up to Cyrus taking the throne. In the sixth chapter of Daniel, we saw Darius challenged to sign a decree that no one could pray to anyone but Darius for 30 days, leading to the situation where Daniel found himself in the lion's den. That event was part of the raging spiritual battle now mentioned by this angel! Who knows what additional challenges for the Jews were averted because of the angel's support of Darius at that time. This makes the warm relationship we saw between Darius and Daniel even more significant. It was the result of great spiritual intercession.

Application — My Notes & Bible Study Questions

14

DANIEL CHAPTER 11
EARTHLY KINGS AT WAR

Daniel's account of the future recorded in chapter 11 is so astonishing in its detail that critics who don't believe in prophecy have no place to go except to claim desperately that it was written after that history took place.

Yet any claim of that nature meets with impossible credibility problems, because copies of Daniel have been found dating earlier than many of the events described in these passages. Not only that, but the book was translated into Greek around 270BC as part of the Septuagint, and that version is identical to Hebrew versions. If you take a book published recently, then find a copy of the same book published much earlier and the two are the same, you cannot claim that someone changed it along the way!

Chapter 11 and 12 work together as one vision, with chapter 10 forming the prelude or introduction. The vision can be divided into 3 parts:

- **Part 1**, though it was future to Daniel, is history to us, because it was completely fulfilled by events now past.
- **Part 2** was fulfilled as a foreshadowing in the second century BC. However, this description will also be fulfilled in the future under a coming world leader.
- **Part 3** is still in the future as far as we're concerned. Some people (generally known as "preterists") insist that all of Daniel relates to events that are now over, but this requires the holder of that view to argue that prophecy is allegorical.

While Daniel was fasting, an angel appeared to him above the water of the Tigris River. This angel, described in terms similar to those used by John several hundred years later in his Revelation of Jesus Christ, has talked about spiritual warfare.

DANIEL 11:1

> 1 And in the first year of Darius the Mede, I took my stand to support and strengthen him.

Continuing his statement begun at the end of chapter 10, the angel says that he took action to support Darius the Mede and protect him from spiritual attack. This spiritual protection paved the way for Cyrus to release the Jews and allow them to return to their homeland, as prophesied by Isaiah almost 200 years earlier.

Part 1:
The Seleucid Wars

Through his vision, Daniel has given us insight into war in the spiritual realm. The angel now describes hundreds of years of future (to Daniel) war between men, in particular the ongoing battles over several generations between the Seleucid empire (the *king of the North*) and the Egyptian empire of Ptolemy (the *king of the South*). These verses of Daniel 11 are clearly historical to us. They can all be matched to events in history with uncanny detail.

DANIEL 11:2

> 2 Now, I tell you the truth: three kings will yet stand up in Persia; and then a fourth who will be far richer than the others. By power gained through his riches he will stir up everyone against the kingdom of Greece.

The three kings are **Cambyses** (Cyrus' elder son) from 529-523; an imposter named **Gaumata** (also named Bardiya), who passed himself off as Cyrus' younger son after having the real son murdered, from 523-522; and **Darius 1** from 522-485. Darius was the son of Hystaspes who murdered the imposter. He was of royal blood, the cousin of Cyrus.

The fourth king is **Xerxes** (Ahasuerus) who ruled during the near-holocaust described in the book of Esther, from 485-464. He would ultimately play a major role in Greece's anger towards the Persians by spending years trying to violently subdue Greece through military might with only partial success.

The angel's earlier account of spiritual warfare with the demonic *kings of Persia* probably related to the battle over protecting the Jews from Haman's attempt to wipe them out through Xerxes. A Jewish Queen named Esther became the source of their salvation in a surprising plot twist. Read the book of Esther for insight.

DANIEL 11:3

> 3 **Then a mighty king will stand up, who will rule with great authority, and do as he pleases.**

This is a reference to **Alexander the Great**. The angel has skipped a number of other Persian kings, moving forward about 120 years.

DANIEL 11:4

> 4 **After he comes, his kingdom will be broken up and divided toward the four winds of heaven. It will not go to his descendants, nor will it have the authority he had, for his kingdom will be plucked up and given to others beside those.**

Alexander died at the height of his power. His half brother, Philip Arrhidaeus, was mentally incapable of leading. Alexander had two sons, too young to take over, who were murdered within 13 years of their father's death. After 22 years of infighting, Alexander's empire was divided up between his four key generals. None of these four were even a shadow of the original.

The two key pieces were that of **Seleucus Nicator**, who took control of Syria, and **Ptolemy I Soter** taking Egypt. These two would battle each other for the next 150 years, continuing until Roman rule was established in the area under Pompey.

Because these power struggles are seen through the lens of Israel, they are described in geographical reference to Israel. Thus, Seleucus who is located north of Israel is "the king of the North" while Ptolemy is "the king of the South."

DANIEL 11:5

> 5 **The king of the south will be strong, but one of his princes will be even stronger and will have great authority and power over his own kingdom.**

Ptolemy reigned Egypt from 323-285BC. However, his successor **Ptolemy II Philadelphus** (285-245BC) became an even stronger king, establishing the great Library of Alexandria and commissioning the Septuagint translation of the Hebrew Scriptures into Greek, the common trade language of the day.

KING OF THE NORTH
After Alexander's death, the Greek empire fell into a state of disarray for over 20 years. Eventually Seleucus Nicator (above) took control of the area then known as Syria (which included today's Israel and Lebanon). He would begin an ongoing battle with Egypt that would last until the birth of the Roman Empire. In Daniel's vision, Seleucus and his descendents represent the "King of the North" while Egypt represents the southerly kingdom.

Ptolemy 1 captured Jerusalem on a Sabbath day in 321BC without resistance, but in 316 lost Israel to his rival Antigonus. After the battle of Baza in 312BC, Ptolemy regained the territory with assistance from Seleucus Nicator (312-281BC). Seleucus established the Seleucid empire, ruling from Babylon.

DANIEL 11:6

> 6 At the end of many years they will join together as allies. The daughter of the king of the south will come to the king of the north to make an agreement, but she will not retain her power and neither will he nor his power stand. At this time she will be handed over, together with the escorts that brought her and her father and the one who supported her.

A political marriage was arranged between **Antiochus II Theos** (262-246BC) and Ptolemy II Philadelphus' daughter **Berenice**. Antiochus had to divorce his wife Laodiceia, which enraged her. She responded by poisoning Antiochus and Berenice, along with their infant son and setting her elder son **Seleucus II Callinicus** on the throne (246-226BC). Note that his happened after the Septuagint was written, containing the complete book of Daniel.

DANIEL 11:7

> 7 But out of her family line will arise one in his estate. He will come with an army, and will enter the fortress of the king of the north. He will fight against them, and will succeed.

The brother of the murdered Berenice, **Ptolemy III Euergetes** (245-221BC) sought revenge. Taking the throne of Egypt, he invaded Syria, seized the port of Antioch and overran Seleucus' empire all the way to Babylon.

DANIEL 11:8

> 8 He will also seize and carry captive into Egypt their gods with molten images and their valuable articles of silver and gold. For certain years he will stay away from the king of the north.

Ptolemy III took huge spoils back to Egypt. These included gold, silver and many idols.

DANIEL 11:9

> 9 Then the king [of the north] will invade the kingdom of the king of the south, but will retreat into his own land.

After two years Seleucus II reorganized and marched south against Egypt, but was soundly defeated and returned to Antioch with only a small force remaining.

Note that your Bible may contain a remarkably different turn of events. There's a good reason for the confusion: the sentence structure in the Hebrew isn't very specific, making it quite easy to misunderstand.

As a result, some Bibles such as the KJV appear to indicate that the king of the south attacks north, while others say that the king of the north invades southward, which is the intended meaning. The exact Hebrew reading goes like this (Hebrew words in bold):

MAN'S ENDLESS STATE OF WAR

War and hate are the by-products of rebellion against God's command to love Him with all our heart and to love our neighbors as ourselves.

Daniel's vision shows hundreds of years of continual war between the empires of Seleucus and Ptolemy. Yet the vision extends far into the future without missing a beat.

After the Christian church is removed, it seems that this continual north-south feud will carry on as if it had never been interrupted.

> **bow** [will invade] [the other] **melek** [kingdom] **negeb** [south] [and will] **shuwb** [turn away from, retreat] [to his own] **adamah** [land]

It's easy to see how challenging it can be to translate from one language to another. If a translator assigns *negeb* (south) as the origin of the invasion rather than the origin of the retreat, he will come up with a different interpretation.

DANIEL 11:10

> 10 But his sons will prepare for war, and will assemble a great army, one that will come and sweep through like a flood. Then he will return, and be stirred up all the way to his fortress.

Seleucus' sons were **Seleucus III Ceraunus** (226-223BC) who was killed in Asia Minor, and **Antiochus III**, also known as **Antiochus The Great**. History books tend to have lots to say about Antiochus the Great (223-187BC) who recovered the fortress of Seleucia along with Tyre, then resumed the war with Egypt.

DANIEL 11:11

> 11 Then the king of the south will be moved with rage, and will come and fight against the king of the north, who will raise a large army, but it will be defeated.

The army of **Ptolemy IV Philopator** (221-203BC) marched against Antiochus III. At the battle of Raphia just south of Gaza, Antiochus was defeated despite his larger army and signed a peace treaty with Ptolemy who then went on a tour of the Holy lands, though he was badly treated in Jerusalem.

DANIEL 11:12

> 12 And when he has carried off the army, the king of the south will be filled with pride and will slaughter many tens of thousands, but he will not be strengthened by it.

Filled with pride and angry about what happened to him in Jerusalem, Ptolemy IV took out his humiliation when he returned to Egypt by murdering thousands of Egyptian Jews.

DANIEL 11:13

> 13 **For the king of the north will return with an even larger army than the previous one. After a few years he will advance with a huge army fully equipped.**

After Ptolemy IV died, his four-year-old son succeeded him as **Ptolemy V Epiphanes** (203-181BC). Some 12 years after his defeat at the Battle of Raphia, Antiochus III set out with a greater army in an attempt to conquer Egypt.

DANIEL 11:14

> 14 **And in those times many will stand up against the king of the south. Violent criminals among your people will raise themselves up to fulfill the vision, but they will not succeed.**

AN EMPIRE DIMINISHED

Once the greatest power on earth, the empire of Egypt gradually diminished in power and influence to become a mere shadow of its former glory. By the time of the Seleucid-Ptolemy feuds, Egypt was struggling to maintain control of the Nile valley and its key cities.

As the Ptolemys began to rely on the Romans to help them against Antiochus IV, they became puppets of the Roman empire, which eventually took control of the region after the death of the last Cleopatra.

Antiochus had an ally in Philip of Macedon, the father of Alexander the Great. In addition, many vassal kings of Egypt opposed Ptolemy V.

In 200BC, an Egyptian Jew named **Scopas** raised up an army of mercenaries and rebels in an attempt to win Judea from Antiochus but he was defeated by Antiochus III's army of 100,000 men at Sidon in 198BC.

DANIEL 11:15-16

15 Then the king of the north will come and build up siege ramps and capture the most fortified cities. The forces of the south will not withstand, not even their best troops, no one will have any strength to resist.

16 But the invader will do as he pleases, and none will be able to stand against him. He will set himself up in the glorious land, and will have the power to destroy it.

In the city that would later be named Caesarea Philippi north of Galilee, Antiochus took control of Palestine from the Egyptians for the last time, soundly defeating them at the Battle of Panium. Meanwhile the Romans were getting a foothold in Greece and working on their naval strength.

DANIEL 11:17

17 He will be determined to enter with the might of his whole kingdom, so this is what he will do: he will give him his daughter in marriage to overthrow the kingdom. But she will not remain loyal to helping him.

Increasing Roman control was beginning to play a role in the conflicts between the Seleucid and Egyptian empires. A peace accord was established in 196BC, which would later be utilized by Antiochus IV when he wrested control of the empire. Anticipating he would need to neutralize Egypt, Antiochus III had entered a marriage alliance, sending his daughter **Cleopatra** to be the bride of Ptolemy V. Because the boy was much too young at the time, the marriage wasn't consummated for several years. Antiochus expected her to be a useful spy, but instead she became loyal to her husband and the plans of Antiochus failed to help him.

DANIEL 11:18-19

> 18 After this will he turn his attention toward the coast lands, and will take many of them. But a prince for his own behalf will put an end to his insolence and will cause it to turn back upon him.
>
> 19 Then he will turn his attention toward the fortresses of his own land, but he will stumble and fall, and will be seen no more.

In 192BC, Antiochus invaded Greece with an army of 10,000 but was soundly defeated a year later at the Battle of Thermopylae. He then took to a sea battle to keep the Romans out of his territory, but lost the fight. He called for 70,000 reinforcements. Legendary Carthinian general Hannibal, to whom he had granted exile, offered advice, but Antiochus refused to take it.

Roman troops under Scipio met those of Antiochus in battle at Magnesia north of Ephesus. Yet despite being about half the numbers, the Roman's superior military training and tactics so badly defeated Antiochus that he was completely wiped out in a humiliating defeat that led to a complete and total surrender. He had to pay a tribute equivalent to 30 million dollars. He was ruined.

DANIEL 11:20

> 20 Then will arise a successor who will send a tax collector to maintain the glory of the kingdom. Within a few years he will be destroyed, but not in anger nor in battle.

Seleucus IV Philopator (187-175BC), a son of Antiochus III sent his treasurer **Heliodorus** to Jerusalem to seize funds in an effort to rebuild the coffers of an empire financially wiped out by war. He oppressed Israel through taxation. After 12 years Seleucus was murdered by Heliodorus who hoped to take over.

Part 2:
Past and future

Now we come to a section of the prophecy that applies partially to our own history, yet will also apply in a strange repetition of events to a future leader. This is known as a "foreshadowing," where biblical prophecy applies to two different times in history.

DANIEL 11:21

> 21 **He will be succeeded by a vile person to whom has not been given the honor of royal position. He will come in peaceably, and seize the kingdom by flattery and deceit.**

Antiochus IV Epiphanes was not the rightful heir to the throne. The brother of Seleucus IV Philopator, he had been held in Rome as a hostage to ensure that Seleucus would pay his tribute. After 12 years he had himself trade places with Seleucus' son Demetrius and was released. On his way to Antioch, his brother Seleucus IV was murdered by Heliodorus, Seleucus IV Philopator's tax collector. There were rumors that Heliodorus was actually working for Antiochus IV when he committed that murder. Antiochus IV, through various flatteries and bribes, took hold of the throne.

He was indeed contemptible, having the goal of converting Jerusalem into a Hellenistic center (a center for Greek culture). He also established a co-regency with his nephew who was still a minor, then had him murdered.

The passages that relate well to Antiochus IV are also a foreshadowing of the coming world leader, who will have many of the same characteristics and will take the same actions described here. In that sense these verses relate to two people at the same time, one in our past and one in our future.

Insight

THE MACCABEAN REVOLT

While Antiochus IV was busy in Egypt, a false rumor spread that he had been killed, leading to events that caused rioting in Jerusalem. On the King's return from Egypt in 167BC, enraged by his defeat, he attacked Jerusalem.

"He ordered his soldiers to cut down without mercy those whom they met and to slay those who took refuge in their houses. There was a massacre of young and old, a killing of women and children, a slaughter of virgins and infants. In the space of three days, eighty thousand were lost, forty thousand meeting a violent death, and the same number being sold into slavery." —2 Maccabees 5:12-14

Antiochus then outlawed Jewish religious rites and traditions observed by orthodox Jews, and decreed the worship of Zeus. He also profaned the temple and dedicated it to Zeus with an idol, even sacrificing a pig on the altar as an offering. He sent an army to enforce his decree, committing great atrocities against the Jews, even having two women hurled off the wall with their babies just for circumcising their children.

A group of Jews sprang into action to end this apostasy and bring order back to Jerusalem.

Five brothers, the sons of Mattathias Maccabeaus, a priest, rose up against Antiochus and led a 3-year revolt that eventually succeeded in recapturing the city.

Exactly three years to the day after Antiochus IV set up the idol, the temple was rededicated in a ceremony called "Hanukkah" (the word means Dedication), which is still celebrated every December 25 to this day.

At the time that Antiochus initially conducted his blasphemous act, December 25 had no historical significance; Christianity wasn't born yet and that day was of no particular importance to the Jews. However, that day now has enormous religious significance for both Jews and Christians. It is possible that the future world leader will desecrate the temple on the same day.

DANIEL 11:22-23

> 22 They will be swept like a flood from before him, and will be destroyed. Yes, even the prince of the covenant.
>
> 23 After making an agreement with him, he will work deceitfully, for he will rise to power and become strong with only a small number of people.

These passages refer to Antiochus' dealings with the priesthood. They appear to refer to the Jewish religious adherence being swept away, as Antiochus would later eliminate all Jewish practices. The *prince of the covenant* probably refers to the **high priest Onias III**. First he had been deposed peacefully. But then his brother Jason offered Antiochus a bribe and was installed as high priest. Later another brother, Menelaus, offered a larger bribe and became high priest instead. In the fall of 171 Onias was murdered.

DANIEL 11:24

> 24 He will invade, on the pretense of peace, even the richest provinces and he will do things that neither his fathers nor his forefathers did. He will distribute among his followers the prey, plunder, loot and wealth. Yes, he will plot the overthrow of fortresses, but only for a time.

Antiochus IV robbed the richest places of the countries under his control, and was known for distributing the loot to gain political power. He also attacked his enemies when they least expected it, after making peace agreements with them.

DANIEL 11:25-26

> 25 He will stir up his power and courage against the king of the south with a great army. And the king of the south will be stirred up to battle with a very great and powerful army, but he will not stand because of the plots devised against him.

> 26 Yes, those who eat from his own provisions will destroy him. His army will be swept away and many will die in battle.

After Cleopatra died, **Ptolemy VI Philometer** (a nephew of Antiochus IV) received bad advice by two officials who were trying to undermine him and was unable to withstand an attack from Antiochus in 169BC. Antiochus took the city of Memphis and Ptolemy surrendered.

DANIEL 11:27

> 27 Both these kings' hearts will be bent on evil, and they will speak lies to each other at the same table. But their plans will not succeed, for the end will still be at the appointed time.

Because Ptolemy VI Philometer was a nephew, he ate at the same table with Antiochus IV as they discussed politics and military strategy. Antiochus, of course, wanted to control all of Egypt and was only using his nephew to gain information he could use to win. Meanwhile, the citizens of Alexandria made Ptolemy's younger brother **Ptolemy Physcon** king instead. Antiochus tried to break the revolt but was unsuccessful and returned to Syria. Ptolemy VI then disavowed his loyalty to Antiochus and was reinstated with his brother in a co-regency of Egypt.

DANIEL 11:28

> 28 Then he [the king of the north] will return to his land with great riches, but his heart will be against the holy covenant. He will take action against it and then return to his own land.

Antiochus IV was unhappy with the events in Egypt and raided the temple treasury. There's disagreement on exactly when this took place. This account, given to Daniel in advance, implied that it happened between the first and second Egyptian invasions.

DANIEL 11:29

> ²⁹ **At the appointed time he will return and invade the south again; but the outcome will not be as it was the previous times.**

In the spring of 168 Antiochus again headed for Egypt with an initial siege of Memphis. He took control of lower Egypt, as he had before, then turned his attention on Alexandria, the city which had defied him on his last attempt. This time the outcome was quite different, as the city appealed for help from a young upstart military power with a naval base just up the cost at Cyprus.

Note the reference that this happened at "the appointed time." No doubt Antiochus IV thought he was calling the schedule of events, but in fact it was entirely under the control of God.

DANIEL 11:30

> ³⁰ **For ships of Chittim [Cyprus] will come against him. Therefore he will be grieved and will turn back, and will vent his rage against the holy covenant. So will he do; he will return and show favor to those who forsake the holy covenant.**

Roman ships from **Cyprus** (also called *Kittim* or *Chittim*) arrived just as Antiochus approached Alexandria. Roman consul Gaius Popillius Laenas met him by the walls of Alexandria and commanded him to leave Egypt. When Antiochus replied that he had to consult with his advisors, the Romans drew a circle in the dirt around him and declared that he had to give his answer before stepping out of the circle. This was probably in July 168. Deeply humiliated by this defeat at the hands of a young military power, he headed home and turned his fury on the Jews.

DANIEL 11:31

> 31 **His armed forces will rise up and they will desecrate the sanctuary of strength, and will take away the daily sacrifice. Then they will place the abomination that causes desolation.**

There was a rumor in Jerusalem that Antiochus IV had been killed in battle. Jason took the opportunity to rise up against Menelaus in an attempt to gain back his position. This further enraged Antiochus IV, who went about his attack in his usual deceitful style. He sent Apollonius with a contingent of soldiers into Jerusalem on the Sabbath day, apparently on a peace mission. But the men suddenly began a merciless slaughter of thousands of Jews.

Antiochus IV then abolished the daily sacrifice and all religious observances, including the reading of Scripture. He slaughtered a pig on the altar. On December 25, 167BC he set up an idol of Zeus in the Holy of Holies and declared the temple officially a temple to the Greek god Zeus. This action is known as *the abomination that causes desolation*. Yet Jesus refers to a future event, imploring us that when we see *the abomination that causes desolation spoken of by the prophet Daniel*, we are to know that the end is near.

Although we focus on Antiochus IV because it is so clearly represented here, we must also keep in mind that this refers also to the actions of a world leader who is yet to come. That ruler will act in the same way and will also banish the sacrifice 3-1/2 years after enforcing a peace treaty with Israel. He will abolish religious observances and slaughter untold numbers of Jews, as well as setting up an idol in the Holy of Holies.

DANIEL 11:32

> 32 Those who have violated the covenant he will corrupt by flatteries, but the people who know their God will be strong, and will take action against him.

There were many non-religious Jews who supported this movement towards Hellenization (converting to Greek culture). In today's world a majority of Jews are non-religious and since this relates both to past and future events, it is not hard to see how the future world leader will corrupt many Jews at that time to his way of thinking.

Part 3: Looking ahead

The verses that follow move away from clear relation to Antiochus IV and seem to refer exclusively to the actions of the future leader, the one often called the Antichrist. This section is open to much debate because, even with the help of visions like these, the future is unknown territory except what we can connect to other passages of Scripture. The vision's similarity to other prophetic passages such as 2 Thessalonians 2 are striking.

DANIEL 11:33-35

> 33 Those who have understanding among the people will instruct many. Yet they will fall by the sword, be burned or captured or plundered for many days.
>
> 34 When they will fall, they will be receive little help, but many will deceitfully come to their side.
>
> 35 Some of the wise will fall, so they may be refined and purged and purified until the time of the end, because it will still come at the appointed time.

These events refer equally well to the time of the Maccabean revolt and the final actions of the Jews opposing the Antichrist.

DANIEL 11:36

> 36 **The king will do as he pleases. He will exalt himself and magnify himself above every god, and will speak unheard-of things against the God of gods. He will prosper until the time of wrath is completed, for what was determined will be done.**

Although it is true that Antiochus referred to himself as *god manifest* (it was even on his coins), these references don't relate well to Antiochus. He did honor Zeus. Note also that this king will prosper until the *time of wrath* is complete. The time of wrath parallels the descriptions of the bowls of wrath in the book of Revelation.

The reference that he will say unheard-of-things means that his blasphemies and accusations against God will go beyond anything a leader of the past would have dared to utter. He will not control his tongue in order to meet standards of public decency.

DANIEL 11:37-38

> 37 **He will show no regard for the God of his fathers, nor the one desired by women, nor will he regard any god, for he will magnify himself above them all.**
>
> 38 **But in his estate he will honor a god of fortresses, and a god unknown to his fathers he will honor with gold and silver, and with precious stones and pleasant things.**

Some scholars believe that the coming world ruler will be a Jew because of this passage and others. He will consider himself divine publicly, magnifying himself above all gods. Yet he will honor a god of some kind with symbolic rituals. This behavior is similar to that of Antiochus IV, who worshipped Zeus despite calling himself divine.

💡 Insight

THE COMING WORLD LEADER: JEW OR GENTILE?

There is much debate about whether the coming world leader will be a Jew or a Gentile. There are reasons to believe he may have Jewish roots, but the evidence is inconclusive.

Jesus referred to the coming world leader in an interesting context: "another will come in his own name and him you will receive" (see John 5:43). Since Jews would not receive a Gentile, this is one reason some scholars believe the coming world leader may have a Jewish background.

Like Antiochus IV, he will claim to be divine, yet honor another god at the same time. Daniel 11:37 says "He will show no regard for the gods of his fathers... nor will he show regard for any other god; for he will magnify himself above them all." Verse 38 goes on to say that he will honor a god his forefathers did not know.

If he shows no regard for any gods of his ancestors, but honors a god unknown to them, then who are his ancestors?

If the future leader is a Gentile, any god he honors is likely to have been recognized in some form by pagan ancestors. If he's of Jewish blood, then the reference to multiple gods could refer to the false gods the Jews worshipped during times of apostasy.

Other passages that seem to point to someone of Jewish descent include Ezekiel 21:25-27; 28:2-10; and Psalm 55.

Some say he's of Assyrian descent, based on Isaiah 14:25 and other passages.

The book of Revelation points out that there are two figures involved. One of these, a spiritual leader, will call for people to worship the other.

Some Bible translations say he will *not desire women* but this is a poor interpretation. The NIV is much more accurate than the KJV on this passage. This reference means that he will not have a regard for *the one desired by* women, which is a reference to women expecting to bear the anticipated Messiah as their son (the role eventually fulfilled by Mary). It is not a reference to homosexuality as some claim. Isaiah had foretold a young woman, a virgin, who would give birth to the promised Messiah. Jewish women for generations had desired to be that highly honored woman of faith.

The reference to *god of fortresses* is interesting. Many scholars believe that this is just a reference to the Akra, the Syrian military garrison attached to the Temple Mount. But it may have deeper meaning. I've been told the word *god* is in the feminine rather than masculine form, but haven't been able to confirm that. Could this be a reference to a goddess? If you look closely at statues or images of Artemis or Diana of Ephesus, their crown includes the image of a fortress. The sentence structure in the Hebrew language also suggests that there are possibly two different gods that will be honored, one the god of fortresses and the other a god unknown to his ancestors. We don't know if this has relevance.

DANIEL 11:39

> 39 He will engage the strongest fortresses with the help of a foreign god, whom he will acknowledge. He will increase in glory and will assign people as rulers over many, and will divide up the land for financial gain.

Like Antiochus IV, he will have military success and will gain power through political maneuvering. But while Antiochus did grant limited power to certain people, there are no historical records of him putting others into positions where they would rule over kingdoms. This refers to the coming world leader, not to Antiochus IV Epiphanes.

DANIEL 11:40

> 40 **At the time of the end the king of the south will attack him in battle, and the king of the north will storm against him like a whirlwind, with chariots, and horsemen and a great fleet of ships. He will invade many countries, and sweep over them like a flood.**

None of this relates to Antiochus IV and his battle against the Ptolemys. His final defeat by the Romans at Alexandria ended any attempt to conquer Egypt. The battle between Syria and Egypt appears to be a continuing one in the future, according to this verse. For this reason and others, some scholars believe this coming world leader will be of Syrian birth.

Antiochus never had a great fleet. This leader has a large naval force. This battle happens in the very end times (*at the time of the end*). The navy may be the result of his conquest of the three nation states described in other parts of Scripture.

WHY THE REFERENCE TO CHARIOTS?

Some people wonder about the references to *chariots* and *horsemen*. They argue that prophecies like these are invalid because they don't mention modern weapons of war. It's a fair point. After all, we know that a future battle is likely to use far more sophisticated modern weapons.

We must recognize that Daniel wasn't shown exact history but a vision designed by God that represents history. It would have made no sense for God to explain or show Daniel battle tanks and supersonic fighter jets, because Daniel would have no frame of reference for such things. He wouldn't have known what to do with them and it would have set his description on a distracting and potentially disastrous side road trying to explain them. Such descriptions might even have ruined his credibility, causing Jewish leaders to dismiss his prophecy instead of embracing it.

So it makes perfect sense for God to show the events in terms that Daniel could understand: chariots instead of tanks.

DANIEL 11:41

> 41 **He will also invade the glorious land. Many countries will be overthrown, but these will escape out of his hand: Edom, Moab, and the leaders of Ammon.**

Daniel is told that the coming world ruler will militarily invade Israel, and that many countries will be overthrown, but that Jordan and some related areas will not be taken. Remember that earlier he enforced a peace treaty. Now he ignores it.

The verse suggests that the country of Jordan will be protected. Ammon, Moab and Edom were located on the east side of the Dead Sea, the area currently occupied by Jordan. When the Israelites prepared to cross the Jordan River, they camped on the plains of Moab.[1] The Bible states that the remnant of Israel that is faithful to God through the Great Tribulation will be given protection in the ancient stone city of Petra.[2] This is in Jordan, related directly to the territories described here.

Yet the descendents of these ancient nations have blended into today's Palestinians, who hate Israel and want to remove it from the map. The land of Edom in particular has long represented a great enemy of the faithful. Under Jehoshaphat, Judah was invaded by a confederacy of Edomites, Moabites and Ammonites. God responded to Jehoshaphat's pleas, telling the king, "the battle is not yours, but God's" and causing the invaders to be so confused they attacked one another and slaughtered themselves.[3] Claims of judgement against these nations are found throughout Scripture.

---
1 Numbers 22:1, Joshua 3:1
2 Genesis 45:7, Isaiah 10:20, Psalms 60:9,108:10, Jeremiah 49:16
3 2 Chronicles 20:1-30

DANIEL 11:42-43

> 42 He will stretch forth his power over many countries. Even the land of Egypt will not escape.
>
> 43 He will gain control over the treasures of gold and of silver and over all the precious things of Egypt, with the Libyans and the Ethiopians in submission to him.

Antiochus IV never did conquer deep into Egypt, and certainly not even close to Libya or other parts of Africa. The extent of his victories over Egypt were the region around the city of Memphis. The future leader will obviously conquer other areas including Libya and North Africa.

DANIEL 11:44

> 44 But reports out of the east and out of the north will trouble him. Therefore he will set out with great fury to destroy and utterly annihilate many.

Reports from the "north" refer to Russia. Including the "east" may be a reference to Iran or China. Several prophecies refer to an attack from the *far north* and *Magog* (the region of Russia).[4] In 1989, Russia and Iran negotiated their first major arms deal, which included pledges of non-interference in each other's domestic affairs.[5] Some experts have said the agreement includes a clause that Russia would protect Iran in any future invasion of Israel. Could this be the *hook in Magog's jaw*?[6] Russia and China have also signed a number of comprehensive arms agreements.

The Bible talks about an invasion of 200 million soldiers from the far east (almost certainly China).[7] Are these the reports referred to here? We can't be sure until those events take place. In any case, these reports of rebellion will enrage the coming world leader into furious activity to annihilate all who oppose him.

---

4   Ezekiel 38:15, 39:2, 39:6; Revelation 20:8
5   The Council on Foreign Relations, *Backgrounder: Russia-Iran Arms Trade*
6   Ezekiel 38:3-5
7   Revelation 9:15-17, 16:12

DANIEL 11:45

> 45 He will pitch the tents of his royal palace between the seas in the glorious holy mountain. Yet he will come to his end, and no one will help him.

Some say this place *between the seas* refers to a location in Jerusalem (between the Dead Sea and the Sea of Galilee). Others say it refers to a location between the Mediterranean and the Sea of Galilee. So which is it? Note that the verse only refers to the *palace* location, not the place where the Antichrist actually meets his end.

The verse says the coming world ruler will build a palace *in the glorious holy mountain*. Daniel has used this reference to the "holy mountain" before (Daniel 9:26). The mountain is almost certainly Mount Moriah, in Jerusalem. Moriah is the location of Abraham's sacrifice of Isaac, and the place where God chose to place his name,[8] eventually becoming the location of the Temple Mount.

One commonly held view is that it means Armageddon (literally *the mountain of Megiddo*). Megiddo, the location of the final battle of Armageddon, is a mountain range located near the Jezreel Valley between the Mediterranean and the Sea of Galilee. We know the Antichrist will come to his end there. This location would not explain why Daniel gives it such holy relevance, as it has no spiritual significance. It is not a 'glorious' holy mountain in any way.

Scripture tells us that when Christ returns, He will stand on the Mount of Olives, splitting the mountain in two.[9] It also stands between the Dead Sea and the Sea of Galilee. But aside from this final relevance and a few other key aspects of biblical history, the Mount of Olives doesn't have special significance.

Because Daniel has used the same phrase twice, the first time very specifically indicating Jerusalem, we can be sure what he means.

---

8   Deuteronomy 12:5
9   Zechariah 14:4

✎ Application My Notes & Bible Study Questions

15

DANIEL
CHAPTER 12
THE END OF THE WORLD

As Daniel prayed and fasted, an angel appeared to him in a vision and blessed him with the most detailed prophecy of all time, rich with specific information about hundreds of years of history yet to come.

Today, we have the benefit of 20/20 hindsight. We can look back and see how every aspect of the historical portion of the vision was actually fulfilled. But when it comes to things that are still in the future, we're in the same boat Daniel was. We can only guess at details such as who is involved and which nations are meant.

The twelfth and final chapter of Daniel's book is a continuation of the vision begun in chapter 10. We have now moved into an area that remains entirely in the future, even for us.

We know this much:

A coming world leader will arise through deceit and political maneuvering. He will enforce a treaty with Israel, ensuring that they can fulfil the Jewish religious observances. Then suddenly, after three and a half years, he will invade Israel with a military force, banning the sacrifice. He will demand to be worshipped by the Jews as if he were God. Their resistance to this outrageous command will lead to war and atrocities that will eventually culminate at the Battle of Armageddon. The world leader will defile the temple by placing an idol inside. An army of 200 million[1] will march towards Israel from the east, across a dry river bed where the Euphrates River used to flow. There will be so much death and destruction that blood will run in the streets like rivers.[2]

As we enter Chapter 12, Daniel continues with his account of the final vision, from the time of the terrible Great Tribulation.

---

1   Revelation 9:16, 16:12
2   Revelation 14:20

DANIEL 12:1

> 1 At that time Michael will arise, the great prince who protects your people. There will be a time of trouble such as never was since the beginning of nations until then. And at that time your people will be delivered, everyone whose name is found written in the book.

Daniel is told about the Great Tribulation, with words almost identical to those shared by Jesus in the Olivet sermon: a time of distress such as has not happened since the beginning of the world. Jesus may even be quoting Daniel.

Michael is described as the prince who protects the Jews (*your people* refers specifically to the Jews). At that time he will spring into new action. The reference to him arising could mean that he will be revealed visibly to those he is protecting, but that's conjecture.

Imagine the setting as the bowls of wrath described in the book of Revelation pour out their various stages of devastation. Every living thing in a third of the world's oceans dies.[3] One third of the ships at sea are destroyed. The sun delivers scorching heat unlike anything in past history, destroying a third of the world and all its green spaces.[4] An earthquake shakes the earth with such magnitude that cities across multiple nations, and even complete mountain ranges, are leveled to the ground.[5] Large numbers will die from drinking poisoned water.[6] The remaining population will wish for death during the torments they endure, and millions will die.[7] Everything builds to a crescendo in preparation for the Battle of Armageddon.

---

[3] Revelation 8:9, 16:3
[4] Revelation 8:7, 16:8
[5] Revelation 16:18
[6] Revelation 8:10
[7] Revelation 9:6

Yet notice the wonderful hope presented so clearly: everyone (not just some) whose name is written in the Lamb's Book of Life will be delivered.[8]

Every person who accepts that Jesus Christ is the promised Messiah and follows Him will be given eternal life. Have you made a decision for Christ, or are you sitting on the fence? If you are a Christian, are you truly living as a believer, obeying the Word of God?

DANIEL 12:2

> 2 Many of them that sleep in the dust of the earth will awake, some to everlasting life, others to shame and everlasting contempt.

This points to a bodily resurrection and judgement after the return of Christ. They will then enter the next phase of existence, according to what they believe. Those whose names are not written in the Lamb's Book of Life will be exposed to shame and contempt before the whole body of heavenly hosts and the saints,[9] when all their sins will be exposed to view and they are led off to everlasting torment.

Rather than judgement and contempt, those who are true followers of Jesus will receive everlasting life in the presence of God.

It is fascinating that the Bible refers to *many* rather than *all* who sleep in the temporary state we call death. This indicates that others who were dead are already risen, supporting the view of a "rapture" of believers who will be raised into the clouds before the final Day of the Lord.

---

8   Revelation 21:27
9   Revelation 20:11-15

DANIEL 12:3

> 3 **Those who are wise will shine as the brightness of the heavens; and those who turn many to righteousness like the stars for ever and ever.**

Daniel says that those who are wise will shine, and those who make a greater impact for the Kingdom will shine even more brightly than others. This is a very specific reference to the rewards talked about in the New Testament. Believers often forget about the rewards promised to us for righteousness. We focus on the fact that we are saved, but so afraid of touching the subject of works that we forget there are specific rewards for the things we do in Christ.

Jesus shared these words with his disciples:

> **"Then the righteous will shine like the sun in the kingdom of their Father. He who has ears, let him hear."**
> —Matthew 13:43 (NIV)

What a marvelous promise for all Christians! Yet there is more to living a life of righteousness. The apostle Paul described the consequences of how we live as Christians:

> **"If any man builds on this foundation [of salvation in Christ] using gold, silver, costly stones, wood, hay or straw, his work will be shown for what it is, because the Day will bring it to light. It will be revealed with fire, and the fire will test the quality of each man's work. If what he has built survives, he will receive his reward. If it is burned up, he will suffer loss; he himself will be saved, but only as one escaping through the flames."** —1 Corinthians 3:12-15 (NIV)

All believers will be saved. Our salvation is *not* dependent upon works, for that would diminish the price God paid. Works have nothing to do with our salvation lest anyone should boast,[10] but works have everything to do with our heavenly reward.

---

10   Ephesians 2:9

All believers are eligible for a reward, yet only some will receive one, because this reward is based on what we have done with our faith. Things you did for the wrong motives will be burned up. If you offered a homeless person a meal, but only because someone important was looking, your effort will be like "straw" in the fire of judgement and will disappear. Only those things done with a motive of genuine love, compassion and faith will be blessed.

It is truly beautiful to see how closely the words of Jesus and the declarations of the New Testament apostles mirror the vision given to Daniel some 500 years earlier.

DANIEL 12:4

> 4 **But you, Daniel, close up the words and seal the book until the time of the end. Many will roam here and there, and knowledge will be increased."**

Once again we see Daniel told to *seal up* the details of the rest of his vision. Scholars are divided on exactly what this means. Certainly we know that sealing up means that the vision is to be written down and completed. But some believe that the reference *until the time of the end* suggests that future documents written by Daniel may eventually come to light at the appointed time. Others say that it means God will reveal additional knowledge or insight at some future time, such as the recent discoveries of the so-called (and controversial) "Bible Codes" of equidistant letter sequences which have revived Jewish interest in the Scriptures.

It is interesting that Daniel was shown a state of the world in which *knowledge will be increased.* For centuries knowledge remained relatively stable, ramping up slightly during the Age of Enlightenment. However, in the past century our knowledge has grown so dramatically it now doubles in mere months.

Some say this passage refers to spiritual knowledge only, meaning the growth in commentaries and books about details of Scripture. Since Jerome's first ground-breaking Bible commentary was published around AD400, we have seen an overwhelming quantity of information to help us better understand the Scriptures. Yet it seems that the vast majority of recent *new* knowledge is heresy or teachings of higher criticism that work against the traditional view of the Bible as being the perfect, inerrant Word of God.

DANIEL 12:5-7

> 5 **Then I, Daniel, looked, and there stood two others, one on this side of the bank of the river, and one on the opposite bank.**
>
> 6 **One of them said to the man clothed in linen, who was upon the waters of the river, "How long will it be to the end of these wondrous things?"**
>
> 7 **The man clothed in linen, who was upon the waters of the river, held up his right hand and his left hand to heaven, and I heard him swear by him who lives forever, saying that "It will be for a time, times, and half a time. When he will have completed breaking the power of the holy people, all these things will be finished."**

There at the banks of the Tigris river, Daniel saw other angels standing opposite each other on either side of the river. This is a good-sized river, not just a meandering stream. This verse supports 1 Peter 1:8-12, as it implies that even the angels are not fully informed about how the prophetic promises of God will be fulfilled and are eager to learn.

> **"Even angels long to look into these things."**
> —Peter 1:12b (NIV)

The phrase *a time, times and half a time* means 3-1/2 years. It represents a single year plus a dual (two years) plus half a year. Other time periods given to Daniel (see Daniel 12:11-12 below) refer to 1,290 days and 1,335 days, the latter including other stages of development in the end times events before the beginning of the millennium rule of Christ brings perfect peace.

The angel who was speaking to Daniel throughout this vision is floating above the river. He tells Daniel that the coming of the Messiah will take place *when the power of the holy people has been finally broken.* This suggests that they are at the end of all hope in a human sense.

At the Battle of Armageddon, though a short event that will end with the sudden return of Christ and the heavenly host, the remaining believers are at the point of total military defeat, no longer able to resist physically the juggernaut gathered against them. The Bible says that the battle would promise to be so completely devastating that if it weren't for the coming of the Messiah no life would be spared.[11] Christ comes just before every single human life would be destroyed. Could that mean a world at the brink of nuclear annihilation? Or some even more devastating weapon that hasn't been invented yet?

DANIEL 12:8-10

8 I heard, but I did not understand. So I asked, "My Lord, what will be the outcome of these things?"

9 He answered, "Go your way, Daniel, for the words are closed up and sealed until the time of the end.

10 Many will be purified and made spotless and refined through trials, but the wicked will continue to do evil. None of the wicked will understand, but the wise will understand.

Daniel is concerned about the Jews and wants to know how these events will ultimately end in hope for the Jewish people. The angel answers that many Jews will be saved, but not all.

---

11   Matthew 24:22

It is distressing that so many Jews today, called as a nation by God and rescued so often by His mighty hand, could be atheists or agnostics, unwilling to embrace Him.

Yet Scripture tells us that even in those last days, as spiritual revival sweeps through Israel and great numbers turn to the truth of God's promises as described in the prophecies of Daniel, Ezekiel and others, many of God's own people — those with whom He has a deep covenant relationship — will remain spiritually cold and unwilling to surrender to His authority.

DANIEL 12:11-13

> 11 **From the time that the daily sacrifice is abolished and the abomination that causes desolation set up, 1,290 days shall occur.**
>
> 12 **Blessed is the one who waits for and comes to the end of the 1,335 days.**
>
> 13 **But go you your way till the end happens. For you will rest, and arise to receive your allotted inheritance at the end of the days."**

THE LONG WAIT

We often get impatient as we await the final "Day of the Lord," especially when we see our world and our nation fall into spiritual decay and increasing wickedness.

But think about how long the wait has been for some believers. First-century Christians were convinced that Jesus Christ would return in their lifetime, yet nearly two millennium later we are still waiting.

The key is to ask what we're doing with that time. Are you using every day to bless those around you? Or are you selfishly hoarding your spiritual knowledge, keeping it to yourself rather than sharing it with the unsaved, and wishing that Jesus will return so you can get out of this messy world?

Daniel is told about three different time periods in the entire account given to him about the last seven years:

- **Time, times and half a time** (3-1/2 years)
- **1,290 days**
- **1,335 days**

These are slightly different time periods, though they overlap. We can't build doctrine on exactly how they all relate, because we lack details. But we can gain some insights from Scripture if we look hard and carefully at the text.

1,290 days are 3 years 7 months, or 43 months based on the 360-day lunar calendar used throughout Scripture.

The third time period given to Daniel is 1,335 days, which represents another 45 days (1,290 + 45 = 1,335). He doesn't say what those days represent, nor how they apply to the Great Tribulation period. Why mention specific numbers at all? These numbers have a reason! Daniel must want us to understand them. It's consistent with everything we've learned about the man.

Some Bible teachers believe that a month and a half are assigned to officially inaugurate Christ to his position on the physical throne of David for the millennium rule of peace promised in Scripture. However, this is challenging to reconcile with the text. Notice that the angel tells Daniel that those who wait until the full 1,335 days are complete will be blessed. If the Messiah comes *before* that time is over, they don't have a choice of waiting during the remaining days, so why would they be especially blessed by waiting?

This 1,335 day period is far from clear and we must wait until God brings more enlightenment before we can fully understand it. But there is a way to reconcile the differences in a general sense, which we shall now explore in detail.

💡 Insight

Believers often forget about the rewards promised to us by Jesus Christ for our faith and righteousness. We focus on the fact that we are saved, but forget that there are specific rewards for the things we do as a direct result of our belief in God and His Son.

Jesus promises a reward for every believer, according to how well he or she has performed as a Christian:

"For the Son of Man is going to come in the glory (majesty, splendor) of His Father with His angels, and then He will render account and reward every man in accordance with what he has done." —Matthew 16:27 (AMP)

"Behold, I am coming soon! My reward is with me, and I will give to everyone according to what he has done." —Revelation 22:12 (NIV)

The apostle Paul gave additional insight into the subject of rewards:

"But on the judgment day, fire will reveal what kind of work each builder has done. The fire will show if a person's work has any value. If the work survives, that builder will receive a reward. But if the work is burned up, the builder will suffer great loss. The builder will be saved, but like someone barely escaping through a wall of flames."
—1 Corinthians 3:13-15 (NLT)

These rewards are not like trophies placed on a mantle where they are forgotten and left to gather dust. They shine forever as part of us, visible as different levels of brightness for all to see throughout eternity!

Isn't this worth saying no to a few temptations in life?

Isn't this worth a few hard decisions and a little effort or sacrifice in your earthly walk?

Isn't this worth taking a few extra moments now and then to do something unexpected for someone in need, out of genuine compassion and love?

Praise God for these promised rewards so rich in undeserved grace and mercy!

RECONCILING THE FINAL EVENTS

This final passage in Daniel, and particularly the timeline given in verse 11, creates an interesting challenge for us. The wording can easily be interpreted in two different ways:

> **1** That the ending of the sacrifice and the idol being set up take place on the same day, with the Great Tribulation ending 1,290 days later.

> **2** That the two are different events, and there are 1,290 days between the ending of the sacrifice and the setting up of the idol. Persecution begins when the sacrifice is ended, but becomes the Great Tribulation after the idol is set up.

The first interpretation is a common viewpoint found in many commentaries, and for good reason. We do know that the *abomination that causes desolation* talked about by Jesus represents the start of a time of intense persecution we refer to as the Great Tribulation. Jesus warned that this event would usher in great horror.

Tradition holds that the desecration of the temple happens on the same day as the ending of the sacrifice. But does it?

Let's take a closer look at several passages to gain a deeper understanding of how we may interpret this sequence:

> His armed forces will rise up and they will desecrate the sanctuary of strength, and will take away the daily sacrifice. Then they will place the abomination that causes desolation. —Daniel 11:31

A chronological sequence is hinted by the use of *then*, but there is no indication how far apart the two events occur. They could happen on the same day, or they could be years apart. Note that the desecration mentioned in the first part of the verse is not the same thing as the abomination of placing the idol.

Let's look at another reference to this same sequence:

> And he will confirm a covenant with the many for one week. In the middle of the week he will put an end to sacrifice and offering, and on a corner of the altar [or wing of the temple] he will set up an abomination that causes desolation, until the end that has been decreed is poured out upon him. —Daniel 9:27

In this prophecy given to Daniel by the angel Gabriel, we see no indication of how much time will elapse between the two events. Based on this passage, they could happen on the same day, or they could be years apart.

Let's go to the New Testament to see what Jesus had to say about those days:

> When you see 'the abomination that causes desolation' standing where it does not belong—let the reader understand—then let those who are in Judea flee to the mountains. Let no one on the roof of his house go down or enter the house to take anything out. Let no one in the field go back to get his cloak. How dreadful it will be in those days for pregnant women and nursing mothers! Pray that this will not take place in winter, because those will be days of distress unequaled from the beginning, when God created the world, until now—and never to be equaled again. If the Lord had not cut short those days, no one would survive. But for the sake of the elect, whom he has chosen, he has shortened them. —Mark 13:14-20 (NIV)

Jesus made no mention of the cancellation of the sacrifice. He referred only to the placing of the idol. But he said that this becomes the beginning of a short and terrible time period which we refer to as the Great Tribulation.

Did Jesus mean the *entire* 3-1/2 year time of persecution, or was he referring only to a final, much more severe, tribulation — perhaps 45 days in length? After all, he did say that God was shortening the time, "for the sake of the elect." Jesus said that the time will be so short we don't even have a chance to grab our coats!

So what does it say in Daniel's exact original Hebrew wording? Looking at a literal interpretation of the Hebrew text in Daniel 12:11, we see the following (Hebrew words in bold):

eth [And from the time] **suwr** [when shall be taken away] **tamiyd** [the regular sacrifice] **nathan** [and set up] **shiqquts** [the abomination] **shamem** [that desolates] **yowm** [days — 'shall be' is implied] **eleph** [a thousand] **meyah** [a hundred doubled to mean two hundred] **tishiym** [ninety]

The Hebrew word **eth** is typically used as an adverb with preposition, relating to a continuation of events after something happens. It is implied in the context that the word **yowm** means this many days *shall be* or *will be* involved. So we are given two events, then told that **from** one **and** the other shall be 1,290 days. Were the two combined, or was he saying from the one *until* the other?

Why mention two different events if they are essentially one and the same, yet leave out what happens at the ending point? The argument has been that the end is assumed, and that's why Daniel doesn't mention it. Yet that seems curiously at odds with his incredible precision in everything he writes and does.

Daniel gives three different time periods, and expects us to understand them, based on the rest of his vision. If these two events are one and the same, that leaves us with a mystery about the 1,335 days. This does not appear to fit with Daniel's character or the context of his writing. He does not like to leave mysteries, and loves to give us specific timelines to work from. So why leave a time period that is never explained, but assumes we understand?

If we take the references to mean the two events are separated by 1,290 days, then the final 45 days are the Great Tribulation. That's a short time period. We are used to thinking of a 3-1/2 year Great Tribulation. Yet it *must* be short! Jesus said so. He warned about the rush to leave homes and clothing behind. He said to pray it isn't in the winter — not just the day of desecration but the "days of distress." If it's 3-1/2 years long, it would cover three winters!

To accept that the final 45 days represent the worst of the tribulation does not mean that the previous 3-1/2 years are easy. It still allows for a very serious time of persecution throughout those years, like we've always known, as the bowls of wrath mentioned in Revelation are poured out one at a time. The final 45 days would merely be the worst of it, when the blood runs to the height of a horse's bridle, as John was shown.[12]

Finally, we need to reflect on Daniel's earlier vision from chapter 9, where he used mathematical precision to indicate a specific day. He was a man of details, blessed by God to be clear in his prophetic proclamations. Thus, it stands to reason that his final vision would also be mathematically accurate. The reference to "time, times and half a time" would reflect 3-1/2 years in a general sense. The next reference of 1,290 days would represent the exact number of days between the end of the sacrifice and the setting up of the idol. The final reference of 1,335 days would represent the time from the end of the sacrifice to the coming of the Messiah.

In chapter 9, Daniel uses the evening sacrifice as a way of measuring time, saying that Gabriel came to him "about the time of the evening sacrifice." He loves what the sacrifice represents. Throughout his life, he has been so focused on the sacrifice that it would be very consistent with his character to use the banning of the sacrifice as the starting point for all three numbers given.

---

12   Revelation 14:20

The beginning of this 1,290 day time period is the day on which the coming world ruler, after securing the Jews access to the sacrifice some 3-1/2 years earlier, takes it away from them and outlaws religious observance. It is in the middle of the final week of 70 weeks of years mentioned in chapter 9, and the start of serious, violent persecution against the saints worldwide.

It may also be the day on which the idol is set up, but of that we cannot be certain.

1,260 days are assigned for two witnesses to preach their prophetic messages in Jerusalem. The overlap does not have to be exactly 30 days on one side. Some events take place after the two witnesses are slain, including their resurrection and ascension 3-1/2 days later.[13] Perhaps their resurrection even ushers in the defiling of the temple, as a final act of revenge beginning a furious rampage against believers lasting 45 days until the return of Christ.

42 months (1,260 days) are specified as the time during which the Gentiles will "trample" Jerusalem, and the time that the beast will exercise his authority over the world.[14]

1,260 days are also decreed in Revelation 12:6 as the time when the saints in Israel (referred to as *the woman*) will flee into the wilderness during persecution. It is believed that they seek sanctuary in the rock city of Petra (in Jordan), where God provides nourishment and protection, since He promises that the territory of Edom and Moab will be protected, and there are references to Petra in the Psalms and elsewhere.[15]

The book of Daniel ends with a promise of resurrection and reward, the inheritance of the saints. It is a fitting conclusion to one of the most remarkable books in all of Scripture.

---

13 Revelation 11:3-12
14 Revelation 11:2, 13:5
15 Psalm 60:9, 108:10, Isaiah 42:11, Ezekiel 39:11

Insight

Top: Traditional view of the final "week of years," in which the sacrifice ends and the temple are defiled on the same day, making the Great Tribulation a 3-1/2 year time period.

■ **Sacrifice Ends AND Temple Defiled**
Coming World Ruler suddenly ends the daily sacrifice and defiles the temple, the **Abomination that Causes Desolation**. Both take place on the same day.

1,290 Days
Great Tribulation
Period of continuous violent persecution as the "bowls of wrath" are poured out on mankind.

Two Witnesses
1,260 days
Two witnesses are given supernatural protection and the ability to hold back the rain while they preach in Jerusalem. After 1,260 days they are killed, then come back to life 3-1/2 days later.

Extra Days
45 days
Daniel refers to an additional 45 days. With this view, it is unclear what these extra days represent. Some say they are for the preparation of the millennial reign of Christ.

■ **Return of Christ**
Traditional view puts return of Christ here, but that leaves us unclear on the remaining days

Time of Peace
Approx 3-1/2 years
Coming World Ruler enforces peace treaty, Israel begins observance of traditional religious rites, including daily sacrifice.

Years: 1 2 3 4 5 6 7
Days: 1260   1260 1335
                              1290

Bottom: An alternate view based on the prophecy of Daniel, in which the ending of the sacrifice and the defiling of the temple are 1,290 days apart, making the worst persecution of the Great Tribulation a short period of 45 days.

1,335 Days

■ **Sacrifice Ends**
Coming World Ruler suddenly ends the daily sacrifice, begins persecution.

1,290 Days
Time of persecution/tribulation
The ending of the sacrifice begins a period of tribulation, as the "bowls of wrath" mentioned in Revelation are poured out on mankind. Then the World Ruler defiles the temple, the **Abomination that Causes Desolation**, exactly 1,290 days after ending the sacrifice.

Two Witnesses
1,260 days
Two witnesses are given supernatural protection and the ability to hold back the rain while they preach in Jerusalem. After 1,260 days they are killed, then come back to life 3-1/2 days later.

■ **Temple Defiled**
Coming World Ruler puts idol in temple.

"Great" Tribulation
45 days
Daniel refers to an additional 45 days. This would be the worst part of the persecution. Jesus said to leave your house without going back for a coat, to run for safety because time was so short.

■ **Return of Christ**
Daniel said he who waits for the 1,335 days will be blessed.

Time of Peace
3-1/2 years
Coming World Ruler enforces peace treaty, Israel begins observance of traditional religious rites, including daily sacrifice.

Years: 1 2 3 4 5 6 7
Days: 1260   1260 1335
                              1290

So what does it mean to "be a Daniel" in today's world? We often hear that phrase thrown around. But what exactly does it mean in our culture? How can we apply his example in real life?

We are in the world, but not of the world.[16] At the same time, we are told to be transformed by the renewing of our minds.[17] Knowing where to stand firm and where to let go is where the Daniels of our times distinguish themselves.

It has never been easy holding firmly to your faith in a multicultural society. Daniel served as the chief of the wise men and astrologers. Yet we know from his character and example that he did not engage in the practices they followed. Despite his faithfulness, he was not universally loved. Even after he saved the lives of the wise men, they sought to have him executed.

Being a Daniel is not about forcing your beliefs on others, but setting a consistent example of love and biblical character that honors God and causes others to reflect on and think about.

The following are key qualities that set Daniel and his friends apart from the surrounding culture:

- **Consistently spending time in God's Word.** The apostle Paul told the church to "devote yourself to the public reading of Scripture, to preaching and to teaching."[18] Scripture is God-breathed and relevant to every aspect of life.[19] Daniel loved God's Word! The Pocket Testament League is a great way to focus on God's Word and read, carry and share it with others. Go to *www.pocketpower.org/7115* to get started.

---

16 John 15:19, 17:14-15
17 Romans 12:2
18 1 Timothy 4:13
19 2 Timothy 3:16

- **Praying regularly.**[20] Prayer is conversation with God and builds our relationship with Him. Daniel had a habit of praying three times a day. Even when doing so became a threat to his life, he did not change this pattern.

- **Trusting God in all circumstances.**[21] God is not only to be praised and worshipped when things are going well, but also when things are going badly. Everything is under His control. Our love and trust should not be dependent on circumstances. Praising Him in adversity, as Daniel and his friends did, is a powerful sign of genuine faith and trust.

- **Showing humility, joy and grace in all situations.** This is tremendous evidence of the Holy Spirit at work in your life.[22] The example of graciousness when mistreated or persecuted has always made a huge impact on others.

- **Demonstrating purity and high ethical standards**, no matter how inconvenient or uncomfortable.[23] When things are unfair, shortcuts and small lies often seem harmless. They're not. The smallest act of dishonesty is a sin and opens the door to other sins. Never give in to temptation.

Jesus said we are the salt of the earth.[24] He went on to point out that if salt loses its saltiness, it has no value. As a Daniel in your world, you are a source of flavor in the midst of bland hopelessness. Hold fast to your faith. Make an effort to apply these principles to your life, and trust God to use your example to impact those around you.

---

20 1 Thessalonians 5:17; 2 Timothy 1:3
21 Romans 4:3, 5, 10:9; 1 Corinthians 1:9
22 Galatians 5:22
23 Philippians 4:8
24 Maatthew 5:13

Application — My Notes & Bible Study Questions

16

RESOURCES MAPS PHOTOS AND TIMELINES

A Nation Divided

David and his son Solomon ruled a united kingdom for more than 70 years. After Solomon's death, civil war split the nation in two. The northern tribes, generally referred to as Israel, chose the rebel Jeroboam as their king, while the southern kingdom, known as Judah, confirmed Solomon's son Rehoboam as its first ruler.

The northern kingdom went through increasingly evil rulers until the nation fell to the Assyrians in 722BC. Judah also had its share of evil kings, but a few good ones kept the nation from judgement until the fall of Jerusalem to the Babylonians in 587BC.

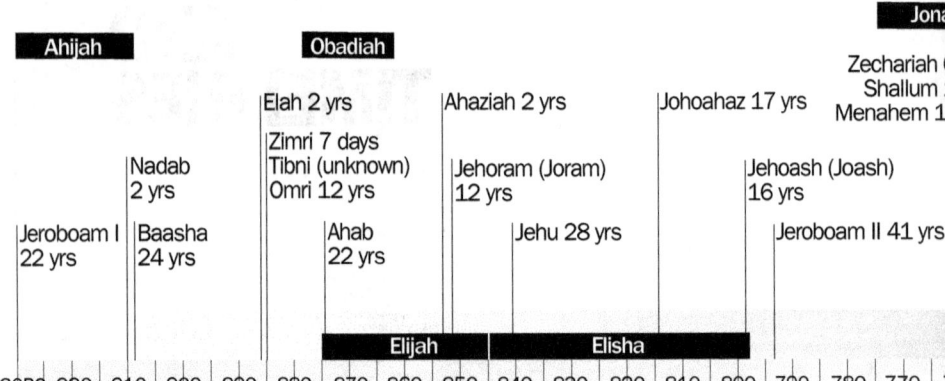

Israel Northern Kingdom

Ahijah | Obadiah | Jona

Zechariah 6
Shallum 1
Menahem 10

Elah 2 yrs | Ahaziah 2 yrs | Johoahaz 17 yrs
Zimri 7 days
Nadab 2 yrs | Tibni (unknown) | Jehoram (Joram) 12 yrs | Jehoash (Joash) 16 yrs
Omri 12 yrs
Jeroboam I 22 yrs | Baasha 24 yrs | Ahab 22 yrs | Jehu 28 yrs | Jeroboam II 41 yrs

Elijah | Elisha

930BC 920 910 900 890 880 870 860 850 840 830 820 810 800 790 780 770 7

Joash (Jehoash) 40 yrs | Uzziah (Azariah) 52 yrs
Asa 41 yrs | Queen Athaliah 6 yrs | Amaziah 29 yrs
Abijah 3 yrs | Ahaziah 1 yr
Rehoboam 17 yrs | Jehoram 8 yrs
Jehoshaphat 25 yrs

Judah Southern Kingdom

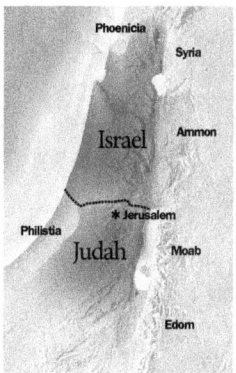

Chronologies for the kings of Israel and Judah can vary by up to 10 years depending on the source. Figures shown here are from E.R. Thiele, *The Mysterious Numbers of the Hebrew Kings* (Grand Rapids, Zondervan, 1983). Note that some reigns overlap.

Prophets are shown in black bars (dates approximate), the position related to whether they served God in Israel or Judah. Some prophets are not shown here because they served primarily after the fall of Jerusalem. These include: Daniel, Ezekiel, Haggai, Zechariah, Joel and Malachi (all serving Judah either in Babylon or in the holy land following the return of the exiles).

Zechariah 6 mo
Shallum 1 mo
Menahem 10 yrs
Pekahiah 2 yrs
Pekah 8 yrs
Hoshea 9 yrs
Fall of Israel to Assyria

Hosea

740 730 720 710 700 690 680 670 660 650 640 630 620 610 600 587BC

Isaiah | Jeremiah

Ahaz 16 yrs
Manasseh 55 yrs
Josiah 31 yrs
Fall of Jerusalem to Babylon
Hezekiah 29 yrs
Amon 2 yrs
Zedekiah 11 yrs
Jotham 16 yrs
Jehoiachin 3 mo
Huldah
Jehoahaz 3 mo
Jehoiakim 11 yrs
Micah
Nahum
Zephaniah
Habakkuk

The Babylonian Exile

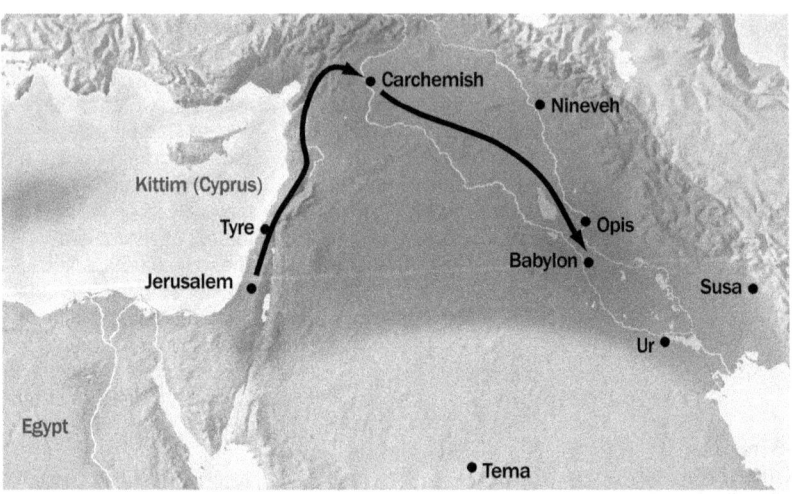

The Jewish people had been warned by the prophets that they would be subject to the Babylonians for ignoring the "Sabbath of the Land."

As an empire, Babylon had existed for over a thousand years, but had been conquered by the Assyrians.

Nabopalassar, Babylon's first Chaldean king, declared independence in 626BC following the death of Assyrian king Ashurbanipal. The Babylonians formed a coalition with the Medes and conquered the Assyrian capital of Nineveh in 612, as had been prophecied by Nahum. Within a short time, Babylon dominated an area nearly the size of the previous Assyrian empire.

Thousands of Jews died in a vain defense of Judah, and Jerusalem surrendered after a siege. Thousands of Jews were deported in three phases before the city was destroyed, the largest group consisting of 18,000 people including warriors and craftsmen (2 Kings 24:14-16).

The exiles trekked an ardous journey of 1,600 km (1,000 miles) through desert regions, first north to Carchemish and then to Babylon, along the trade route. It would have been a difficult, exhausting trip, filled with physical and mental abuse, hunger and disease. No doubt many perished along the way. It must have been exceptionally challenging for children.

Jeremiah told the exiles, in a letter, to prosper and multiply. He encouraged them and prophecied that they would be released after 70 years, a prophecy fulfilled by Cyrus.

Nebuchadnezzar's Babylon

Based on archeological evidence, this graphic shows the overall structure of the city of Babylon.

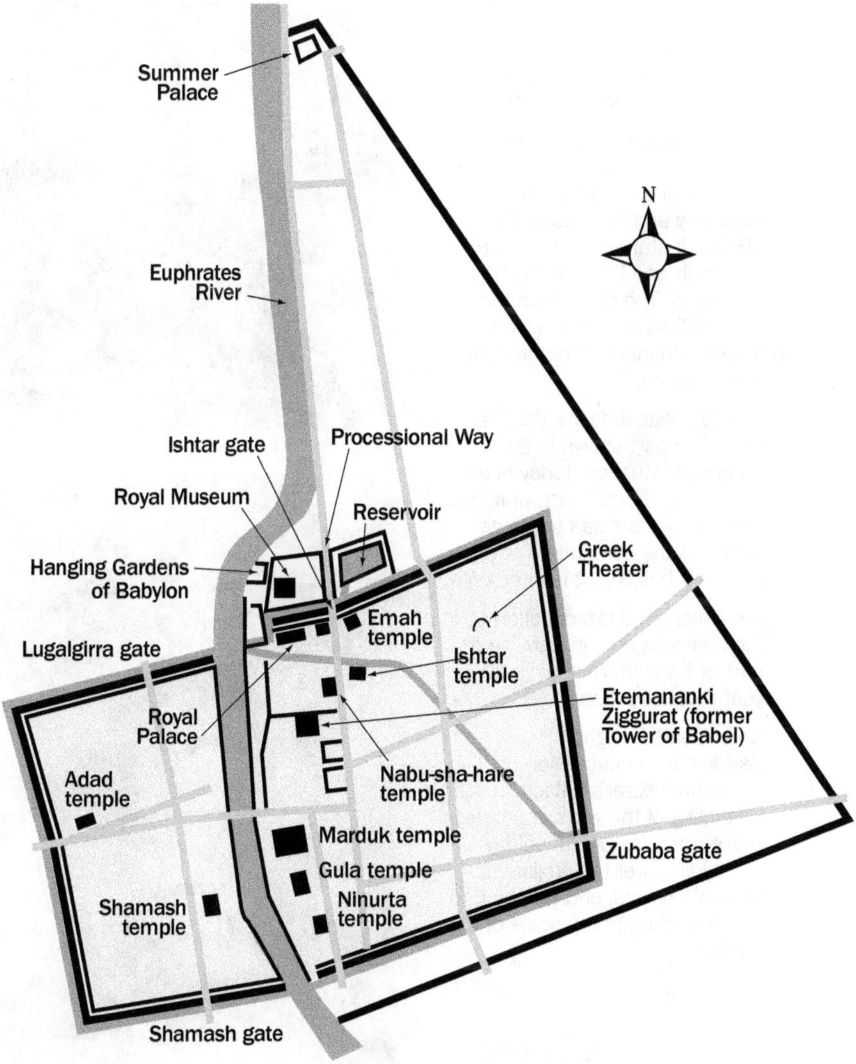

Images of Babylon

The Ishtar Gate (right) was dedicated to the Babylonian goddess Ishtar, constructed of blue glazed tiles with alternating rows of bas-relief images of various gods of Babylon. It was the main gate into the city, situated at the north end near Nebuchadnezzar's palace and just past the hanging gardens.

A reconstruction was built at the Pergamon Museum in Berlin out of material excavated by Robert Koldewey and finished in the 1930s. It stands 14 meters (47 feet) high and 30 meters (100 feet) wide. The excavation ran from 1902-1914. During that time the foundation of the gate was uncovered.

The gate was in fact a double gate. The part shown in the Pergamon Museum today is only the smaller frontal part, while the larger back part was too large to fit into the constraints of the museum building. It is in storage.

A smaller-sized reproduction of the gate was built in Babylon as part of Saddam Hussein's 20-year reconstruction project.

Shown bottom right is Saddam's reconstruction of Nebuchadnezzar's palace. This rebuilding of the walls and palace broke the rules of archeology by building over the original excavation area, and was built to only a fraction of the scale of the original.

Below a scale model of the original Processional Way and Ishtar Gate. This represented only one small part of the world's most impressive fortress city.

To the right is a painting of what the famous Hanging Gardens of Babylon may have looked like. They were one of the seven wonders of the ancient world.

At the bottom is today's scaled-down partial city reconstruction built by Saddam Hussein. Even at it's reduced size, the walls are imposing. Imagine what those walls would have looked like at their actual size back in the ancient culture of sixth century BC.

Alexander's Conquest of the World

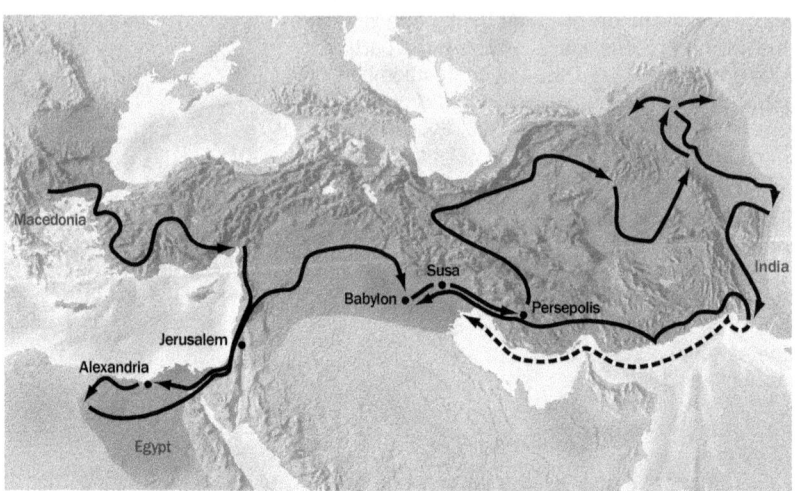

Alexander the Great's rise to power was nothing short of spectacular.

When he was just 20 years old, he took the Macedonian throne following the assassination of his father, Philip II. He quickly proved to be an adept leader. Alexander began his reign by bringing Greek states mired in revolt under control.

Two years later, in 334BC, he led his army across the Hellespont to drive the Persians out of Asia Minor (modern day Turkey). He won a decisive victory even though his men were outnumbered three to one. Two years after his campaign began, he had already taken Egypt, declaring himself Pharaoh, and now moved east towards Babylon.

Alexander's military route of conquest covered 22,500 km (14,000 miles) in just 11 years.

As had been prophecied to Daniel, he shattered the Persian empire with a furious passion. He burned the magnificent palace of Darius the Great in Persepolis, in retaliation for the Persian's destruction of the Parthenon in Athens years earlier.

Ancient writers such as Xenophon and Isocrates scornfully commented that the Persians had become used to luxury and soft, making them easy to overcome in battle.

In 326 Alexander defeated the most skillful foe he had met, King Porus of India. His beloved horse died here.

His army war weary by that time, he returned to Babylon by a difficult land passage, with some of his army returning by sea.

In 323, now only 32 years of age, the brilliant but savage young leader took a fever and died.

Daniel's 70 Weeks

Daniel Chapter 9 describes a vision given to Daniel, in which he is told that "70 weeks of years" are decreed before the end of the world. This includes a gap of unknown length between the end of the 69th week of years and the start of the 70th week. The removal of the church can take place at any time, after which God completes His plan for the Jews.

69 weeks of years	Gap of unknown length	70th week
7 + 62 = 69	Jesus: "Times of the Gentiles" Gentiles in control of Jerusalem	Final 7 years
Artaxerxes decree 1st of Nisan, 445BC	**Messiah the King** April 6, AD32 (Palm Sunday)	**Church removed** The "Rapture" can happen anytime, which will begin the final events described in many parts of Scripture
Time span 69 x 7 = 483 biblical years, or 173,880 days	**Messiah "cut off"** Jesus crucified, Passover AD32	
	Temple destroyed AD70 by Titus	

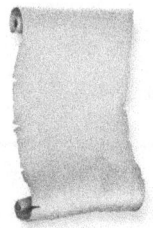

Peace in Israel — 3.5 yrs | 3.5 yrs
World Ruler negotiates enforcement of peace treaty, Jewish religious rites once again take place.

Sacrifice ends, persecution begins
World ruler suddenly ends sacrifices, bans religious observance and begins persecution of believers.

Two Witnesses preach in Jerusalem
Two witnesses preach for 1260 days in Jerusalem, then are killed. 3-1/2 days later they are resurrected and ascend to heaven.

Extra days: worst of Tribulation period?
Daniel refers to additional days, their meaning not specified.

Timeline of Daniel's Life

This timeline covers Daniel's life, but does not take into account possible minor differences based on partial years. Timelines for biblical events are difficult to determine. Some historical dates use the secular calendar, beginning with the month of Tishri, while others use the religious Jewish calendar, which begins with Nisan.

In addition, Babylonian and Jewish reckoning of a a king's reign are different. The Jews of Judah counted the first year of his reign, while Babylonians ignored it and referred only to the first **complete** year as the first year of his reign. The months prior to that were called **the year year of ascension** or **the year he became king**.

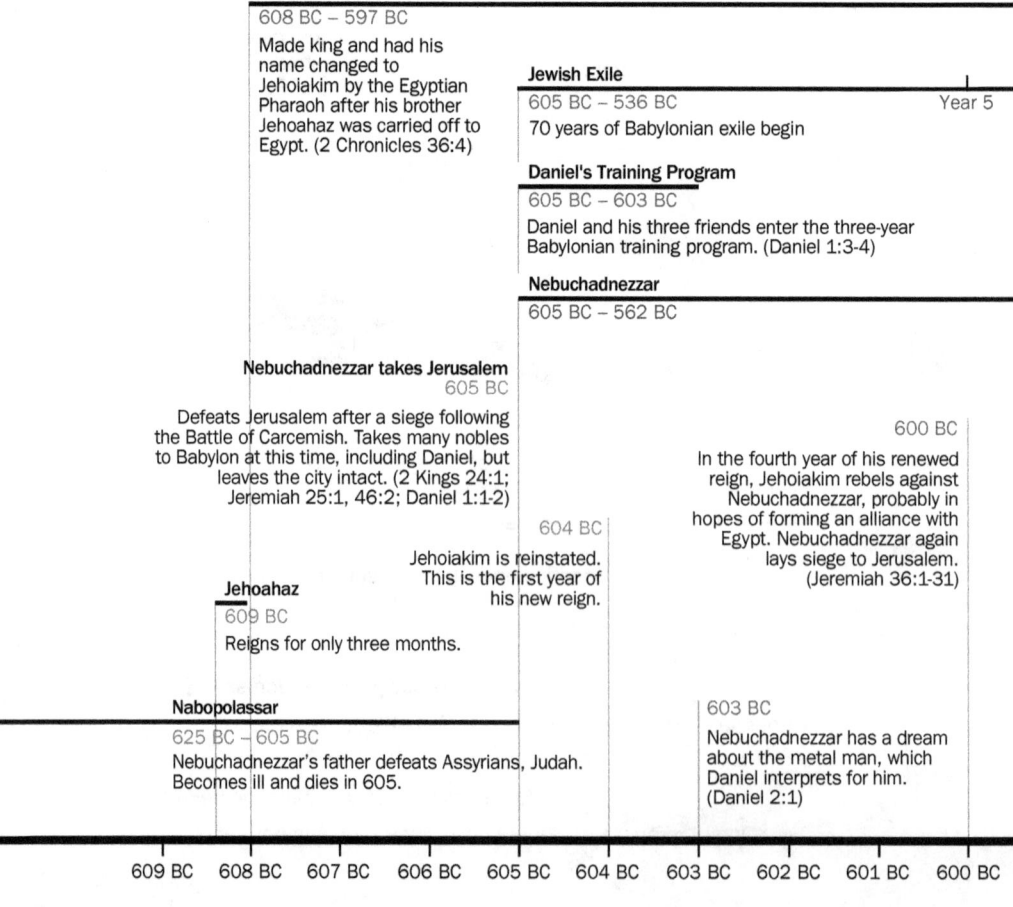

Eliakim
608 BC – 597 BC
Made king and had his name changed to Jehoiakim by the Egyptian Pharaoh after his brother Jehoahaz was carried off to Egypt. (2 Chronicles 36:4)

Jewish Exile
605 BC – 536 BC   Year 5
70 years of Babylonian exile begin

Daniel's Training Program
605 BC – 603 BC
Daniel and his three friends enter the three-year Babylonian training program. (Daniel 1:3-4)

Nebuchadnezzar
605 BC – 562 BC

Nebuchadnezzar takes Jerusalem
605 BC
Defeats Jerusalem after a siege following the Battle of Carcemish. Takes many nobles to Babylon at this time, including Daniel, but leaves the city intact. (2 Kings 24:1; Jeremiah 25:1, 46:2; Daniel 1:1-2)

604 BC
Jehoiakim is reinstated. This is the first year of his new reign.

600 BC
In the fourth year of his renewed reign, Jehoiakim rebels against Nebuchadnezzar, probably in hopes of forming an alliance with Egypt. Nebuchadnezzar again lays siege to Jerusalem. (Jeremiah 36:1-31)

Jehoahaz
609 BC
Reigns for only three months.

Nabopolassar
625 BC – 605 BC
Nebuchadnezzar's father defeats Assyrians, Judah. Becomes ill and dies in 605.

603 BC
Nebuchadnezzar has a dream about the metal man, which Daniel interprets for him. (Daniel 2:1)

609 BC 608 BC 607 BC 606 BC 605 BC 604 BC 603 BC 602 BC 601 BC 600 BC

Daniel was now in Babylon, serving Nebuchadnezzar, but many Jews were still in Jerusalem, as the city remained standing. When Nebuchadnezzar replaced Jehoiakim with Zedekiah, he took another 18,000 people captive, including the prophet Ezekiel.

Eliakim (renamed Jehoiakim)
608 BC – 597 BC

Jewish Exile
605 BC – 535 BC
70 years of Babylonian exile

Year 10

Year 15

Nebuchadnezzar
605 BC – 562 BC

Zedekiah
597 BC – 587 BC
Nebuchadnezzar installs Jehoiachin's uncle Mattaniah as a vassal king and changes his name, making him swear an oath of loyalty. 18,000 more people are taken to Babylon as captives, including the prophet Ezekiel. (2 Kings 24:17-18; 2 Chronicles 36:11; Jeremiah 37:1)

594 BC
Jeremiah sends a letter to the Jews in Babylon with a number of officials when king Zedekiah is summoned there by Nebuchadnezzar. (Jeremiah 51:59-60)

593 BC
Ezekiel sees a prophecy while in the city of Babylon. (Ezekiel 1:1-3)

Jehoiachin
597 BC
Reigned 3 months, 10 days. Declared "childless" by God because of his evil ways. (2 Kings 24:12; 2 Chron 36:8-10)

600 BC 599 BC 598 BC 597 BC 596 BC 595 BC 594 BC 593 BC 592 BC 591 BC 590 BC

Jeremiah warned king Zedekiah against his futile effort to rebel against the Babylonian king, but Zedekiah refused to listen and put the prophet in prison.

But just as prophecied, Nebuchadnezzar returned and destroyed the city, punishing Zedekiah by having his sons killed before him and then putting out his eyes.

Jewish Exile
605 BC – 535 BC
70 years of Babylonian exile

| Year 20 | Year 25 |

588 BC
Zedekiah puts Jeremiah in prison to shut him up, but he is eventually rescued. The Babylonians abandon their siege to deal with Pharaoh Hophra at the border of Judah. (Jeremiah 32:1-3, 34:21-22, 37:5)

Nebuchadnezzar
605 BC – 562 BC

Zedekiah
597 BC – 587 BC

Jerusalem destroyed
587 BC
The Babylonians are victorious against the Egyptian Pharaoh, then return to Judah. Enraged, Nebuchadnezzar destroys Jerusalem on Tisha B'Av (the 9th day of the month of Av). 4,600 Jews are taken captive. (2 Kings 25:8-9; Jeremiah 1:3, 39:1-2)

Siege of Tyre
586 BC – 573 BC
Nebuchadnezzar besieges the city of Tyre for 13 years. Historians aren't certain exactly which years this took place, but this period seems most likely.

589 BC
Zedekiah rebels against his oath of loyalty to Nebuchadnezzar, who then comes up against Jerusalem and besieges the city for two and a half years. (2 Kings 25:1-2)

590 BC 589 BC 588 BC 587 BC 586 BC 585 BC 584 BC 583 BC 582 BC 581 BC 580 BC

This decade was relatively quiet, but a civil uprising has been identified in archeological records. It took place around 577-576BC, making 576 a likely time for Nebuchadnezzar's construction of the idol designed to bring unity to the empire.

Jewish Exile
605 BC – 535 BC
70 years of Babylonian exile

Year 30 — Year 35

Nebuchadnezzar
605 BC – 562 BC

Nebuchadnezzar's Idol
576 BC

Some scholars believe this was the time Nebuchadnezzar set up the 90-foot idol covered in gold, requiring people to worship the image or be thrown into a furnace. It corresponds to the end of a civil uprising in Babylonia that would make such a proclamation politically meaningful. (Daniel 3:1)

Siege of Tyre
586 BC – 573 BC

Nebuchadnezzar besieges the city of Tyre for 13 years. Historians are not certain exactly which years.

571 BC

Some scholars believe this was the year in which Nebuchadnezzar had his vision of seven years of insanity, which Daniel interprets for him. (Daniel 4:4-17)

580 BC — 579 BC — 578 BC — 577 BC — 576 BC — 575 BC — 574 BC — 573 BC — 572 BC — 571 BC — 570 BC

We don't know when Nebuchadnezzar experienced his seven years of insanity. Scholars have identified two different time periods as likely. Of these, the later period, from 570-583 seem to be the most plausible, as the event probably took place closer to the end of the king's life. It is believed that he wrote his testimony shortly before he died in 562BC.

Jewish Exile
605 BC – 535 BC
70 years of Babylonian exile

Year 40

Year 45

Nebuchadnezzar
605 BC – 562 BC

Nebuchadnezzar's Insanity?
570 BC – 563 BC

There is some disagreement among scholars about when Nebuchadnezzar's seven years of insanity took place, but this period seems the most likely. During these seven years, shortly before he died, there are no historical records about Nebuchadnezzar's activities as king. (Daniel 4:28-33)

563 BC
Nebuchadnezzar's kingdom is restored to him, greater than it was before. It is believed he published his testimony shortly before he died. (Daniel 4:36)

Evil Merodach
562 BC – 560 BC
Evil Merodach, whose Babylonian name was Amel-Marduk, takes the throne. (Jeremiah 52:31; 2 Kings 25:27)

570 BC | 569 BC | 568 BC | 567 BC | 566 BC | 565 BC | 564 BC | 563 BC | 562 BC | 561 BC | 560 BC

After Nebuchadnezzar died, the kingdom went through many challenges as increasingly weak kings mismanaged everything from the military to the economy. Nabonidus became increasingly unpopular because of his emphasis on a non-traditional god, causing the Babylonian priests to oppose him. He retreated to Tema in Arabia, putting Belshazzar in charge of Babylon. Nabonidus didn't return to Babylon until years later, when the Persians made their military advances into the Chaldean empire.

Jewish Exile
605 BC – 535 BC
70 years of Babylonian exile

Year 50

Year 55

Nabonidus
556 BC – 539 BC

Belshazzar
553 BC – 539 BC
Nabonidus appoints his son Belshazzar as co-regent over Babylon. The date is not certain, but 553 seems plausible. Sir Robert Anderson puts the date at 551.

552 BC
Daniel has a dream of the same four kingdoms shown previously to Nebuchadnezzar, but with different metaphors as it represents God's view of those kingdoms rather than man's view. (Daniel 7:1)

551 BC
Cyrus defeats his relative, king Astyages of Media, to assume the throne of the Medo-Persian empire east of Babylon. He may have been assisted by Nabonidus.

Neriglissar
560 BC – 556 BC
Neriglissar (also named Nergal-Sharezer; his name means "Nergal, protect the king") murders his brother-in-law Evil Merodach and takes over the kingdom. (Jeremiah 39:13-14)

Labashi-Marduk
556 BC – 555 BC
Neriglissar's son Labashi-Marduk succeeds him but is murdered by Nabonidus after nine months.

560 BC 559 BC 558 BC 557 BC 556 BC 555 BC 554 BC 553 BC 552 BC 551 BC 550 BC

As Babylon continued to weaken under the poor leadership of Nabonidus and his co-regent, Belshazzar, Cyrus began to flex his muscles in Persia, beginning an aggressive expansion campaign that eventually moved into the Chaldean empire. One by one, the cities north of Babylon fell to the Persian onslaught.

Jewish Exile
605 BC – 535 BC
70 years of Babylonian exile

Year 60

Year 65

Nabonidus
556 BC – 539 BC

Belshazzar
553 BC – 539 BC

550 BC
Daniel sees a vision of the coming Greek empire. This vision takes place in the Persian city of Susa, with Daniel standing beside the Ulai Canal. (Daniel 8:1-2)

547 BC
East of Babylon, in Persia, Cyrus expands his empire. He reconquers most of Parthia, Sogdiana, Bactria and Arachosia, which were attempting to establish independence.

546 BC
Cyrus consolidates his conquests into a single empire, known as the Archaemenid Empire, after Archemaenides, an earlier king of the Persians from whom Cyrus traced his descent.

541 BC
Cyrus moves westward into the Babylonian empire, taking the cities north of Babylon.

550 BC 549 BC 548 BC 547 BC 546 BC 545 BC 544 BC 543 BC 542 BC 541 BC 540 BC

Persian king Cyrus, having conquered the surrounding cities, turned his attention to Babylon in October 539. His army dug channels to divert the river, which dropped to the height of a man's thigh during the night, and the army slipped under the gates to take Babylon without a battle.

Within the next year (based on Jewish reckoning of a king's reign), Daniel was given his vision of the 70 weeks of years. When Cyrus took the throne, he released the Jews, as Jeremiah had foretold. Historians disagree on the year this took place, but 535 corresponds with the 70 years of exile prophecied and confirmed by Jeremiah, Daniel and others.

Jewish Exile
605 BC – 535 BC
70 years of Babylonian exile

Nabonidus
556 BC – 539 BC

Belshazzar
553 BC – 539 BC

Babylon Falls
539 BC

While Belshazzar throws a party, Persian general Ugbaru diverts the Euphrates river to lower the water level and enters the 'unconquerable' city of Babylon without a battle. (Daniel 5:30-31)

Darius the Mede
539 BC – 536 BC

Cyrus installs Darius the Mede as Viceroy of Babylonia, with royal powers. Darius is 62 years old at the time.

537 BC
Daniel has a revelation that the Jews will be released, followed by his vision of the 70 weeks of years. This takes place in the 'first year' of Darius (the second year since being crowned). (Daniel 9:1)

Year 70

Cyrus the Persian
536 BC – 531 BC

Cyrus takes the throne of Babylon and releases the Jews, allowing them to return to Jerusalem. (Ezra 5:13; 2 Chronicles 36:22-23)

534 BC
It appears that Daniel leaves the city of Babylon around this time, but we don't know where he went. From his continued presence in the region we know that he did not return to Palestine with the release of the Jews, probably because of his age. (Daniel 1:21)

533 BC
Daniel is given his final prophetic vision after three weeks of mourning. He says he is beside the Tigris river (Babylon is on the Euphrates). Daniel would have been approaching 90 years of age. (Daniel 10:1-5)

532 BC
It is generally believed from language structure that Daniel finished his memoirs around this time.

540 BC | 539 BC | 538 BC | 537 BC | 536 BC | 535 BC | 534 BC | 533 BC | 532 BC | 531 BC | 530 BC

Bibliography of Primary Sources

Abingdon's Strong's Exhaustive Concordance
ISBN 0-687-40030-9

Alexander: The Boy Soldier Who Conquered the World
Simon Adams
ISBN 0-7922-3660-2

Baker's Bible Atlas
Charles F. Pfeiffer
ISBN 60-15536

Baker's Bible Handbook
Edited by Walter A. Elwell
ISBN 0-8010-3203-2

Bible Teacher's Commentary
Lawrence O. Richards, Published 2002
Formerly *The Victor Bible Background Commentary*
Cook Communications Ministries

The Coming Prince
Sir Robert Anderson

Eerdman's Bible Dictionary
Edited by Allen C. Myers
ISBN 0-8028-2402-1

Encyclopedia of Mysterious Places
Robert Ingpen & Philip Wilkinson
ISBN 0-88665-583-8

Expositional Commentary of Daniel
Chuck Missler

The Harper Atlas of the Bible
ISBN 0-06-181883-6

Hebrew-Greek Key Study Bible, NASB
edited by Spiros Zodhiates, Th.D.
ISBN 0-89957-690-7

The Interlinear Bible in Hebrew, Aramaic, Greek, English

The IVP Bible Background Commentary of the Old Testament
John H Walton, Victor H. Matthews & Mark W. Chavalas
ISBN 0-8308-1419-1

Jesus Freaks Vols 1 & 2
DC Talk and The Voice of the Martyrs
ISBN 1-57778-072-8 / 0-7642-2746-7

Josephus: The Essential Works
translated by Paul L. Maier
ISBN 0-8254-3260-X

Great books of the Western World Vol 6, Herodotus & Thucydides
Robert Maynard Hutchins, editor in chief

The Life and Times of Jesus the Messiah
Alfred Edersheim
ISBN 0-943575-83-4

Nave's Topical Bible
edited by John R. Kohlenberger III
ISBN 0-310-57950-3

Pagans and Christians
Robin Lane Fox
ISBN 0-394-55495-7

The Rise and Fall of the Great Empires
Andrew Taylor
ISBN 978-1-84724-513-7

The Stones Cry Out
Randall Price
ISBN 1-56507-640-0

The Temple
Alfred Edersheim
ISBN 1-56563-136-6

Today's Handbook of Bible Characters
E.M. Blaiklock
ISBN 0-87123-948-5

Today's Handbook of Bible Times and Customs
William L. Coleman
ISBN 0-87123-594-3

Vanished Civilizations
Reader's Digest Books
ISBN 0-949819-18-2

Index

70 Weeks of years, diagram 299

A
Abednego 59, 97-105, 148
abomination that causes desolation 224, 261, 279-280, 282-287
Afghanistan 179
Ahasuerus 248
Akkadian 39
Alexander the Great 17, 78, 173, 190–202, 248
Alexander the Great, map 298
angels 230, 239
Antichrist 81, 176, 198, 199, 224, 272, 280, 282-287
Antiochus III (Antiochus The Great) 252-255
Antiochus II Theos 250
Antiochus IV 224
Antiochus IV Epiphanes 194, 196, 200, 256–269
anti-Semitism 21, 83, 241
Aramaic 168
Arioch 71, 73
Armageddon 269
Artexerxes 218
Ashpenaz 56
Astyages 131
atonement 213

B
Babylon 32–49
Babylonian empire 79, 170
Babylonian Exile 294
Babylon, map of 295
Babylon, photos of 32-33, 296-297
Battle of Armageddon 272, 278
Battle of Carcemish 43
Battle of Thermopylae 255
Belshazzar 27, 131–144, 169, 190, 202, 305
Berenice 250
bigotry 156
Book of Evil Deeds 178
Book of Life *see Lamb's Book of Life*
Book of Remembrance 178

Book of Truth 179, 240
bowls of wrath 273
Brussels Treaty Powers 80

C
Caesarea Philippi 254
Cambyses 247
Cassander 172
Chaldean empire 32
China 268
Cleopatra 254
Club of Rome 175
cuneiform writing 28
Cyprus (Chittim) 260
Cyrus 131-144, 161, 191, 231, 247, 306

D
Darius 157, 159, 207
Darius 1 247
Darius the Mede 148, 240, 247
dreams 62, 66-83, 113
divided kingdom 292-293

E
Egypt 179
Egyptian empire 247-269, 253
Elisha 228
Emperor Tiberius 216
Esther 241, 248
eunuch (saris) 57
European Union 80
Evil-Merodach (Amel-Marduk) 130
Ezekiel 26, 178, 212, 301

F
furnace 101

G
Gabriel 198, 210-211
Gaumata 247
Governors 93, 102
Great Tribulation 184, 202, 273, 280, 282-287
Greece 179
Greek (Macedonian) empire 79, 190, 298
Gubaru 149

H

Hanukkah 257
heavenly thrones 180
Heliodorus 255, 256
Hezekiah 228, 237
Hystaspes 247

I

idol 91
innerancy of Scripture 20
Iran 179, 268
Iraq 179

J

Jason 194, 261
Jehoahaz 42
Jehoiachin (Jekoniah/Coniah) 44-46
Jehoiakim 43, 55
Jeremiah 43, 206, 293
Jordan 179
Josiah 41
Judas Maccabeas, Hanukkah 196

K

king of Aram 228

L

Labashi-Marduk 130
Lacanthropy, Boanthropy 124
Lamb's Book of Life 178, 274
Lebanon 179
lions' den 152
Lysimachus 172

M

Maccabean revolt 257, 263
magi 58, 104, 201
Magog, Russia 268
Man of metal 77
Marduk 35, 37, 56
martyrs 153
Mattaniah 46
Mattathias Maccabeaus 257
Mediterranean Sea (Great Sea) 169, 269
Medo-Persian empire 78, 170, 192

Menelaus 194
menorah (lamp stand) 136
Meshach 59, 97-105, 148
Messiah the King 22, 76, 215, 217, 223
Messianic prophecy 117–118
Michael the Archangel 230, 240-241, 273
Mount Moriah 269
Mount of Olives 215, 269
music, musical instruments 95

N
Nabonidus 27, 130, 169, 190, 191, 202, 305-306
Nabopolassar 37, 54
Nebuchadnezzar 27, 34, 37, 54–63, 66–83, 90–106, 108–128, 130, 300-304
Nebuzaradan 47
Neco 42, 43
Neriglissar 130
Nisan vs Tishri 232

O
Onias III 194, 197, 258

P
Pakistan 179
Pax Romana 175
Persian empire 78, 135, 152, 171, 193
Persian wars 171
Petra 183, 267, 281
Philip of Macedon 253
Post-modern textual criticism 19
Prefects 93, 102
pride, sin of 108
Ptolemy 172
Ptolemy II Euergetes 250
Ptolemy II Philadelphus 249
Ptolemy I Soter 248
Ptolemy IV Philopator 252
Ptolemy V Epiphanes 253-254
Ptolemy VI Philometer 259

R
Rapture 219, 299
resurrection 274
rewards for faithfulness 275-276, 281

Rock of salvation 84–85
Roman empire 79, 173, 174, 175, 177, 182, 184, 185
Rosh Hashana 232

S
Sabbath of the land 42, 210
Satraps 93, 102, 149
Scopas 253
Seleucid empire, Seleucid wars 247–269
Seleucus 172
Seleucus III Ceraunus 252
Seleucus IV Philopator 255
Seleucus Nicator 248, 249
Sennacherib 228
Seventy weeks of years 212–226, 287, 299
Shadrach 59, 97-105, 148
Simhat Torah 233
spiritual warfare 228
Susa 28, 191

T
ten toes of Roman empire 80
Theophany 102, 104, 235
Tigris river 162, 234, 277
Tigris River 246
Timeline of Daniel's life 300-307
times of the Gentiles 222
Tisha B' Av 49
Titus 222, 223
Tower of Babel 35, 58
Turkey 179

W
watchman angel 115
Western European Union 80
writing on the wall 134–144

X
Xerxes 171, 193, 248

Z
Zedekiah 37, 46-48
Zeus 175, 195, 196, 224, 263

WANT TO POWER UP YOUR LIFE?

Would you like to study the Bible and learn how to be a lion of faith like Daniel? Want to share your faith, but aren't sure how to start? The Pocket Testament League can help. Inspired by the vision of a teenage girl, League members pledge to Read, Carry and Share God's Word.

Membership is free, and just takes a moment. You'll be able to order Gospels and other publications, sign up for free daily devotionals and other Bible reading programs, take free training courses to learn how to share your faith, and more.

Since 1893, members of The Pocket Testament League have made it a goal of their life to read a portion of God's Word each day, carry it with them, and give it to others as God provides opportunities. Over 110 million Gospels of John have been shared with the lost!

As a member of the League, you'll be motivated and encouraged to:

- **Read** God's Word each day;
- **Carry** God's Word with you wherever you go
- **Share** God's Word with others as He gives opportunities

www.pocketpower.org/7115

THE POCKET TESTAMENT LEAGUE
PO Box 800
Lititz, PA 17543
(717) 626-1919
www.pocketpower.org

How to really wear your faith on your sleeve

Visit the Illuminosity Press store for a variety of products that show your commitment to your faith. Featuring modern graphic design and quality construction, these powerful items let you share what matters to you, and can challenge people in your life to consider and investigate the truth of Scripture for themselves.

www.illuminositypress.com/store/

ILLUMIN●SITY

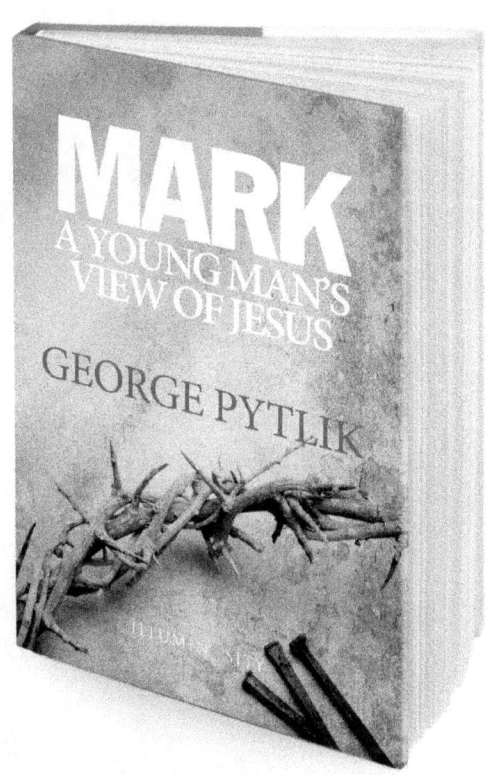

Enjoyed Daniel? Look for Mark coming soon!

In production for seven years, this study of the gospel of Mark features the same ground-breaking style of the Daniel commentary. Discover fascinating insights that will give you a new appreciation of Mark's detailed, youthful look at the life of Jesus. Maps, charts, and timelines make this one of the most comprehensive studies of Mark ever published. Sign up at **www.illuminositypress.com** to receive E-mail updates on Mark and other upcoming releases.

ILLUMIN✺SITY